5 INGREDIENT RECIPES

TASTE OF HOME BOOKS • RDA ENTHUSIAST BRANDS, LLC • MILWAUKEE, WI

P. 26

Taste of Home

ISBN: 978-1-61765-835-8
**LIBRARY OF CONGRESS CONTROL
NUMBER:** 2019931315

DEPUTY EDITOR: Mark Hagen
SENIOR ART DIRECTOR: Raeann
Thompson
EDITOR: Hazel Wheaton
ART DIRECTOR: Maggie Conners
DESIGNER: Jazmin Delgado
COPY CHIEF: Deb Warlaumont Mulvey

COVER
PHOTOGRAPHER: Dan Roberts
SET STYLIST: Stacey Genaw
FOOD STYLIST: Josh Rink

PICTURED ON FRONT COVER:
Fettuccine with Sausage & Fresh Tomato
Sauce, p. 114

PICTURED ON TITLE PAGE:
Broccoli-Cheddar Beef Rolls, p. 100

Printed in China
1 3 5 7 9 10 8 6 4 2

CONTENTS

P. 240

P. 122

P. 89

P. 123

GET SOCIAL WITH US

LIKE US: facebook.com/tasteofhome | **PIN US:** pinterest.com/taste_of_home

FOLLOW US: @tasteofhome | **TWEET US:** twitter.com/tasteofhome

TO FIND A RECIPE:
tasteofhome.com

TO SUBMIT A RECIPE:
tasteofhome.com/submit

TO FIND OUT ABOUT OTHER
***TASTE OF HOME* PRODUCTS:**
shoptasteofhome.com

NO LONG SHOPPING LISTS— AND NO LONG SHOPPING TRIPS!

For today's busy home cooks, saving time is nearly as important as saving money...and can sometimes seem even harder to do. Luckily, it doesn't take a lot of time or a whole shopping cart full of expensive ingredients to create irresistible homemade meals. Every recipe in this book requires no more than five ingredients and comes together with no fuss, no hassle and no wasted effort.

Whether you're serving up dinner on a busy weeknight, setting out a tasty breakfast to start the day right or even planning a party for friends, you'll find everything you're looking for in this new collection. Submitted by savvy home cooks across North America, the 290 recipes in this book will help you create delicious meals your family will love, while keeping your shopping budget under control. What's more, there are 150 recipes here that take 30 minutes or less to make, so it's easy to budget your time as well. Every recipe has been tested and approved by the *Taste of Home* Test Kitchen, so you know they'll come out right the first time.

Homemade breakfasts, satisfying soups and sandwiches, hearty entrees, delicious sides and salads, and lots of tantalizing sweets— they're all here. Dig in today and discover your family's new favorite meals!

P. 139

P. 135

P. 84

P. 137

P. 22

SHORT ON TIME?

Keep an eye out for that handy clock-watching icon!
It identifies all the recipes in this book that can be made
in 30 minutes (or less!), from the time you open the fridge
to when you put the meal on the table!

P. 200

P. 234

P. 176

HOW DO YOU COUNT TO 5?

You'll notice throughout this book that some recipe lists run longer than five lines. That's because there are a few items that we don't include in our five-ingredient counts. These are essentials that are so basic we feel comfortable assuming every kitchen always has them on hand. What are they? There are four items on the list, some of which you can customize as you wish.

1. WATER

2. SALT

When we say "salt," we're referring to traditional table salt, and we don't count it. Many cooks regularly use kosher salt instead, preferring it for its more predictable "pinch" measure—feel free to do so. But if a particular recipe requires kosher salt, we'll name it specifically, and include it in our count.

3. PEPPER

Black pepper is a go-to kitchen staple, and we don't count it. However, if a recipe demands freshly cracked black pepper, we will name it and count it. Cracked pepper gives the freshest flavor, but not everyone owns a pepper mill.

4. OIL

Three oils make our "don't count" list: Vegetable oil, canola oil and regular olive oil. Vegetable and canola oil are highly versatile and can be used interchangeably. They don't have a strong flavor and do have a high smoke point, which makes them ideal for frying, sauteing and baking. Regular olive oil adds a hint of fruity flavor and can be used for light sauteing, roasting, and dressings and sauces. Extra virgin olive oil, on the other hand, has more specialized uses due to its low smoke point, and will be specified (and counted!) when it's needed for the recipe.

We also don't include optional items when counting ingredients. We view these items as suggestions—either as garnishes or as a complement—but they aren't necessary to make the recipe, so you can easily leave them out. Also, you can always swap them out for your own preferred finishing touches.

5 TIPS FOR MAKING THE MOST OF 5 INGREDIENTS

1. THINK FRESH. Many of the most famous classic dishes have short ingredient lists and rely on a few distinctive flavors to carry the day. Start with good-quality ingredients and don't overcook, and you won't need a lot of extras.

2. CONSIDER COMMERCIALLY AVAILABLE INGREDIENTS THAT PILE ON THE FLAVOR. Jarred sauces, packaged rice mixes, seasoning blends, tomatoes with herbs, and canned soups let you get a head start.

3. USE MIXES IN NEW WAYS. A cake mix can be a good basis for cookies or bars. Biscuit and cookie mixes can also provide inspiration for a new recipe.

4. CHECK OUT PREPARED FOODS. Just because food is already cooked doesn't mean you need to serve it as is! Cakes from the bakery section, rotisserie chicken from the deli—use these as the starting point for your own dishes.

5. MAKE CONVENIENCE PRODUCTS YOUR OWN. Rice, stuffing and pasta mixes are ideal for experimentation. Try adding chopped fresh apple, celery and onion to a stuffing mix, for example, or add shrimp to a rice mix. Take a second look at convenience breads, such as crescent rolls, biscuits and frozen bread dough. You don't have to just make bread with them—they also work with some well-chosen ingredients to make appetizers, casseroles or calzones.

Stocking Your Pantry

Key to the magic of being able to pull together a great meal on short notice (and prevent an unexpected grocery run) is to have a well-stocked pantry. If you cover your bases, you'll always have some things in the cupboard that will work well together. Here are some suggestions for a few basic ingredients to always have on hand.

Chicken stock or broth • vinegar (red wine, white wine and/or balsamic) • eggs • milk • condensed soup (cream of mushroom and/or chicken) • salsa • all-purpose flour • a selection of herbs and spices • lemons • garlic • pastas • tomato sauce or paste • canned tomatoes (diced) • canned beans (garbanzo beans, white beans, kidney beans and/or black beans) • bread or rolls • rice mixes • onions • shredded cheese (cheddar, Italian blend or Mexican blend) • butter • frozen vegetables (mixed veggies, frozen peas, spinach) • prepared salad dressings • rice • bacon • honey • hot sauce/Tabasco sauce • bread crumbs • prepared mustard • bacon

BREAKFAST

TOAD IN THE HOLE BACON SANDWICH
P. 10

1

2

3

4

5

SERVE UP A DELICIOUS HOMEMADE
BREAKFAST WITHOUT LOTS OF
EARLY-MORNING PREP WORK!

RISE & SHINE PARFAIT

This fruit, yogurt and granola parfait is so easy to make. You can use whichever of your favorite fruits are in season.
—Diana Laskaris, Chicago, IL

Takes: 15 min. • **Makes:** 4 servings

- 4 cups fat-free vanilla yogurt
- 2 medium peaches, chopped
- 2 cups fresh blackberries
- ½ cup granola without raisins or Kashi Go Lean Crunch cereal

Layer half the yogurt, peaches, blackberries and granola into 4 parfait glasses. Repeat layers. Serve immediately or refrigerate until ready to serve.

1 parfait: 259 cal., 3g fat (0 sat. fat), 7mg chol., 6mg sod., 48g carb. (27g sugars, 7g fiber), 13g pro.

TOAD IN THE HOLE BACON SANDWICH

(PICTURED ON P. 8)

Switch up the cheese—pepper jack gives a nice kick—or use sliced kielbasa, ham or sausage instead of bacon in this versatile grilled-cheese breakfast sandwich.
—Kallee Krong-McCreery, Escondido, CA

Takes: 15 min. • **Makes:** 1 serving

- 2 slices sourdough bread
- 1 Tbsp. mayonnaise
- 1 large egg
- 1 slice cheddar cheese
- 2 cooked bacon strips

1. Using a biscuit cutter or round cookie cutter, cut out the center of one slice of bread (discard the center or save for another use). Spread mayonnaise on one side of each bread slice. In a large skillet coated with cooking spray, lightly toast the cutout slice, mayonnaise side down, over medium-low heat. Flip slice; crack an egg into the center. Add the remaining bread slice to the skillet, mayonnaise side down; layer with cheese and bacon.
2. Cook, covered, until egg white is set, yolk is soft-set and cheese begins to melt. If needed, flip slice with egg to finish cooking. To assemble sandwich, use solid slice as bottom and cutout slice as top.

1 sandwich: 610 cal., 34g fat (11g sat. fat), 240mg chol., 1220mg sod., 46g carb. (4g sugars, 2g fiber), 30g pro.

RISE & SHINE PARFAIT

BREAKFAST PIZZA

I used to make this for the morning drivers when I worked at a pizza delivery place. It's a quick and easy eye-opener that appeals to all.
—Cathy Shortall, Easton, MD

Takes: 30 min. • **Makes:** 8 servings

- 1 tube (13.8 oz.) refrigerated pizza crust
- 2 Tbsp. olive oil, divided
- 6 large eggs
- 2 Tbsp. water
- 1 pkg. (3 oz.) bacon bits
- 1 cup shredded Monterey Jack cheese
- 1 cup shredded cheddar cheese

1. Preheat oven to 400°. Unroll and press dough onto bottom and ½ in. up sides of a greased 15x10x1-in. pan. Prick thoroughly with a fork; brush with 1 Tbsp. oil. Bake until crust is lightly browned, 7-8 minutes.

2. Meanwhile, whisk together eggs and water. In a nonstick skillet, heat remaining oil over medium heat. Add the eggs; cook and stir just until thickened and no liquid egg remains. Spoon over the crust. Sprinkle with bacon bits and cheeses.

3. Bake until cheese is melted, 5-7 minutes.

1 piece: 352 cal., 20g fat (8g sat. fat), 169mg chol., 842mg sod., 24g carb. (3g sugars, 1g fiber), 20g pro.

BREAKFAST PIZZA

MARMALADE FRENCH TOAST SANDWICHES

MARMALADE FRENCH TOAST SANDWICHES

I change up these warm, filling sandwiches by using sweet or savory jellies, depending on my mood. Try hot pepper jelly when you want a little morning sizzle.
—Danielle Loring, Lewiston, ME

Takes: 25 min. • **Makes:** 6 servings

 1 container (8 oz.) whipped cream cheese
 12 slices sourdough bread
 ¾ cup orange marmalade
 4 large eggs
 2 Tbsp. 2% milk
  Maple syrup, optional

1. Spread cream cheese over six slices of bread; top with marmalade and the remaining bread. In a shallow bowl, whisk eggs and milk.
2. Lightly grease a griddle; heat over medium heat. Dip both sides of the sandwiches into the egg mixture. Place sandwiches on griddle; toast 2-3 minutes on each side or until golden brown. If desired, serve with syrup.
1 sandwich: 447 cal., 16g fat (9g sat. fat), 151mg chol., 628mg sod., 65g carb. (28g sugars, 2g fiber), 13g pro.

BERRY-FILLED DOUGHNUTS

Just four ingredients are all you'll need for this treat. Friends and family will never guess that refrigerated buttermilk biscuits are the base for these golden, jelly-filled doughnuts.
—Ginny Watson, Broken Arrow, OK

Takes: 25 min.
Makes: 10 doughnuts

  Oil for deep-fat frying
 2 tubes (6 oz. each) small refrigerated flaky biscuits (5 count)
 ½ cup seedless strawberry jam
 ¾ cup confectioners' sugar

1. In an electric skillet or deep fryer, heat oil to 350°. Separate the biscuits; press each to flatten slightly. Fry the biscuits, a few at a time, until golden brown, 1-1¼ minutes per side. Drain on paper towels.
2. Cut a small hole in the tip of a pastry bag; insert a small pastry tip. Fill bag with jam. With a small knife, pierce a hole into the side of each doughnut; fill with jam.
3. Toss with confectioners' sugar. Serve warm.
1 doughnut: 190 cal., 7g fat (1g sat. fat), 0 chol., 360mg sod., 30g carb. (17g sugars, 0 fiber), 2g pro.

BERRY-FILLED
DOUGHNUTS

PULL-APART CARAMEL COFFEE CAKE

PULL-APART CARAMEL COFFEE CAKE

The first time I made this delightful breakfast treat for a brunch party, it was a huge hit. Now I get requests every time family or friends do anything around the breakfast hour! I always keep the four simple ingredients on hand.
—Jaime Keeling, Keizer, OR

Prep: 10 min. • **Bake:** 25 min.
Makes: 16 servings

2   tubes (12 oz. each) refrigerated buttermilk biscuits
1   cup packed brown sugar
½   cup heavy whipping cream
1   tsp. ground cinnamon

1. Preheat oven to 350°. Cut each biscuit into four pieces; arrange evenly in a 10-in. fluted tube pan coated with cooking spray. In a small bowl, mix the remaining ingredients until blended; pour over the biscuits.

2. Bake for 25-30 minutes or until golden brown. Cool in pan for 5 minutes before inverting onto a serving plate.

5 pieces : 204 cal., 8g fat (3g sat. fat), 10mg chol., 457mg sod., 31g carb. (16g sugars, 0 fiber), 3g pro.

BAKED OMELET ROLL

This hands-off omelet bakes in the oven, so you don't have to keep a constant eye on it as you do eggs that cook on the stovetop.
—Susan Hudon, Fort Wayne, IN

Takes: 30 min. • **Makes:** 6 servings

 6 large eggs
 1 cup whole milk
 ½ cup all-purpose flour
 ½ tsp. salt
 ¼ tsp. pepper
 1 cup shredded cheddar
      cheese
      Thinly sliced green onions,
      optional

1. Preheat oven to 375°. Place eggs and milk in a blender. Add the flour, salt and pepper; cover and process until smooth. Pour into a greased 13x9-in. baking pan. Bake until the eggs are set, 20-25 minutes.
2. Sprinkle with cheese. Roll up omelet in pan, starting with a short side. Place with seam side down on a serving platter. Cut into ¾-in. slices. If desired, sprinkle with green onions.
2 slices: 204 cal., 12g fat (6g sat. fat), 238mg chol., 393mg sod., 11g carb. (3g sugars, 0 fiber), 13g pro.

DILLY ASPARAGUS FRITTATA

A frittata is an easy breakfast or brunch entree. Unlike scrambled eggs and omelets, they don't require any stirring or flipping.
—*Taste of Home* Test Kitchen

Takes: 30 min. • **Makes:** 4 servings

 2 Tbsp. butter
 8 large eggs
 1 cup cooked chopped
      asparagus
 1 cup shredded cheddar
      cheese, divided
 ½ tsp. dill weed
 ½ tsp. salt
 ⅛ tsp. pepper

1. Preheat oven to 425°. In an 8-in. ovenproof skillet, melt the butter. In a large bowl, beat eggs. Stir in the asparagus, ¾ cup of cheese, the dill, salt and pepper. Pour into skillet. Cook, without stirring, over medium-low heat for 8 minutes.
2. Remove from the heat; sprinkle with the remaining cheese. Bake for 6-8 minutes or until a knife inserted in the center comes out clean. Cut into wedges.
1 wedge: 307 cal., 24g fat (13g sat. fat), 470mg chol., 650mg sod., 4g carb. (2g sugars, 1g fiber), 19g pro.

BAKED OMELET ROLL

SHEEPHERDER'S
BREAKFAST

SHEEPHERDER'S BREAKFAST

My sister-in-law always made this delicious breakfast dish when we were camping. Casseroles like this were a big help while I was raising my nine children.
—Pauletta Bushnell, Albany, OR

Takes: 30 min. • **Makes:** 8 servings

- ¾ lb. bacon strips, finely chopped
- 1 medium onion, chopped
- 1 pkg. (30 oz.) frozen shredded hash brown potatoes, thawed
- 8 large eggs
- ½ tsp. salt
- ¼ tsp. pepper
- 1 cup shredded cheddar cheese

1. In a large skillet, cook bacon and onion over medium heat until the bacon is crisp. Drain, reserving ¼ cup of drippings in the pan.
2. Stir in hash browns. Cook, uncovered, over medium heat until bottom is golden brown, about 10 minutes. Turn potatoes. With the back of a spoon, make 8 evenly spaced wells in the potato mixture. Break an egg into each well. Sprinkle with salt and pepper.
3. Cover and cook on low until the eggs are set and the potatoes are tender, about 10 minutes. Sprinkle with cheese; let stand until cheese is melted.
1 serving: 354 cal., 22g fat (9g sat. fat), 222mg chol., 617mg sod., 22g carb. (2g sugars, 1g fiber), 17g pro.

PEANUT BUTTER OATMEAL

PEANUT BUTTER OATMEAL

My son and I eat this every day for breakfast. It's a hearty, healthy way to jump-start our day.
—Elisabeth Reitenbach, Terryville, CT

Takes: 15 min. • **Makes:** 2 servings

- 1¾ cups water
- ⅛ tsp. salt
- 1 cup old-fashioned oats
- 2 Tbsp. creamy peanut butter
- 2 Tbsp. honey
- 2 tsp. ground flaxseed
- ½ to 1 tsp. ground cinnamon
  Chopped apple, optional

In a small saucepan, bring water and salt to a boil. Stir in oats; cook for 5 minutes over medium heat, stirring occasionally. Transfer oatmeal to bowls; stir in the peanut butter, honey, flaxseed, cinnamon and, if desired, apple. Serve immediately.
¾ cup: 323 cal., 12g fat (2g sat. fat), 0 chol., 226mg sod., 49g carb. (19g sugars, 6g fiber), 11g pro.

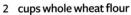

WHOLE WHEAT PANCAKES

This fuss-free recipe calls for whole wheat flour and buttermilk, which make the pancakes filling but also very light. Serve them with hot chocolate for a breakfast that's sure to delight little ones.
—Line Walter, Wayne, PA

Takes: 25 min.
Makes: 20 pancakes

2 cups whole wheat flour
½ cup toasted wheat germ
1 tsp. baking soda
½ tsp. salt
2 large eggs
3 cups buttermilk
1 Tbsp. canola oil

1. In a large bowl, combine the flour, wheat germ, baking soda and salt. In another bowl, whisk eggs, buttermilk and oil. Stir into dry ingredients just until blended.

2. Pour batter by ¼ cupfuls onto a hot griddle coated with cooking spray; turn when bubbles form on top. Cook until the second side is golden brown.

Freeze option: Freeze cooled pancakes between layers of waxed paper in an airtight freezer container. To use, place pancakes on an ungreased baking sheet, cover with foil, and reheat in a 375° oven for 6-10 minutes. Or, place a stack of three pancakes on a microwave-safe plate and microwave on high until heated through, 45-90 seconds.

2 pancakes: 157 cal., 4g fat (1g sat. fat), 45mg chol., 335mg sod., 24g carb. (4g sugars, 4g fiber), 9g pro. **Diabetic exchanges:** 1½ starch, 1 fat.

★ ★ ★ ★ ★ **READER REVIEW**

"This was the first time I'd made pancakes in 30 years—I usually fix waffles. This is a great recipe! They are very light and we'll definitely have them again."

OHBEEONE TASTEOFHOME.COM

WHOLE WHEAT PANCAKES

EGG BURRITOS

Zap one of these frozen burritos in the microwave and you'll stave off hunger all morning. My family loves this combo, but I sometimes use sausage instead of bacon.
—Audra Niederman, Aberdeen, SD

Takes: 25 min.
Makes: 10 burritos

- 12 bacon strips, chopped
- 12 large eggs
- ½ tsp. salt
- ¼ tsp. pepper
- 10 flour tortillas (8 in.), warmed
- 1½ cups shredded cheddar cheese
- 4 green onions, thinly sliced

1. In a large heavy skillet, cook the bacon until crisp; drain on paper towels. Remove all but 1-2 Tbsp. of the drippings from the pan.
2. Whisk together the eggs, salt and pepper. Heat skillet over medium heat; pour in the egg mixture. Cook and stir until the eggs are thickened and no liquid egg remains; remove from heat.
3. Spoon about ¼ cup of the egg mixture onto the center of each tortilla; sprinkle with cheese, bacon and green onions. Roll into burritos.

Freeze option: Cool eggs before making burritos. Individually wrap burritos in paper towels and foil; freeze in an airtight container. To use, remove foil; place the paper towel-wrapped burrito on a microwave-safe plate. Microwave on high until heated through, turning once. Let stand for 15 seconds before unwrapping completely.

1 burrito: 376 cal., 20g fat (8g sat. fat), 251mg chol., 726mg sod., 29g carb. (0 sugars, 2g fiber), 19g pro.

EGG BURRITOS

STUFFED HAM & EGG BREAD

GRANDMOTHER'S TOAD IN A HOLE

I have such fond memories of my grandmother's puffy Yorkshire pudding wrapped around little sausages—a dish my kids called "the boat."
—Susan Kieboam, Amherstburg, ON

Prep: 10 min. + standing
Bake: 25 min. • **Makes:** 6 servings

- 3   large eggs
- 1   cup 2% milk
- ½   tsp. salt
- 1   cup all-purpose flour
- 1   pkg. (12 oz.) uncooked maple breakfast sausage links
- 3   Tbsp. olive oil
     Butter and maple syrup, optional

1. Preheat oven to 400°. In a small bowl, whisk eggs, milk and salt. Whisk flour into egg mixture until blended. Let stand 30 minutes. Meanwhile, cook the sausage according to package directions; cut each of the sausage links into three pieces.
2. Place oil in a 12-in. nonstick ovenproof skillet. Place in oven until hot, 3-4 minutes. Stir batter and pour into prepared skillet; top with sausage. Bake until golden brown and puffed, 20-25 minutes. Remove from skillet; cut into wedges. If desired, serve with butter and syrup.

1 wedge: 336 cal., 22g fat (6g sat. fat), 126mg chol., 783mg sod., 20g carb. (2g sugars, 1g fiber), 14g pro.

STUFFED HAM & EGG BREAD

My son, Gus, is a lover of all things ham-and-eggs, so I created this comforting stuffed bread with him in mind. I later added tomatoes to the recipe, and he still gives it a big thumbs-up.
—Karen Kuebler, Dallas, TX

Prep: 25 min. • **Bake:** 20 min.
Makes: 8 servings

- 2   tsp. canola oil
- 1   can (14½ oz.) diced tomatoes, drained
- 6   large eggs, lightly beaten
- 2   cups chopped fully cooked ham
- 1   tube (11 oz.) refrigerated crusty French loaf
- 2   cups shredded sharp cheddar cheese

1. Preheat oven to 400°. In a large nonstick skillet, heat oil over medium heat. Add the tomatoes; cook and stir until the juices have evaporated, 12-15 minutes. Add eggs; cook and stir until they are thickened and and no liquid egg remains, 3-4 minutes. Remove from heat; stir in the ham.
2. Unroll dough onto a greased baking sheet. Sprinkle cheese lengthwise down one half of the dough to within 1 in. of edges. Top with egg mixture. Fold dough over filling, pinching to seal; tuck the ends under.
3. Bake until deep golden brown, 17-20 minutes. Cut into slices.

1 slice: 321 cal., 17g fat (7g sat. fat), 188mg chol., 967mg sod., 22g carb. (3g sugars, 1g fiber), 22g pro.

GRANDMOTHER'S TOAD IN A HOLE

CRANBERRY CHIP PANCAKES

CRANBERRY CHIP PANCAKES

A few simple ingredients make for pancakes so luscious you may not reach for the syrup!
—Aris Gonzalez, Deltona, FL

Takes: 25 min.
Makes: 6 pancakes

- ½ cup fresh or frozen cranberries
- 1 cup water, divided
- 1 cup complete pancake mix
- 1 tsp. grated orange zest
- ¼ cup orange juice
- ¼ cup white baking chips

1. In a small saucepan, cook the cranberries and ½ cup water over medium heat until berries pop, about 10 minutes.

2. Meanwhile, in a large bowl, combine the pancake mix, orange zest, orange juice and the remaining water just until moistened. Fold in chips. Drain cranberries; fold into the batter.

3. Pour batter by ¼ cupfuls onto a greased hot griddle; turn when bubbles form on top. Cook until second side is golden brown.

3 pancakes: 368 cal., 9g fat (4g sat. fat), 4mg chol., 853mg sod., 66g carb. (24g sugars, 3g fiber), 8g pro.

★ ★ ★ ★ ★ **READER REVIEW**

"This has fast become one of my favorites. Easy and great flavor."

COPELAH TASTEOFHOME.COM

SOUTHERN SUNSHINE EGGS

This creamy, comforting egg dish is just right for a brunch or light supper for two. It's a perfect meal in one—with or without the bacon, if you prefer!
—Carol Forcum, Marion, IL

Prep: 20 min. • **Bake:** 20 min.
Makes: 2 serving

- 4   bacon strips
- 4   large eggs
- ⅓   cup half-and-half cream
- ⅛   tsp. pepper
- ½   cup shredded cheddar cheese
- 2   green onions, chopped

1. Cook bacon over medium heat until cooked but not crisp. Remove to paper towels to drain.
2. Whisk 2 eggs, cream and pepper. Wrap two bacon strips around the inside edge of each of two 8-oz. ramekins coated with cooking spray.
3. Sprinkle half the cheese and onions in each ramekin. Divide egg mixture between ramekins. Break an egg into each. Sprinkle with remaining cheese and onion. Bake at 350° for 18-22 minutes or until eggs are completely set.
1 serving: 380 cal., 28g fat (14g sat. fat), 486mg chol., 521mg sod., 5g carb. (3g sugars, 0 fiber), 24g pro.

SOUR CREAM BLUEBERRY MUFFINS

When we were growing up, Mom made these warm, delicious muffins on chilly mornings. I'm now in college and enjoy baking them for friends.
—Tory Ross, Cincinnati, OH

Prep: 15 min. • **Bake:** 20 min.
Makes: 1 dozen

- 2   cups biscuit/baking mix
- ¾   cup plus 2 Tbsp. sugar, divided
- 2   large eggs
- 1   cup sour cream
- 1   cup fresh or frozen blueberries

1. Preheat oven to 375°. In a large bowl, combine the biscuit mix and ¾ cup of sugar. In a small bowl, combine eggs and sour cream; stir into the dry ingredients just until combined. Fold in the blueberries.
2. Fill greased muffin cups three-fourths full. Sprinkle with the remaining sugar. Bake until a toothpick inserted in a muffin comes out clean, 20-25 minutes. Cool 5 minutes before removing muffins from pan to a wire rack.
Note: If using frozen blueberries, use without thawing to avoid discoloring the batter.
1 serving: 195 cal., 7g fat (3g sat. fat), 48mg chol., 272mg sod., 29g carb. (16g sugars, 1g fiber), 3g pro.

SOUTHERN SUNSHINE EGGS

LOADED
BREAKFAST
POTATOES

LOADED BREAKFAST POTATOES

My kids love loaded potatoes in restaurants, so I modified them to make at home. Using the microwave will save you about 10 minutes. I also use thin-skinned red potatoes instead of russets to save on peeling time.
—Tena Kropp, Aurora, IL

Takes: 30 min. • **Makes:** 6 servings

- 1½ lbs. red potatoes, cubed
- ¼ lb. bacon strips, chopped
- ¾ cup cubed fully cooked ham
- 1 cup shredded cheddar cheese
- ½ tsp. salt
- ¼ tsp. pepper
- Sour cream

1. Place potatoes in a microwave-safe dish and cover with water. Cover and microwave on high for 4-5 minutes or until tender.
2. In a large skillet, cook bacon over medium heat until crisp. Remove to paper towels with a slotted spoon. Drain potatoes; saute in bacon drippings until lightly browned. Add the ham, cheese, salt, pepper and bacon. Cook and stir over medium heat until the cheese is melted. Serve with sour cream.

¾ cup: 273 cal., 16g fat (8g sat. fat), 45mg chol., 776mg sod., 19g carb. (1g sugars, 2g fiber), 13g pro.

BREAKFAST SKEWERS

BREAKFAST SKEWERS

These spicy-sweet kabobs are an unexpected offering for a brunch. They're a great companion to any egg dish.
—Bobi Raab, St. Paul, MN

Takes: 20 min. • **Makes:** 5 servings

- 1 pkg. (7 oz.) frozen fully cooked breakfast sausage links, thawed
- 1 can (20 oz.) pineapple chunks, drained
- 10 medium fresh mushrooms
- 2 Tbsp. butter, melted
- Maple syrup

1. Cut sausages in half; on five metal or soaked wooden skewers, alternately thread the sausages, pineapple and mushrooms. Brush with butter and syrup.
2. Grill, uncovered, over medium heat, turning and basting with syrup, for 8 minutes or until the sausages are lightly browned and the fruit is heated through.

1 skewer: 246 cal., 20g fat (8g sat. fat), 37mg chol., 431mg sod., 13g carb. (12g sugars, 1g fiber), 7g pro.

MAPLE TOAST & EGGS

SWEET BROILED GRAPEFRUIT

I was never a fan of grapefruit until I had it broiled at a restaurant—it was so tangy and delicious! I now make it often for my whole family.
—Terry Bray, Auburndale, FL

Takes: 15 min. • **Makes:** 2 servings

- 1 large grapefruit
- 2 Tbsp. butter, softened
- 2 Tbsp. sugar
- ½ tsp. ground cinnamon

Preheat broiler. Cut grapefruit crosswise in half; if desired, cut a thin slice from the bottom of each so that they sit level. Cut around each grapefruit section to loosen fruit. Place on a baking sheet. Top with butter. Mix sugar and cinnamon; sprinkle over fruit. Broil 4 in. from heat until sugar is bubbly.

½ grapefruit: 203 cal., 12g fat (7g sat. fat), 31mg chol., 116mg sod., 26g carb. (24g sugars, 2g fiber), 1g pro.

★ ★ ★ ★ ★ **READER REVIEW**

"This is the best way to make grapefruit. I never really liked grapefruit until I tried this recipe!"

KDBUGG22 TASTEOFHOME.COM

MAPLE TOAST & EGGS

I live in the country, right next door to my sister and her family. They enjoy this dish each time I serve it—as breakfast, lunch or even a special evening meal.
—Susan Buttel, Plattsburgh, NY

Prep: 20 min. • **Bake:** 20 min.
Makes: 12 cups

- 12 bacon strips, diced
- ½ cup maple syrup
- ¼ cup butter
- 12 slices firm-textured white bread
- 12 large eggs
  Salt and pepper to taste

1. Preheat oven to 400°. In a large skillet, cook bacon over medium heat until crisp. Using a slotted spoon, remove to paper towels to drain. In a small saucepan, heat syrup and butter until the butter is melted; set aside.

2. Trim crust from bread; flatten slices with a rolling pin. Brush one side generously with the syrup mixture; press each slice into a greased muffin cup with the syrup side down. Divide the bacon among the muffin cups.

3. Carefully break one egg into each cup. Sprinkle with salt and pepper. Cover with foil. Bake until the egg whites are completely set and the yolks begin to thicken but are not hard, 18-20 minutes. Serve immediately,

2 egg cups: 671 cal., 46g fat (18g sat. fat), 476mg chol., 805mg sod., 44g carb. (20g sugars, 1g fiber), 21g pro.

CINNAMON FRUIT BISCUITS

These sweet treats are so easy, I'm almost embarrassed when people ask me for the recipe. They're a snap to make with refrigerated biscuits, sugar, cinnamon and your favorite fruit preserves.
—Ione Burham, Washington, IA

Prep: 15 min.
Bake: 15 min. + cooling
Makes: 10 servings

½ cup sugar
½ tsp. ground cinnamon
1 tube (12 oz.) refrigerated buttermilk biscuits, separated into 10 biscuits
¼ cup butter, melted
10 tsp. strawberry preserves

1. Preheat oven to 375°. Combine sugar and cinnamon. Dip top and sides of biscuits in butter, then in cinnamon-sugar.

2. Place on ungreased baking sheets. With the end of a wooden spoon handle, make a deep indentation in the top of each biscuit; fill with 1 tsp. preserves.

3. Bake 15-18 minutes or until golden brown. Cool 15 minutes before serving (filling will be hot).

1 biscuit: 178 cal., 5g fat (3g sat. fat), 12mg chol., 323mg sod., 31g carb. (14g sugars, 0 fiber), 3g pro. **Diabetic exchanges:** 2 starch, 1 fat.

CINNAMON FRUIT BISCUITS

BREAKFAST SWEET POTATOES

BREAKFAST SWEET POTATOES

Baked sweet potatoes aren't just for dinner! Top them with breakfast favorites to power up your morning.
—*Taste of Home* Test Kitchen

Prep: 10 min. • **Bake:** 45 min.
Makes: 4 servings

- 4 medium sweet potatoes (about 8 oz. each)
- ½ cup fat-free coconut Greek yogurt
- 1 medium apple, chopped
- 2 Tbsp. maple syrup
- ¼ cup toasted unsweetened coconut flakes

1. Preheat oven to 400°. Place sweet potatoes on a foil-lined baking sheet. Bake until tender, 45-60 minutes.
2. With a sharp knife, cut an X in each potato. Fluff pulp with a fork. Top with remaining ingredients.

1 stuffed sweet potato: 321 cal., 3g fat (2g sat. fat), 0 chol., 36mg sod., 70g carb. (35g sugars, 8g fiber), 7g pro.

TEST KITCHEN TIP
To microwave the potatoes, scrub them and pierce with a fork; place on a microwave-safe plate. Microwave, uncovered, on high for 12-14 minutes or until tender, turning once.

BACON & EGG BUNDLES

BACON & EGG BUNDLES

This is a fun way to serve both bacon and eggs in one bite! The recipe can easily be doubled.
—Edith Landinger, Longview, TX

Prep: 20 min. • **Bake:** 15 min.
Makes: 6 servings

- 12 to 18 bacon strips
- 1 tsp. butter
- 6 large eggs
  Freshly ground pepper, optional

1. Preheat oven to 325°. In a large skillet, cook bacon over medium heat until partially cooked but not crisp. Drain on paper towels.
2. Lightly grease six muffin cups with 1 tsp. butter. Cut six bacon strips crosswise in half; leave the rest whole. Line the bottom of each muffin cup with two bacon halves. Line sides of each muffin cup with one or two whole bacon strips. Break an egg into each cup.
3. Bake until the egg whites are completely set and the egg yolks begin to thicken but are not hard, 12-18 minutes. If desired, sprinkle with pepper.

1 bundle: 311 cal., 28g fat (9g sat. fat), 225mg chol., 447mg sod., 1g carb. (1g sugars, 0 fiber), 13g pro.

APPETIZERS

& BEVERAGES

**ROOT BEER
PULLED PORK NACHOS
P. 32**

1

2

3

4

5

YOU'LL BE READY FOR A PARTY
BEFORE YOU KNOW IT WITH THESE
EASY-TO-ASSEMBLE DRINKS, APPS
AND SMALL-PLATE SPECIALS!

PIZZA ROLL-UPS

This has been a regular after-school snack in my house since I first got the recipe through 4-H Club. These bite-sized pizza treats, made with refrigerated crescent rolls, are especially good served with spaghetti sauce for dipping.
—Donna Klettke, Wheatland, MO

Prep: 20 min. • **Bake:** 15 min.
Makes: 2 dozen

- ½ **lb. ground beef**
- 1 **can (8 oz.) tomato sauce**
- ½ **cup shredded part-skim mozzarella cheese**
- ½ **tsp. dried oregano**
- 2 **tubes (8 oz. each) refrigerated crescent rolls**

1. Preheat oven to 375°. In a large skillet, cook beef over medium heat until no longer pink; drain. Remove from the heat. Add the tomato sauce, mozzarella cheese and oregano.
2. Separate crescent dough into eight rectangles, pinching seams together. Place about 3 Tbsp. of meat mixture along one long side of each rectangle. Roll up, jelly-roll style, starting with a long side. Cut each roll into three pieces.
3. Place, seam side down, 2 in. apart on greased baking sheets. Bake rolls 15 minutes or until golden brown.

2 pieces: 122 cal., 7g fat (2g sat. fat), 13mg chol., 265mg sod., 8g carb. (2g sugars, 0 fiber), 6g pro.

PIZZA ROLL-UPS

ROOT BEER PULLED PORK NACHOS

(PICTURED ON P. 30)

I count on my slow cooker to do the honors when I have a house full of summer guests. Teenagers especially love DIY nachos. Try cola, ginger ale or lemon-lime soda if you're not into root beer.
—James Schend,
Pleasant Prairie, WI

Prep: 20 min. • **Cook:** 8 hours
Makes: 12 servings

- 1 **boneless pork shoulder butt roast (3 to 4 lbs.)**
- 1 **can (12 oz.) root beer or cola**
- 12 **cups tortilla chips**
- 2 **cups shredded cheddar cheese**
- 2 **medium tomatoes, chopped Pico de gallo, chopped green onions and sliced jalapeno peppers, optional**

1. In a 4- or 5-qt. slow cooker, combine pork roast and root beer. Cook, covered, on low until the meat is tender, 8-9 hours.
2. Remove roast; cool slightly. When cool enough to handle, shred meat with two forks. Return pork to slow cooker; keep warm.
3. To serve, drain pork. Layer tortilla chips with pork, cheese, tomatoes and, if desired, any or all of the optional toppings. Serve immediately.

1 serving: 391 cal., 23g fat (8g sat. fat), 86mg chol., 287mg sod., 20g carb. (4g sugars, 1g fiber), 25g pro.

MINI FETA PIZZAS

We usually have lots basil from our garden, and like to use it to make pesto for our mini pizzas. We often add extra feta once they're done.
—Nicole Filizetti, Stevens Point, WI

Takes: 20 min. • **Makes:** 4 servings

- 2 **whole wheat English muffins, split and toasted**
- 2 **Tbsp. reduced-fat cream cheese**
- 4 **tsp. prepared pesto**
- ½ **cup thinly sliced red onion**
- ¼ **cup crumbled feta cheese**

1. Preheat oven to 425°. Place muffins on a baking sheet.
2. Mix cream cheese and pesto; spread over the muffins. Top with onion and feta cheese. Bake until lightly browned, 6-8 minutes.

1 mini pizza: 136 cal., 6g fat (3g sat. fat), 11mg chol., 294mg sod., 16g carb. (4g sugars, 3g fiber), 6g pro. **Diabetic exchanges:** 1 starch, 1 fat.

CHOCOLATE BISCUIT PUFFS

I know my favorite snack is fun for kids because I dreamed it up when I was 9 years old! The puffs are shaped to keep the chocolate inside a tasty surprise.
—Joy Clark, Seabeck, WA

Takes: 20 min.
Makes: 10 servings

- 1 **tube (12 oz.) refrigerated buttermilk biscuits**
- 1 **milk chocolate candy bar (1.55 oz.)**
- 2 **tsp. cinnamon sugar**

1. Preheat oven to 450°. Flatten each biscuit into a 3-in. circle. Break the candy bar into pieces; place a piece on each biscuit. Bring up the edges to enclose the candy; pinch to seal.
2. Place puffs seam side down on an ungreased baking sheet. Sprinkle with cinnamon sugar. Bake for 8-10 minutes or until golden brown.

1 puff: 127 cal., 5g fat (2g sat. fat), 1mg chol., 284mg sod., 18g carb. (5g sugars, 0 fiber), 2g pro.

MINI FETA PIZZAS

LIKE 'EM HOT WINGS

SWEET POTATO FRIES WITH BLUE CHEESE

I hated sweet potatoes when I was a child—because they came out of a can! When I learned of their health benefits, my husband and I began trying fresh sweet potatoes. At some point, we discovered how absolutely awesome they are with blue cheese!
—Katrina Krumm,
Apple Valley, MN

Takes: 25 min. • **Makes:** 2 servings

- 1   Tbsp. olive oil
- 2   medium sweet potatoes (about 1¼ lbs.), peeled and cut into ½-in.-thick strips
- 1   Tbsp. apricot preserves
- ¼   tsp. salt
- 3   Tbsp. crumbled blue cheese

In a large skillet, heat oil over medium heat. Add the sweet potatoes; cook until tender and lightly browned, turning occasionally, 12-15 minutes. Add the preserves, stirring to coat; sprinkle with salt. Top with blue cheese.

1 serving: 246 cal., 11g fat (3g sat. fat), 9mg chol., 487mg sod., 34g carb. (15g sugars, 3g fiber), 5g pro.

LIKE 'EM HOT WINGS
These spicy chicken wings are wonderfully seasoned. They're an easy snack everyone enjoys.
—Myra Innes, Auburn, KS

Prep: 10 min. • **Bake:** 30 min.
Makes: about 2 dozen

- 2½   lbs. chicken wings
- 1   bottle (2 oz.) hot pepper sauce (about ¼ cup)
- 1   to 2 garlic cloves, minced
- 1½   tsp. dried rosemary, crushed
- 1   tsp. dried thyme
- ¼   tsp. salt
- ¼   tsp. pepper
    Celery sticks, carrot sticks and blue cheese salad dressing, optional

1. Preheat oven to 425°. Cut chicken wings into three sections; discard the wing tips. In a large bowl, combine the hot pepper sauce, garlic and seasonings. Add chicken wings; toss to evenly coat. Transfer to a well-greased 13x9-in. baking dish.
2. Bake, uncovered, until chicken juices run clear, 30-40 minutes, turning every 10 minutes. Serve with celery, carrots and blue cheese dressing if desired.
Note: Uncooked chicken wing sections (wingettes) may be substituted for whole chicken wings.
1 wing: 43 cal., 3g fat (1g sat. fat), 12mg chol., 51mg sod., 0 carb. (0 sugars, 0 fiber), 4g pro.

SWEET
POTATO FRIES
WITH BLUE
CHEESE

PIZZA RING

PIZZA RING

My 7-year-old, Sarah, loves pizza. This is a recipe she came up with, and it was a huge success!
—Tricia Richardson, Springdale, AR

Takes: 30 min. • **Makes:** 8 servings

- 1   lb. bulk Italian sausage
- 1   can (15 oz.) pizza sauce, divided
- 1½ cups shredded part-skim mozzarella cheese, divided
- 4   oz. Canadian bacon, chopped
- 2   tubes (8 oz. each) refrigerated crescent rolls

1. Preheat oven to 375°. In a large skillet over medium heat, cook sausage until no longer pink; drain. Stir in ½ cup pizza sauce, 1 cup cheese and the Canadian bacon.

2. Unroll the crescent dough and separate into triangles. On an ungreased 14-in. pizza pan, arrange the triangles in a ring with the points toward the outside and the wide ends overlapping at the center, leaving a 4-in. opening. Press the overlapping dough to seal.

3. Spoon the filling onto the wide end of the triangles. Fold the pointed ends of the triangles over the filling, tucking the points under to form a ring (filling will be visible).

4. Bake for 12-15 minutes or until golden brown and heated through. Sprinkle with remaining cheese. Bake 5 minutes longer or until the cheese is melted. Serve with the remaining pizza sauce.

1 slice with 2 Tbsp. pizza sauce: 214 cal., 13g fat (4g sat. fat), 22mg chol., 593mg sod., 13g carb. (4g sugars, 0 fiber), 10g pro.

CHEESE STRAWS

Just a few on-hand ingredients go into these long, crisp cracker sticks. The delicate, hand-held snacks are great for parties.
—Elizabeth Robinson, Conroe, TX

Prep: 20 min.
Bake: 15 min. + cooling
Makes: 2½ dozen

- ½ cup butter, softened
- 2 cups shredded sharp cheddar cheese
- 1¼ cups all-purpose flour
- ½ tsp. salt
- ¼ tsp. cayenne pepper

1. Preheat oven to 350°. In a large bowl, beat butter until light and fluffy. Beat in the cheese until blended. Combine flour, salt and cayenne; stir into the cheese mixture until a dough forms. Roll into a 15x6-in. rectangle. Cut into thirty 6-in. strips. Gently place strips 1 in. apart on ungreased baking sheets.

2. Bake until lightly browned, 15-20 minutes. Cool 5 minutes before removing from pans to wire racks to cool completely. Store in an airtight container.

1 straw: 72 cal., 5g fat (4g sat. fat), 16mg chol., 106mg sod., 4g carb. (0 sugars, 0 fiber), 2g pro.

HOMEMADE GUACAMOLE

Nothing is better than fresh guacamole when you're eating something spicy. It's easy to whip together in a matter of minutes.
—Joan Hallford, North Richland Hills, TX

Takes: 10 min. • **Makes:** 2 cups

- 3 medium ripe avocados, peeled and cubed
- 1 garlic clove, minced
- ¼ to ½ tsp. salt
- 2 medium tomatoes, seeded and chopped, optional
- 1 small onion, finely chopped
- ¼ cup mayonnaise, optional
- 1 to 2 Tbsp. lime juice
- 1 Tbsp. minced fresh cilantro

Mash avocados with garlic and salt. Stir in remaining ingredients.
¼ cup: 90 cal., 8g fat (1g sat. fat), 0 chol., 78mg sod., 6g carb. (1g sugars, 4g fiber), 1g pro. **Diabetic exchanges:** 1½ fat.

HOMEMADE GUACAMOLE

CHEESY
QUESADILLAS

CHEESY QUESADILLAS

You can slice these into thin wedges to use as party appetizers or dippers for chili, or serve them with extra salsa and sour cream as a main dish.
—Terri Keeney, Greeley, CO

Takes: 15 min. • **Makes:** 6 servings

- 4 flour tortillas (8 in.), warmed
- 1½ cups shredded Mexican cheese blend
- ½ cup salsa

1. Place the tortillas on a greased baking sheet. Combine the cheese and salsa; spread over half of each tortilla. Fold over.
2. Broil 4 in. from the heat for 3 minutes on each side or until golden brown. Cut into wedges.
1 serving: 223 cal., 11g fat (5g sat. fat), 25mg chol., 406mg sod., 21g carb. (1g sugars, 1g fiber), 9g pro.
Turkey Quesadillas: Sprinkle ½ cup diced cooked turkey over cheese mixture. Proceed as directed.
Two-Cheese Quesadillas: Reduce cheese to 1 cup; combine with 1 cup shredded part-skim mozzarella cheese. If you like, top with your choice of veggies, such as 1 cup finely chopped tomatoes, ½ cup finely chopped green pepper and ¼ cup chopped onion. Proceed as directed. Serve with salsa.

PALOMA

PALOMA

Soon after I learned about this cocktail, I brought the ingredients to a family dinner at my parents'. The next time we got together, my dad had the fixings already set out and ready to go by the time I arrived!
—Ian Cliffe, Milwaukee, WI

Takes: 5 min. • **Makes:** 1 serving

- Dash salt
- 1½ oz. tequila
- ½ oz. lime juice
- ½ cup grapefruit soda or sparkling peach citrus soda
- Lime wedge

In a highball glass filled with ice, combine the salt, tequila and lime juice. Top with soda. Garnish with lime.
1 serving: 148 cal., 0 fat (0 sat. fat), 0 chol., 163mg sod., 14g carb. (13g sugars, 0 fiber), 0 pro.

BEER DIP

GREEK DELI KABOBS

For an easy Mediterranean-style appetizer, marinate broccoli and mozzarella, then skewer with sweet red peppers and salami. Everybody loves food on a stick!
—Vikki Spengler, Ocala, FL

Prep: 30 min. + marinating
Makes: 2 dozen

- 1 **lb. part-skim mozzarella cheese, cut into 48 cubes**
- 24 **fresh broccoli florets (about 10 oz.)**
- ½ **cup Greek vinaigrette**
- 24 **slices hard salami**
- 2 **jars (7½ oz. each) roasted sweet red peppers, drained and cut into 24 strips**

1. In a large resealable plastic bag, combine cheese, broccoli and vinaigrette. Seal bag and turn to coat; refrigerate for 4 hours or overnight.
2. Drain cheese and broccoli, reserving the vinaigrette. On 24 appetizer skewers, alternately thread cheese, salami, broccoli and peppers. Brush with the reserved vinaigrette.
1 kabob: 109 cal., 7g fat (4g sat. fat), 19mg chol., 374mg sod., 2g carb. (1g sugars, 0 fiber), 8g pro.

BEER DIP

You can make this dip in nothing flat. It's packed with shredded cheese and perfect with pretzels. Be aware, though—it's addictive. Once you start eating it, it's hard to stop! This easy recipe will work with any type of beer, including nonalcoholic.
—Michelle Long, New Castle, CO

Takes: 5 min. • **Makes:** 3½ cups

- 2 **pkg. (8 oz. each) cream cheese, softened**
- ⅓ **cup beer**
- 1 **envelope ranch salad dressing mix**
- 2 **cups shredded cheddar cheese**
  Pretzels

In a large bowl, beat the cream cheese, beer and dressing mix until smooth. Stir in cheddar cheese. Serve with pretzels.
2 Tbsp.: 89 cal., 8g fat (5g sat. fat), 26mg chol., 177mg sod., 1g carb. (0 sugars, 0 fiber), 3g pro.

CHILI-LIME ROASTED CHICKPEAS

Looking for a lighter snack that will appeal to everyone? You've found it! These zesty, crunchy chickpeas will have all your guests happily munching away.
—Julie Ruble, Raleigh, NC

Prep: 10 min.
Bake: 40 min. + cooling
Makes: 2 cups

- 2 cans (15 oz. each) chickpeas or garbanzo beans, rinsed, drained and patted dry
- 2 Tbsp. olive oil
- 1 Tbsp. chili powder
- 2 tsp. ground cumin
- 1 tsp. grated lime zest
- 1 Tbsp. lime juice
- ¾ tsp. sea salt

1. Preheat oven to 400°. Line a 15x10x1-in. baking sheet with foil. Spread the chickpeas in a single layer over foil, removing any loose skins. Bake until very crunchy, 40-45 minutes, stirring every 15 minutes.
2. Meanwhile, whisk the remaining ingredients. Remove chickpeas from oven; let cool 5 minutes. Drizzle with the oil mixture; shake pan to coat. Cool completely. Store in an airtight container.

⅓ cup: 178 cal., 8g fat (1g sat. fat), 0mg chol., 463mg sod., 23g carb. (3g sugars, 6g fiber), 6g pro.

★ ★ ★ ★ ★ **READER REVIEW**

"My new favorite snack! The lime gives it the tiniest hint of sweetness."

LISA TASTEOFHOME.COM

CHILI-LIME ROASTED CHICKPEAS

ORANGE JUICE SPRITZER

BBQ CHICKEN BITES

Chicken bites wrapped in bacon get an added kick from Montreal steak seasoning and sweetness from barbecue sauce. We love the mix of textures.
—Kathryn Dampier, Quail Valley, CA

Takes: 25 min. • **Makes:** 1½ dozen

- 6 bacon strips
- ¾ lb. boneless skinless chicken breasts, cut into 1-in. cubes (about 18)
- 3 tsp. Montreal steak seasoning
- 1 tsp. prepared horseradish, optional
- ½ cup barbecue sauce

1. Preheat oven to 400°. Cut the bacon crosswise into thirds. Place bacon on a microwave-safe plate lined with paper towels. Cover the bacon with additional paper towels; microwave on high until partially cooked but not crisp, 3-4 minutes.
2. Place chicken in a small bowl; sprinkle with steak seasoning and toss to coat. Wrap a bacon piece around each chicken cube; secure with a toothpick. Place chicken on a parchment-lined baking sheet.
3. Bake 10 minutes. If desired, add horseradish to barbecue sauce; brush over wrapped chicken. Bake until chicken is no longer pink and bacon is crisp, 5-10 minutes.

1 appetizer: 47 cal., 2 g fat (0 sat. fat), 13 mg chol., 249 mg sod., 3 g carb. (3 g sugars, 0 fiber), 5 g pro.

ORANGE JUICE SPRITZER

This refreshing and pretty spritzer is a nice light wake-me-up drink and an easy way to give a twist to an ordinary glass of orange juice. Most people appreciate that it is not overly sweet.
—Michelle Krzmarzick, Torrance, CA

Takes: 5 min.
Makes: 8 servings

- 4 cups orange juice
- 1 liter ginger ale, chilled
- ¼ cup maraschino cherry juice
  Orange wedges and maraschino cherries, optional

In a 2-qt. pitcher, mix orange juice, ginger ale and cherry juice. Serve over ice. If desired, top servings with orange wedges and cherries.
1 cup: 103 cal., 0 fat (0 sat. fat), 0 chol., 9mg sod., 25g carb. (23g sugars, 0 fiber), 1g pro.

CHICKEN CHILI WONTON BITES

CHICKEN CHILI WONTON BITES

Everyone needs a surefire grab-and-go party recipe. Wonton wrappers filled with chicken and spices make these bites flavorful and fun—perfect for picnics and tailgate parties.
—Heidi Jobe, Carrollton, GA

Takes: 30 min. • **Makes:** 3 dozen

- 36 **wonton wrappers**
- ½ **cup buttermilk ranch salad dressing**
- 1 **envelope reduced-sodium chili seasoning mix**
- 1½ **cups shredded rotisserie chicken**
- 1 **cup shredded sharp cheddar cheese**
   Sour cream and sliced green onions, optional

1. Preheat oven to 350°. Press wonton wrappers into greased miniature muffin cups. Bake until lightly browned, 4-6 minutes.
2. Mix the salad dressing and seasoning mix; add chicken and toss to coat. Spoon 1 Tbsp. filling into each wonton cup. Sprinkle with cheese.
3. Bake until heated through and wrappers are golden brown,

8-10 minutes longer. Serve warm. If desired, top with sour cream and green onions.

1 appetizer: 67 cal., 3g fat (1g sat. fat), 10mg chol., 126mg sod., 6g carb. (0 sugars, 0 fiber), 3g pro.

Mini Reuben Cups: Prepare and bake wonton cups as directed. Mix ½ pound chopped deli corned beef, ½ cup sauerkraut (rinsed and well drained), and ½ cup Thousand Island salad dressing; spoon into wonton cups. Sprinkle with 1 cup shredded Swiss cheese. Bake as directed.

SMOKED SAUSAGE APPETIZERS

A tangy sauce with a touch of currant jelly glazes these miniature sausages. They're an excellent party starter. Make a big batch because they won't last long!
—Kathryn Bainbridge, Pennsylvania Furnace, PA

Takes: 25 min. • **Makes:** 6½ dozen

- ¾ **cup red currant jelly**
- ¾ **cup barbecue sauce**
- 3 **Tbsp. prepared mustard**
- 1 **pkg. (28 oz.) miniature smoked sausages**

In a large saucepan, combine jelly, barbecue sauce and mustard. Cook, uncovered, over medium heat until blended, 15-20 minutes, stirring occasionally. Stir in the sausages; cook, covered, until heated through, about 5 minutes.
3 sausages: 106 cal., 7g fat (3g sat. fat), 17mg chol., 345mg sod., 6g carb. (6g sugars, 0 fiber), 4g pro.

BLUE CHEESE & BACON STUFFED PEPPERS

Grilling is a huge summer highlight for my family. Whenever I put out a plate of these cute little grilled appetizers, people come flocking.
—Tara Cruz, Kersey, CO

Takes: 20 min. • **Makes:** 1 dozen

- 3 **medium sweet yellow, orange or red peppers**
- 4 **oz. cream cheese, softened**
- ½ **cup crumbled blue cheese**
- 3 **bacon strips, cooked and crumbled**
- 1 **green onion, thinly sliced**

1. Cut peppers into quarters. Remove and discard stems and seeds. In a small bowl, mix cream cheese, blue cheese, bacon and green onion until blended.
2. Grill peppers, covered, over medium-high heat or broil 4 in. from heat until slightly charred, 2-3 minutes on each side.
3. Remove peppers from grill; fill each with about 1 Tbsp. of the cheese mixture. Grill until cheese is melted, 2-3 minutes longer.
1 appetizer: 73 cal., 6g fat (3g sat. fat), 17mg chol., 136mg sod., 3g carb. (0 sugars, 0 fiber), 3g pro.

BLUE CHEESE & BACON STUFFED PEPPERS

EASY SMOKED SALMON

EASY SMOKED SALMON

This has become my favorite way to prepare salmon—it's incredibly easy, and yet makes an elegant and impressive appetizer. Set it on a buffet with a selection of crackers, and guests will rave!
—Norma Fell, Boyne City, MI

Prep: 10 min. + marinating
Bake: 35 min. + chilling
Makes: 16 servings

- 1 salmon fillet (about 2 lbs.)
- 2 Tbsp. brown sugar
- 2 tsp. salt
- ½ tsp. pepper
- 1 to 2 Tbsp. liquid smoke
   Capers and lemon wedges, optional

1. Place salmon, skin side down, in an 11x7-in. baking pan coated with cooking spray. Sprinkle with brown sugar, salt and pepper. Drizzle with liquid smoke. Cover and refrigerate for 4-8 hours.
2. Drain and discard liquid. Bake salmon, uncovered, at 350° until the fish flakes easily with a fork, 35-45 minutes. Let cool to room temperature, then cover and refrigerate 8 hours or overnight.
2 oz. cooked salmon: 110 cal., 6g fat (1g sat. fat), 33mg chol., 327mg sod., 2g carb. (0 sugars, 1g fiber), 11g pro. **Diabetic exchanges:** 2 lean meat.

ICED HONEYDEW MINT TEA

ICED HONEYDEW MINT TEA

In this tea, I blend two of my favorite beverages—Moroccan mint tea and honeydew agua fresca—and use fresh mint I grow in the garden on my balcony.
—Sarah Batt Throne, El Cerrito, CA

Takes: 20 min.
Makes: 10 servings

- 4 cups water
- 24 fresh mint leaves
- 8 individual green tea bags
- ⅔ cup sugar
- 5 cups diced honeydew melon, divided
- 3 cups ice cubes, divided
   Additional ice cubes

1. In a large saucepan, bring water to a boil; remove from heat. Add mint leaves and tea bags; steep, covered, 3-5 minutes according to taste, stirring occasionally. Discard mint and tea bags. Stir in sugar.
2. Place 2½ cups of honeydew, 2 cups of tea and 1½ cups of ice in a blender; cover and process until blended. Serve over additional ice. Repeat with the remaining ingredients.
1 cup: 83 cal., 0 fat (0 sat. fat), 0 chol., 15mg sod., 21g carb. (20g sugars, 1g fiber), 0 pro. **Diabetic exchanges:** 1 starch, ½ fruit.

ROASTED SWEET POTATO WEDGES

RASPBERRY-WALNUT BRIE

Just a few ingredients are needed to make this creamy and elegant appetizer. It's perfect for a family movie night or an evening spent with friends. The stone-ground wheat crackers are perfect for this recipe; the flavor won't fight with the sweet-tart fruit jam and the tangy cheese.
—Janet Edwards, Beaverton, OR

Takes: 10 min.
Makes: 16 servings

- ¼ cup seedless raspberry jam
- 2 rounds (8 oz. each) Brie cheese
- 1 pkg. (11½ oz.) stone ground wheat crackers, divided
- ½ cup finely chopped walnuts
- 1 Tbsp. butter, melted

1. In a small microwave-safe bowl, microwave jam on high until melted, 15-20 seconds; brush over the Brie.
2. Crush nine crackers. In a small bowl, combine the cracker crumbs, nuts and butter; press into the jam. Serve with the remaining crackers.
2 Tbsp.: 236 cal., 15g fat (6g sat. fat), 30mg chol., 367mg sod., 18g carb. (5g sugars, 1g fiber), 9g pro.

ROASTED SWEET POTATO WEDGES

Sweet potatoes roasted with curry and smoked paprika delight everybody at our table. Mango chutney makes a tangy dip.
—Maitreyi Jois, Streamwood, IL

Takes: 25 min. • **Makes:** 4 servings

- 2 medium sweet potatoes (about 1 lb.), cut into ½-in. wedges
- 2 Tbsp. olive oil
- 1 tsp. curry powder
- ½ tsp. salt
- ½ tsp. smoked paprika
- ⅛ tsp. coarsely ground pepper

Minced fresh cilantro
Mango chutney, optional

1. Preheat oven to 425°. Place sweet potatoes in a large bowl. Mix oil and seasonings; drizzle over sweet potatoes and toss to coat. Transfer to an ungreased 15x10x1-in. baking pan.
2. Roast 15-20 minutes or until tender, turning occasionally. Sprinkle with cilantro. If desired, serve with chutney.
1 serving: 159 cal., 7g fat (1g sat. fat), 0 chol., 305mg sod., 23g carb. (9g sugars, 3g fiber), 2g pro.
Diabetic exchanges: 1½ starch, 1½ fat.

PEAR-APPLE COCKTAIL

Ah, the memories we made when we went to Hawaii and concocted this delicious drink for our first toast on the island! That makes this recipe special.
—Noelle Appel, Arlington, TX

Takes: 5 min. • **Makes:** 6 servings

- 6 cups unsweetened apple juice, chilled
- ¾ cup pear-flavored vodka, chilled
  Ice cubes
  Cubed fresh pineapple

In a pitcher, mix apple juice and vodka. Serve over ice. Garnish with pineapple.

1 cup: 178 cal., 0 fat (0 sat. fat), 0 chol., 10mg sod., 28g carb. (24g sugars, 1g fiber), 0 pro.

SEAFOOD CHEESE DIP

This cheesy recipe has a nice combination of seafood flavors and clings beautifully to slices of bread. I serve it with toasted French baguettes.
—Michelle Domm, Atlanta, NY

Prep: 15 min. • **Cook:** 1½ hours
Makes: 5 cups

- 1 pkg. (32 oz.) process cheese (Velveeta), cubed
- 2 cans (6 oz. each) lump crabmeat, drained
- 1 can (10 oz.) diced tomatoes and green chiles, undrained
- 1 cup frozen cooked salad shrimp, thawed
  French bread baguettes, sliced and toasted

In a greased 3-qt. slow cooker, combine the process cheese, crabmeat, tomatoes and shrimp. Cover and cook on low until the cheese is melted, 1½-2 hours, stirring occasionally. Serve with baguette slices.
¼ cup: 172 cal., 12g fat (7g sat. fat), 77mg chol., 791mg sod., 4g carb. (3g sugars, 0 fiber), 12g pro.

SEAFOOD CHEESE DIP

RISOTTO BALLS

RISOTTO BALLS

My Italian grandma made these for me when I was growing up. I still ask for them when I visit her, and so do my children. They also freeze well, so I make them ahead of time.
—Gretchen Whelan, San Francisco, CA

Prep: 35 min. • **Bake:** 25 min.
Makes: about 3 dozen

- 1½ cups water
- 1 cup uncooked arborio rice
- 1 tsp. salt
- 2 large eggs, lightly beaten
- ⅔ cup sun-dried tomato pesto
- 2 cups panko (Japanese) bread crumbs, divided
  Marinara sauce, warmed

1. Preheat oven to 375°. In a large saucepan, combine water, rice and salt; bring to a boil. Reduce heat; simmer, covered, until liquid is absorbed and rice is tender, 18-20 minutes. Let rice stand, covered, 10 minutes. Transfer to a large bowl; cool slightly. Add eggs and pesto; stir in 1 cup of the bread crumbs.
2. Place the remaining bread crumbs in a shallow bowl. Shape the rice mixture into 1¼-in. balls. Roll in the bread crumbs, patting to help coating adhere. Place on greased 15x10x1-in. baking pans. Bake until golden brown, 25-30 minutes. Serve risotto balls with marinara sauce.
1 appetizer: 42 cal., 1g fat (0 sat. fat), 10mg chol., 125mg sod., 7g carb. (1g sugars, 0 fiber), 1g pro.
Diabetic exchanges: ½ starch.

WALNUT & FIG GOAT CHEESE LOG

WALNUT & FIG GOAT CHEESE LOG

This simple yet sophisticated spread is so easy to put together. The honey is optional, but the touch of sweetness complements the tang of the goat cheese.
—Ana-Marie Correll, Hollister, CA

Prep: 10 min. + chilling
Makes: 1⅓ cups

- 2 logs (4 oz. each) fresh goat cheese
- 8 dried figs, finely chopped
- ½ cup finely chopped walnuts, toasted, divided
- ¾ tsp. pepper
- 1 Tbsp. honey, optional
  Assorted crackers

In a small bowl, crumble cheese. Stir in figs, ¼ cup of the walnuts, pepper and, if desired, honey. Shape the mixture into a log about 6 in. long. Roll in the remaining walnuts. Refrigerate for 4 hours or overnight. Serve with crackers.
2 Tbsp.: 93 cal., 7g fat (2g sat. fat), 15mg chol., 92mg sod., 6g carb. (3g sugars, 1g fiber), 3g pro.

ROASTED VEGETABLE DIP

STRAWBERRY-BASIL REFRESHER

Fresh strawberries and basil are everywhere in the early summer—put them together in a cooler and its pure sunshine! Garnish with basil leaves and sip it in the shade.
—Carolyn Turner, Reno, NV

Takes: 10 min.
Makes: 12 servings

⅔ cup lemon juice
½ cup sugar
1 cup sliced fresh strawberries
  Ice cubes
1 to 2 Tbsp. chopped fresh basil
1 bottle (1 liter) club soda, chilled

1. Place the lemon juice, sugar, strawberries and 1 cup of ice cubes in a blender; cover and process until blended. Add basil; pulse 1 or 2 times to combine.
2. Divide the strawberry mixture between 12 cocktail glasses. Fill with ice; top with club soda.
1 serving: 40 cal., 0 fat (0 sat. fat), 0 chol., 18mg sod., 10g carb. (9g sugars, 0 fiber), 0 pro.
Diabetic exchanges: ½ starch.

TEST KITCHEN TIP
In ice cube tray squares, place strawberries or fresh basil leaves, or petals from flowers such as pansies or roses that have not been treated with chemicals. Cover with water and freeze. Ta-da! Beautiful ice.

ROASTED VEGETABLE DIP

While my children were always good eaters, I came up with this recipe to get them to eat more veggies and like it. Roasted veggies account for more than half the volume of this dip, which means fewer calories, less saturated fat and more nutrients—not to mention amazing flavor. The dip never lasts long in our house!
—Sarah Vasques, Milford, NH

Prep: 15 min.
Bake: 25 min. + cooling
Makes: 20 servings

2 large sweet red peppers
1 large zucchini
1 medium onion
1 Tbsp. olive oil
½ tsp. salt
¼ tsp. pepper
1 pkg. (8 oz.) reduced-fat cream cheese
  Assorted crackers or fresh vegetables

1. Preheat oven to 425°. Cut vegetables into 1-in. pieces. Place in a 15x10x1-in. baking pan coated with cooking spray; toss with oil, salt and pepper. Roast until tender, stirring occasionally, 25-30 minutes. Cool completely.
2. Place the cooled vegetables and cream cheese in a food processor; process until blended. Transfer to a bowl; refrigerate, covered, until serving. Serve with crackers or fresh vegetables.
2 Tbsp. dip: 44 cal., 3g fat (2g sat. fat), 8mg chol., 110mg sod., 3g carb. (2g sugars, 1g fiber), 2g pro.

TERIYAKI SALMON BUNDLES

I serve these little salmon bundles on skewers for easy dipping. For a lovely presentation, stand them in a small vase filled with table salt.
—Diane Halferty,
Corpus Christi, TX

Prep: 30 min. • **Bake:** 20 min.
Makes: 32 appetizers
(¾ cup sauce)

- 4 **Tbsp. reduced-sodium teriyaki sauce, divided**
- ½ **tsp. grated lemon zest**
- 2 **Tbsp. lemon juice**
- 1¼ **lbs. salmon fillet, cut into 1-in. cubes**
- 1 **pkg. (17.3 oz.) frozen puff pastry, thawed**
- ⅔ **cup orange marmalade**

1. Preheat oven to 400°. In a large bowl, whisk 2 Tbsp. teriyaki sauce, lemon zest and lemon juice. Add salmon; toss to coat. Marinate at room temperature 20 minutes.
2. Drain salmon, discarding the marinade. Unfold puff pastry. Cut each sheet lengthwise into ½-in.-wide strips; cut crosswise in half. Overlap two strips of pastry, forming an X. Place a salmon cube in the center of the X. Wrap the pastry over the salmon; pinch ends to seal. Place on a greased baking sheet, seam side down. Repeat with remaining salmon and pastry. Bake until golden brown, 18-20 minutes.
3. In a small bowl, mix marmalade and the remaining teriyaki. Serve with the salmon bundles.

1 appetizer with about 1 tsp. sauce: 120 cal., 6g fat (1g sat. fat), 9mg chol., 93mg sod., 13g carb. (4g sugars, 1g fiber), 4g pro.

TERIYAKI SALMON
BUNDLES

SLOPPY JOE NACHOS

SLOPPY JOE NACHOS

When my kids were little, they adored this snack they could eat with their fingers. It makes a great quick meal, tailgate food or just a simple treat when you have the munchies.
—Janet Rhoden, Hortonville, WI

Takes: 15 min. • **Makes:** 6 servings

- 1 lb. ground beef
- 1 can (15½ oz.) sloppy joe sauce
- 1 pkg. (12 oz.) tortilla chips

- ¾ cup shredded cheddar cheese
- ¼ cup sliced ripe olives, optional

1. In a large skillet, cook the beef over medium heat until no longer pink; drain. Add sloppy joe sauce; cook, uncovered, for 5 minutes or until heated through.
2. Arrange the chips on a serving plate. Top with meat mixture, cheese and, if desired, olives.
1 serving: 482 cal., 23g fat (8g sat. fat), 52mg chol., 790mg sod., 45g carb. (5g sugars, 3g fiber), 21g pro.

SAVORY POTATO SKINS

For a simple hot snack on your party buffet, put together a plate of these crisp potato skins.
—Andrea Holcomb, Torrington, CT

Prep: 1¼ hours • **Broil:** 5 min.
Makes: 32 appetizers

- 4 large baking potatoes (about 12 oz. each)
- 3 Tbsp. butter, melted
- 1 tsp. salt
- 1 tsp. garlic powder
- 1 tsp. paprika
  Sour cream and chives, optional

1. Preheat oven to 375°. Scrub potatoes; pierce several times with a fork. Place on a greased baking sheet; bake until tender, 1-1¼ hours. Cool slightly.
2. Cut each potato lengthwise in half. Scoop out pulp, leaving ¼-in.-thick shells (save the pulp for another use).
3. Cut each half shell lengthwise into quarters; return to the baking sheet. Brush insides of each shell with butter. Mix the seasonings; sprinkle over buttered shells.
4. Broil 4-5 in. from heat until golden brown, 5-8 minutes. If desired, mix the sour cream and chives and serve with the potato skins.
1 potato skin: 56 cal., 2g fat (1g sat. fat), 6mg chol., 168mg sod., 8g carb. (0 sugars, 1g fiber), 1g pro.

TOASTED RAVIOLI PUFFS

TOASTED RAVIOLI PUFFS

I call toasted ravioli a fan favorite because it always disappears faster than I can make it. This is how you get the party started—with just five ingredients!
—Kathy Morgan, Temecula, CA

Takes: 30 min. • **Makes:** 2 dozen

- 24 refrigerated cheese ravioli
- 1 Tbsp. reduced-fat Italian salad dressing
- 1 Tbsp. Italian-style panko (Japanese) bread crumbs
- 1 Tbsp. grated Parmesan cheese
  Warm marinara sauce

1. Preheat oven to 400°. Cook ravioli according to the package directions; drain. Transfer to a greased baking sheet. Brush with the salad dressing. In a small bowl, mix the bread crumbs and cheese; sprinkle over the ravioli.
2. Bake until ravioli are golden brown, 12-15 minutes. Serve with marinara sauce.
1 ravioli: 21 cal., 1g fat (0 sat. fat), 3mg chol., 43mg sod., 3g carb. (0 sugars, 0 fiber), 1g pro.

SWEDISH ROSÉ SPRITZ

This blushing springtime spritz pairs the delicate flavors of lemon and elderflower liqueur.
—*Taste of Home* Test Kitchen

Takes: 5 min. • **Makes:** 1 serving

- 3 oz. dry rosé wine
- 1 oz. elderflower liqueur
  Lemon seltzer water

Fill a wine glass or tumbler three-fourths full of ice. Add the wine and elderflower liqueur. Top with a splash of lemon seltzer; stir gently.
Note: For testing, we used St-Germain Elderflower Liqueur.
1 serving: 189 cal., 0 fat (0 sat. fat), 0 chol., 7mg sod., 19g carb. (14g sugars, 0 fiber), 0 pro.

SAUSAGE PINWHEELS

These spirals are simple to make but look so special on a buffet. Our guests eagerly help themselves— and sometimes the eye-catching pinwheels never even make it to their plates!
—Gail Sykora, Menomonee Falls, WI

Takes: 30 min. • **Makes:** 1 dozen

- 1   tube (8 oz.) refrigerated crescent rolls
- ½   lb. uncooked bulk pork sausage
- 2   Tbsp. minced chives

1. Preheat the oven to 375°. Unroll the crescent dough onto a lightly floured surface; press the perforations to seal. Roll into a 14x10-in. rectangle.
2. Spread the sausage to within ½ in. of edges. Sprinkle with chives. Roll up carefully jelly-roll style, starting with a long side; pinch seam to seal. Cut into 12 slices; place 1 in. apart in an ungreased 15x10x1-in. pan.
3. Bake until golden brown and the sausage is cooked through, 12-16 minutes.

1 pinwheel: 132 cal., 9g fat (3g sat. fat), 13mg chol., 293mg sod., 8g carb. (1g sugars, 0 fiber), 4g pro.

FONTINA ASPARAGUS TART

This lemony tart is loaded with fontina cheese and fresh asparagus. Be advised...your guests will be vying for the last tasty slice.
—Heidi Meek, Grand Rapids, MI

Prep: 15 min. • **Bake:** 20 min.
Makes: 16 servings

- 1   lb. fresh asparagus, trimmed
- 1   sheet frozen puff pastry, thawed
- 2   cups shredded fontina cheese
- 1   tsp. grated lemon zest
- 2   Tbsp. lemon juice
- 1   Tbsp. olive oil
- ¼   tsp. salt
- ¼   tsp. pepper

1. Preheat oven to 400°. In a large skillet, bring 1 in. of water to a boil; add asparagus. Cook, covered, until crisp-tender, 3-5 minutes. Drain and pat dry.
2. On a lightly floured surface, roll pastry sheet into a 16x12-in. rectangle. Transfer pastry to a parchment-lined large baking sheet. Bake until golden brown, about 10 minutes.
3. Sprinkle 1½ cups cheese over the pastry to within ½ in. of the edges. Place the asparagus over top; sprinkle with the remaining cheese. Mix the remaining ingredients; drizzle over top. Bake until the cheese is melted, 10-15 minutes. Serve warm.

1 piece: 142 cal., 9g fat (4g sat. fat), 16mg chol., 202mg sod., 10g carb. (1g sugars, 1g fiber), 5g pro.

SAUSAGE PINWHEELS

SALADS

& DRESSINGS

MINTY WATERMELON SALAD
P. 60

1

2

3

ATHENOS
FETA
CHEESE
CRUMBLED
TRADITIONAL

4

5

Reese
DOUBLE MARTINI
Sour Cocktail
Onions

QUICK AND TASTY, FRESH AND
DELICIOUS, THESE SALADS AND
HOMEMADE DRESSINGS ARE JUST THE
THING AS A MAIN COURSE OR A SIDE!

**BALSAMIC
CUCUMBER SALAD**

MINTY WATERMELON SALAD

(PICTURED ON P. 58)

My twin grandchildren love to cook with me. Last summer, the three of us were experimenting with watermelon and cheese, and that's where this recipe began. It's great for picnics, neighborhood gatherings or as a healthy snack on a hot summer day.
—Gwendolyn Vetter, Rogers, MN

Prep: 20 min. + chilling
Makes: 8 servings

6 cups cubed watermelon
½ cup thinly sliced fennel bulb
⅓ cup crumbled feta cheese
2 Tbsp. minced fresh mint
2 Tbsp. thinly sliced pickled onions
½ tsp. pepper

In a large bowl, combine all the ingredients. Refrigerate, covered, for at least 1 hour.
¾ cup: 45 cal., 1g fat (1g sat. fat), 2mg chol., 65mg sod., 11g carb. (10g sugars, 1g fiber), 1g pro.
Diabetic exchanges: ½ fruit.

BALSAMIC CUCUMBER SALAD

This fast, fresh salad makes for an easygoing side dish for kabobs, chicken or anything else that's hot off the grill.
—Blair Lonergan, Rochelle, VA

Takes: 15 min. • **Makes:** 6 servings

1 large English cucumber, halved and sliced
2 cups grape tomatoes, halved
1 medium red onion, halved and thinly sliced
½ cup balsamic vinaigrette
¾ cup crumbled reduced-fat feta cheese

In a large bowl, combine the cucumber, tomatoes and onion. Add vinaigrette; toss to coat. Refrigerate, covered, until serving. Just before serving, stir in cheese. Serve with a slotted spoon.
¾ cup: 90 cal., 5g fat (1g sat. fat), 5mg chol., 356mg sod., 9g carb. (5g sugars, 1g fiber), 4g pro.
Diabetic exchanges: 1 vegetable, 1 fat.

CUCUMBER & RED ONION SALAD

My go-to salad for parties and picnics uses the bumper crop of cucumbers from my garden. I pile it on sandwiches and burgers, too.
—Brynn Steckman,
New Albany, OH

Prep: 15 min. + chilling
Makes: 4 servings

- 2 small English cucumbers, thinly sliced
- 1 cup thinly sliced red onion
- 2 Tbsp. white wine vinegar or rice vinegar
- 1 Tbsp. white vinegar
- ¼ tsp. salt
- ¼ tsp. pepper
- ¼ tsp. sesame oil

Place all the ingredients in a bowl; toss to combine. Refrigerate, covered, for about 1 hour. Serve with a slotted spoon.
¾ cup: 31 cal., 0 fat (0 sat. fat), 0 chol., 151mg sod., 7g carb. (2g sugars, 1g fiber), 1g pro.
Diabetic exchanges: 1 vegetable.

**CUCUMBER &
RED ONION SALAD**

ITALIAN HERB SALAD DRESSING

I like to keep this delicious dressing on hand for topping a variety of salad greens.
—Dan Wright, San Jose, CA

Takes: 5 min. • **Makes:** 10 servings

- ¾ cup olive oil
- ½ cup red wine vinegar
- 1 Tbsp. grated Parmesan or Romano cheese
- 1 garlic clove, minced
- ½ tsp. salt
- ½ tsp. sugar
- ½ tsp. dried oregano
  Pinch pepper

Place all the ingredients in a jar with a tight-fitting lid; shake well. Refrigerate until serving. Shake dressing again just before serving.
2 Tbsp.: 150 cal., 16g fat (2g sat. fat), 0 chol., 127mg sod., 1g carb. (0 sugars, 0 fiber), 0 pro. **Diabetic exchanges:** 3 fat.

JEWELED ENDIVE SALAD

My friends have a huge potluck party every year at Christmas. I wanted to bring something distinctive, so I topped off endive and watercress with jewel-toned pomegranate seeds.
—Alysha Braun, St. Catharines, ON

Takes: 15 min. • **Makes:** 8 servings

- 1 bunch watercress (4 oz.)
- 2 heads endive, halved lengthwise and thinly sliced
- 1 cup pomegranate seeds (about 1 pomegranate)
- 1 shallot, thinly sliced

DRESSING
- ⅓ cup olive oil
- 3 Tbsp. lemon juice
- 2 tsp. grated lemon zest
- ¼ tsp. salt
- ⅛ tsp. pepper

1. In a large bowl, combine the watercress, endive, pomegranate seeds and shallot.
2. In a small bowl, whisk the dressing ingredients. Drizzle over the salad; toss to coat.
1 cup: 121 cal., 9g fat (1g sat. fat), 0 chol., 109mg sod., 9g carb. (4g sugars, 4g fiber), 2g pro. **Diabetic exchanges:** 2 fat, 1 vegetable.

ITALIAN HERB SALAD DRESSING

**JEWELED
ENDIVE SALAD**

JICAMA CITRUS SALAD

Jicama is a crunchy Mexican turnip I use in this salad with tangerines and shallots. The sweet and sour flavors, the crunch, it's all yum!
—Crystal Jo Bruns, Iliff, CO

Takes: 15 min.
Makes: 10 servings

8   tangerines, peeled, quartered and sliced
1   lb. medium jicama, peeled and cubed
2   shallots, thinly sliced
2   Tbsp. lemon or lime juice
¼   cup chopped fresh cilantro
½   tsp. salt
½   tsp. pepper

Combine all the ingredients in a bowl; refrigerate until serving.

¾ cup: 76 cal., 0 fat (0 sat. fat), 0 chol., 123mg sod., 19g carb. (11g sugars, 4g fiber), 1g pro. **Diabetic exchanges:** 1 vegetable, ½ fruit.

LOW-FAT TANGY TOMATO DRESSING

This zesty blend is delicious over greens, pasta or fresh garden vegetables. I love that it's a healthier alternative to the oil-heavy versions sold in stores.
—Sarah Eiden, Enid, OK

Takes: 5 min. • **Makes:** 2 cups

1 can (14½ oz.) no-salt-added diced tomatoes, undrained
1 envelope Italian salad dressing mix
1 Tbsp. cider vinegar
1 Tbsp. olive oil

Place all ingredients in a blender; cover and process until blended.
2 Tbsp.: 15 cal., 1g fat (0 sat. fat), 0 chol., 170mg sod., 2g carb. (1g sugars, 0 fiber), 0 pro.

LOW-FAT TANGY TOMATO DRESSING

CUCUMBER SHELL SALAD

Ranch dressing is the mild coating for this pleasant pasta salad full of crunchy cucumber, onion and green peas. Wherever I take it, I'm always asked for the recipe.
—Paula Ishii, Ralston, NE

Prep: 20 min. + chilling
Makes: 16 servings

1 pkg. (16 oz.) medium pasta shells
1 pkg. (16 oz.) frozen peas, thawed
1 medium cucumber, halved and sliced
1 small red onion, chopped
1 cup ranch salad dressing

Cook pasta according to package directions; drain and rinse in cold water. In a large bowl, combine the pasta, peas, cucumber and onion. Add dressing; toss to coat. Cover and chill for at least 2 hours before serving.
¾ cup: 165 cal., 1g fat (0 sat. fat), 0 chol., 210mg sod., 33g carb. (0 sugars, 3g fiber), 6g pro.
Diabetic exchanges: 2 starch.

TEST KITCHEN TIP
If you'd prefer to seed the cucumber before slicing it for this salad, a melon baller makes the task quick and painless.

ASPARAGUS
NICOISE SALAD

ASPARAGUS NICOISE SALAD

I've used my Nicoise as both an appetizer and a main-dish salad, and it's a winner every time I put it on the table. Here's to a colorful, do-ahead sure thing.
—Jan Meyer, St. Paul, MN

Takes: 20 min. • **Makes:** 4 servings

- 1 lb. small red potatoes (about 10), halved
- 1 lb. fresh asparagus, trimmed and halved crosswise
- 3 pouches (2½ oz. each) albacore white tuna in water
- ½ cup pitted Greek olives, halved, optional
- ½ cup zesty Italian salad dressing

1. Place the potatoes in a large saucepan; add water to cover by 2 in. Bring to a boil. Reduce heat; cook, uncovered, until tender, 10-12 minutes, adding asparagus during the last 2-4 minutes of cooking. Drain the potatoes and asparagus; immediately drop into ice water.

2. Drain potatoes and asparagus; pat dry and divide among four plates. Add tuna and, if desired, olives. Drizzle with dressing.

1 serving: 233 cal., 8g fat (0 sat. fat), 22mg chol., 583mg sod., 23g carb. (4g sugars, 3g fiber), 16g pro. **Diabetic exchanges:** 2 lean meat, 1½ starch, 1½ fat, 1 vegetable.

CUCUMBERS WITH DRESSING

CUCUMBERS WITH DRESSING

It wouldn't be summer if Mom didn't make lots of these creamy cucumbers. Just a few simple ingredients dress up slices of this crisp garden vegetable.
—Michelle Beran, Claflin, KS

Prep: 10 min. + chilling
Makes: 6 servings

- 1 cup mayonnaise
- ¼ cup sugar
- ¼ cup white vinegar
- ¼ tsp. salt
- 4 cups thinly sliced cucumbers

In a large bowl, mix first four ingredients; toss with cucumbers. Refrigerate, covered, 2 hours.

¾ cup: 283 cal., 27g fat (4g sat. fat), 3mg chol., 286mg sod., 11g carb. (10g sugars, 0 fiber), 0 pro.

★ ★ ★ ★ ★ **READER REVIEW**

"My grandmother made her cucumber salad with sour cream. When I saw this recipe using mayonnaise instead, I just had to try it. I'm so glad I did! Five stars for sure!"

BICKTASW TASTEOFHOME.COM

ROASTED RED POTATO SALAD

2. Transfer to a large bowl; add onion, eggs, bacon, mayonnaise, salt and pepper. Toss to coat. Cover and refrigerate for several hours or overnight. If desired, sprinkle with paprika and parsley.

1 serving: 355 cal., 27g fat (5g sat. fat), 120mg chol., 412mg sod., 20g carb. (3g sugars, 2g fiber), 7g pro.

EASY ASIAN-STYLE CHICKEN SLAW

The very first time I made this chicken dish, I knew it was a winner because the bowl came back to the kitchen scraped clean.
—Bess Blanco, Vail, AZ

Takes: 15 min. • **Makes:** 8 servings

- 1 pkg. (3 oz.) ramen noodles
- 1 rotisserie chicken, skin removed, shredded
- 1 pkg. (16 oz.) coleslaw mix
- 6 green onions, finely chopped
- 1 cup reduced-fat Asian toasted sesame salad dressing

Discard the seasoning packet from the noodles or save for another use. Break the noodles into small pieces; place in a large bowl. Add chicken, coleslaw mix and green onions. Drizzle with salad dressing; toss to coat.

1½ cups: 267 cal., 10g fat (3g sat. fat), 70mg chol., 405mg sod., 18g carb. (8g sugars, 2g fiber), 26g pro. **Diabetic exchanges:** 3 lean meat, 1 starch, ½ fat.

ROASTED RED POTATO SALAD

I learned how to cook from the two best cooks I know—my mom, Arline, and my Grandma Etta. I got this recipe from my sister-in-law. It's quick and easy, just what I need in my busy life!
—Ginger Cusano, Sandusky, OH

Prep: 40 min. + chilling
Makes: 8 servings

- 2 lbs. red potatoes, cut into 1-in. cubes
- 1 medium onion, chopped
- 4 large hard-boiled eggs, sliced
- 6 bacon strips, cooked and crumbled
- 1 cup mayonnaise
- ½ tsp. salt
- ¼ tsp. pepper
  Paprika and minced fresh parsley, optional

1. Preheat oven to 400°. Place potatoes in a greased 15x10x1-in. baking pan. Bake, uncovered, until tender and golden brown, stirring occasionally, 25-30 minutes. Cool for 15 minutes.

WATERMELON-BLUEBERRY SALAD

People love the combination of flavors in the dressing that tops this seasonal fruit salad. It's so refreshing on a hot summer evening.

—Jenni Sharp, Milwaukee, WI

Takes: 5 min. • **Makes:** 2 servings

1 Tbsp. honey
¾ tsp. lemon juice
½ tsp. minced fresh mint
1 cup seeded chopped watermelon
½ cup fresh blueberries

In a small bowl, combine the honey, lemon juice and mint. Add watermelon and blueberries; toss gently to coat. Chill until serving.

¾ cup: 78 cal., 0 fat (0 sat. fat), 0 chol., 2mg sod., 20g carb. (17g sugars, 1g fiber), 1g pro. **Diabetic exchanges:** 1 fruit, ½ starch.

✳

TEST KITCHEN TIP
A curved grapefruit knife is the best tool for removing the rind from slices of watermelon.

WATERMELON-BLUEBERRY SALAD

**SHREDDED KALE &
BRUSSELS SPROUTS
SALAD**

SHREDDED KALE & BRUSSELS SPROUTS SALAD

This salad gets even better in the fridge, so I make it ahead. I use honey mustard dressing, but any type works fine.
—Alexandra Weisser,
New York, NY

Takes: 15 min. • **Makes:** 6 servings

- 1 small bunch kale (about 8 oz.), stemmed and thinly sliced (about 6 cups)
- ½ lb. fresh Brussels sprouts, thinly sliced (about 3 cups)
- ½ cup pistachios, coarsely chopped
- ½ cup honey mustard salad dressing
- ¼ cup shredded Parmesan cheese

Toss together all ingredients.
1 cup: 207 cal., 14g fat (2g sat. fat), 8mg chol., 235mg sod., 16g carb. (5g sugars, 4g fiber), 7g pro.
Diabetic exchanges: 3 fat, 2 vegetable, ½ starch.

RED POTATO SALAD DIJON

My mother made the best warm potato salad, and now it's a tradition at all our tables. I'll sometimes use Yukon Gold potatoes to make it even prettier.
—Patricia Swart, Galloway, NJ

Prep: 25 min. • **Cook:** 15 min.
Makes: 12 servings

- 3½ lbs. red potatoes (about 12 medium), cubed
- ¼ cup Dijon-mayonnaise blend
- 3 Tbsp. seasoned rice vinegar
- 3 Tbsp. olive oil
- 4 tsp. minced fresh tarragon
- 1½ tsp. salt
- ¾ tsp. pepper
- 6 green onions, thinly sliced

1. Place potatoes in a Dutch oven; add water to cover. Bring to a boil. Reduce heat; cook, uncovered, 10-15 minutes or until tender. Drain; transfer to a large bowl.
2. In a small bowl, mix mayonnaise blend, rice vinegar, oil, tarragon, salt and pepper. Drizzle over the potatoes; toss to coat. Gently stir in green onions. Serve warm. Refrigerate leftovers.
¾ cup: 139 cal., 4g fat (1g sat. fat), 0 chol., 557mg sod., 24g carb. (3g sugars, 2g fiber), 3g pro.
Diabetic exchanges: 1½ starch, 1 fat.

RED POTATO
SALAD DIJON

SWIFT STRAWBERRY SALAD

SWIFT STRAWBERRY SALAD

A simple blend of syrup, orange juice and caramel topping forms the light dressing for fresh berries and crunchy cashews.
—*Taste of Home* Test Kitchen

Takes: 10 min. • **Makes:** 6 servings

- 4 **cups sliced fresh strawberries**
- 2 **Tbsp. caramel ice cream topping**
- 2 **Tbsp. maple syrup**
- 1 **Tbsp. orange juice**
- ⅓ **cup salted cashew halves**

Place strawberries in a large bowl. Mix caramel topping, syrup and orange juice; drizzle over the strawberries. Top with cashews.
⅔ cup: 116 cal., 4g fat (1g sat. fat), 0 chol., 59mg sod., 20g carb. (14g sugars, 3g fiber), 2g pro.

ORANGE & ONION SALAD

I serve this refreshing dish year-round. The almonds in the salad give it extra flair.
—Jean Ann Perkins, Newburyport, MD

Prep: 10 min. + chilling
Makes: 4 servings

- 1 **head Boston lettuce, separated into leaves**
- 1 **medium red onion, thinly sliced into rings**
- 1 **can (11 oz.) mandarin oranges, drained**
  Sliced almonds
  Bottled poppy seed dressing

Arrange the lettuce leaves, onion and oranges on salad plates. Chill. Just before serving, sprinkle with almonds. Serve with poppy seed dressing.
1 cup: 77 cal., 0 fat (0 sat. fat), 0 chol., 19mg sod., 19g carb. (16g sugars, 3g fiber), 2g pro.

BACON-TOMATO SALAD

This wonderful salad tastes like a piled-high BLT without the time, effort or carbs. Plus, you can make it hours ahead and keep it in the fridge until serving time.

—Denise Thurman, Columbia, MO

Takes: 15 min. • **Makes:** 6 servings

- 1   pkg. (12 oz.) iceberg lettuce blend
- 2   cups grape tomatoes, halved
- ¾   cup coleslaw salad dressing
- ¾   cup shredded cheddar cheese
- 12 bacon strips, cooked and crumbled

In a large bowl, combine the lettuce blend and the tomatoes. Drizzle with dressing; sprinkle with cheese and bacon.

1¼ cups: 268 cal., 20g fat (6g sat. fat), 41mg chol., 621mg sod., 11g carb. (9g sugars, 1g fiber), 10g pro.

★ ★ ★ ★ ★ **READER REVIEW**

"Great and easy to make! We had this with grilled chicken for lunch. I will definitely be making it again."

DVIERZEN TASTEOFHOME.COM

LEMONY ZUCCHINI RIBBONS

Fresh zucchini gets a shave and a drizzle of lemony goodness in this fabulous salad. Sprinkle on the goat cheese or feta and dive right in.

—Ellie Martin Cliffe, Milwaukee, WI

Takes: 15 min. • **Makes:** 4 servings

- 1   Tbsp. olive oil
- ½   tsp. grated lemon zest
- 1   Tbsp. lemon juice
- ½   tsp. salt
- ¼   tsp. pepper
- 3   medium zucchini
- ⅓   cup crumbled goat or feta cheese

1. For the dressing, in a small bowl, mix the first five ingredients. Using a vegetable peeler, shave zucchini lengthwise into very thin slices; arrange on a serving plate.
2. To serve, drizzle with dressing and toss lightly to coat. Top with crumbled cheese.

¾ cup: 83 cal., 6g fat (2g sat. fat), 12mg chol., 352mg sod., 5g carb. (3g sugars, 2g fiber), 3g pro.
Diabetic exchanges: 1 vegetable, 1 fat.

BACON-TOMATO SALAD

NECTARINE
& BEET SALAD

NECTARINE & BEET SALAD

Sliced beets and nectarines sprinkled with feta cheese make a scrumptious new blend for a mixed green salad. It may sound like an unlikely combination, but I guarantee it will become one of your favorite salads.
—Nicole Werner, Ann Arbor, MI

Takes: 10 min. • **Makes:** 8 servings

- 2 pkg. (5 oz. each) spring mix salad greens
- 2 medium nectarines, sliced
- ½ cup balsamic vinaigrette
- 1 can (14½ oz.) sliced beets, drained
- ½ cup crumbled feta cheese

CANDY BAR APPLE SALAD

On a serving dish, toss greens and nectarines with vinaigrette. Top with beets and cheese; serve immediately.
1 cup: 84 cal., 4g fat (1g sat. fat), 4mg chol., 371mg sod., 10g carb. (6g sugars, 3g fiber), 3g pro.
Diabetic exchanges: 2 vegetable, ½ fat.

CANDY BAR APPLE SALAD

This creamy, sweet Snickers salad with crisp apple crunch is amazing. The recipe makes a lot, which is good, because it will go fast!
—Cyndi Fynaardt, Oskaloosa, IA

Takes: 15 min.
Makes: 12 servings

- 1½ cups cold 2% milk
- 1 pkg. (3.4 oz.) instant vanilla pudding mix
- 1 carton (8 oz.) frozen whipped topping, thawed
- 4 large apples, chopped (about 6 cups)
- 4 Snickers candy bars (1.86 oz. each), cut into ½-in. pieces

In a large bowl, whisk the milk and pudding mix for 2 minutes. Let stand until soft-set, about 2 minutes. Fold in the whipped topping. Fold in apples and candy bars. Refrigerate until serving.
¾ cup: 218 cal., 9g fat (6g sat. fat), 6mg chol., 174mg sod., 31g carb. (24g sugars, 2g fiber), 3g pro.

✱ TEST KITCHEN TIP
Use crisp, tart apples like Granny Smiths to balance the sweetness in this salad. For a pretty presentation and extra crunch, sprinkle chopped peanuts over the top.

SALAMI & PROVOLONE PASTA SALAD

toss to coat. Refrigerate, covered, for at least 1 hour. If desired, stir in some additional dressing to moisten and sprinkle with basil before serving.

¾ cup: 244 cal., 12g fat (5g sat. fat), 24mg chol., 575mg sod., 23g carb. (2g sugars, 1g fiber), 11g pro.

LEMON DIJON DRESSING

With lemon juice and Dijon mustard, this super fast dressing has a nice tang that's balanced by a hint of sweetness. Try it on a spinach salad or mixed greens with cucumber and tomatoes.
—Bryan Braack, Eldridge, IA

Takes: 10 min.
Makes: about 1 cup

- ½ cup lemon juice
- ⅓ cup light corn syrup
- ¼ cup canola oil
- 1 Tbsp. finely chopped red onion
- 2 tsp. Dijon mustard
- ½ tsp. salt

Place all the ingredients in a jar with a tight-fitting lid; shake well. Just before serving, shake the dressing and drizzle over salad; toss to coat.

2 Tbsp.: 94 cal., 6g fat (0 sat. fat), 0 chol., 165mg sod., 11g carb. (4g sugars, 0 fiber), 0 pro.

SALAMI & PROVOLONE PASTA SALAD

This quick and easy pasta salad has all the flavors of your favorite Italian sub! It's the perfect dish when you want something that's fast, light and cool.
—Jill Donley, Warsaw, IN

Prep: 25 min. + chilling
Makes: 8 servings

- 3 cups uncooked cellentani pasta or elbow macaroni
- 1 medium sweet red pepper, chopped
- 4 oz. provolone cheese, cubed (about 1 cup)
- 4 oz. hard salami, cubed (about 1 cup)
- ⅓ cup prepared Italian salad dressing
  Additional Italian salad dressing and minced fresh basil, optional

1. Cook pasta according to the package directions. Meanwhile, in a large bowl, combine pepper, cheese and salami.
2. Drain pasta and rinse in cold water. Add to the pepper mixture. Drizzle with ⅓ cup dressing and

ROASTED GREEN BEAN SALAD

A tangy dill and Dijon vinaigrette coats crisp-tender beans without overpowering them so the flavor comes through.
—Kathy Shell, San Diego, CA

Prep: 10 min. • **Bake:** 30 min.
Makes: 6 servings

- 2 lbs. fresh green beans, trimmed
- 3 Tbsp. olive oil, divided
- ¾ tsp. salt, divided
- 2 Tbsp. white wine vinegar
- 2 Tbsp. snipped fresh dill or 2 tsp. dill weed
- 1½ tsp. Dijon mustard
- 1½ tsp. sugar
- ¼ tsp. pepper

1. Preheat oven to 400°. In a large bowl, toss beans with 1 Tbsp. oil and ½ tsp. salt. Place beans in a single layer on two ungreased 15x10x1-in. baking pans.
2. Roast 30-35 minutes or until the beans are tender and lightly browned, stirring occasionally.
3. In a small bowl, whisk vinegar, dill, mustard, sugar, pepper and the remaining oil and salt until blended. Transfer the beans to a large bowl. Drizzle with vinaigrette and toss to coat.

1 serving: 108 cal., 7g fat (1g sat. fat), 0 chol., 335mg sod., 11g carb. (4g sugars, 5g fiber), 3g pro.
Diabetic exchanges: 1½ fat, 1 vegetable.

ROASTED GREEN BEAN SALAD

BASIL VINAIGRETTE

MANGO & GRILLED CHICKEN SALAD

We live in the hot South, and this fruity chicken salad is a weeknight standout. I buy salad greens and add veggies for color and crunch.
—Sherry Little, Sherwood, AR

Takes: 25 min. • **Makes:** 4 servings

- 1 lb. chicken tenderloins
- ½ tsp. salt
- ¼ tsp. pepper

SALAD

- 6 cups torn mixed salad greens
- ¼ cup raspberry or balsamic vinaigrette
- 1 medium mango, peeled and cubed
- 1 cup fresh sugar snap peas, halved lengthwise

1. Toss the chicken with salt and pepper. Grill chicken, covered, on an oiled grill over medium heat or broil 4 in. from the heat on each side or until no longer pink, 3-4 minutes. Cut into 1-in. pieces.
2. Divide the greens among four plates; drizzle with vinaigrette. Top with chicken, mango and peas; serve immediately.
1 serving: 210 cal., 2g fat (0 sat. fat), 56mg chol., 447mg sod., 22g carb. (16g sugars, 4g fiber), 30g pro. **Diabetic exchanges:** 3 lean meat, 2 vegetable, ½ starch, ½ fat.

BASIL VINAIGRETTE

This delicate dressing lets the goodness of fresh spring greens shine. It's excellent drizzled over ripe tomatoes.
—Vivian Haen, Menomonee Falls, WI

Takes: 10 min. • **Makes:** ¼ cup

- ¼ cup olive oil
- 4½ tsp. red wine vinegar
- ¼ tsp. ground mustard
- ¼ tsp. dried basil
- ⅛ tsp. garlic powder
  Salt and pepper to taste

In a jar with a tight-fitting lid, combine all ingredients; shake well. Serve over salad greens.
2 Tbsp.: 241 cal., 27g fat (4g sat. fat), 0 chol., 1mg sod., 1g carb. (0 sugars, 0 fiber), 0 pro.

BLACK BEAN SALAD

This salad goes wonderfully with chicken and Mexican main dishes and a great choice when you need something quick for a potluck.
—Peg Kenkel-Thomsen, Iowa City, IA

Prep: 5 min. + chilling
Makes: 8 servings

- 2 cans (15 oz. each) black beans, rinsed and drained
- 1½ cups salsa or pico de gallo
- 2 Tbsp. minced fresh parsley or cilantro

Combine all ingredients in a bowl. Chill 15 minutes before serving.
½ cup: 99 cal., 0 fat (0 sat. fat), 0 chol., 411mg sod., 17g carb. (2g sugars, 6g fiber), 5g pro.
Diabetic exchanges: 1 starch.

MANGO & GRILLED CHICKEN SALAD

SANDWICHES

TORTELLINI PRIMAVERA SOUP
P. 82

1

2

3

4

5

PAIRED UP OR ON THEIR OWN, SOUPS &
SANDWICHES ARE MAGIC. THESE
NO-FUSS RECIPES ARE YOUR TICKET TO
YEAR-ROUND COMFORT FOOD.

WEEKNIGHT CHICKEN MOZZARELLA SANDWICHES

WEEKNIGHT CHICKEN MOZZARELLA SANDWICHES

My husband is a big garlic fan, so we use garlic bread crumbs and garlic sauce for our baked chicken sandwiches. They're so comforting on a chilly day!
—Bridget Snyder, Syracuse, NY

Takes: 30 min. • **Makes:** 4 servings

- 4 boneless skinless chicken breast halves (6 oz. each)
- 1 cup garlic bread crumbs
- 1 cup garlic and herb pasta sauce
- 1 cup shredded part-skim mozzarella cheese
  Grated Parmesan cheese, optional
- 4 kaiser rolls, split

1. Preheat oven to 400°. Pound chicken with a meat mallet to ½-in. thickness. Place the bread crumbs in a shallow bowl. Add chicken, a few pieces at a time, and toss to coat. Transfer to a greased 15x10x1-in. baking pan.
2. Bake, uncovered, until no longer pink, 15-20 minutes. Spoon pasta sauce over chicken. Top with mozzarella cheese and, if desired, Parmesan cheese. Bake until cheese melts, 2-3 minutes longer. Serve on rolls.
1 sandwich: 509 cal., 13g fat (5g sat. fat), 112mg chol., 1125mg sod., 46g carb. (5g sugars, 3g fiber), 50g pro.

TORTELLINI PRIMAVERA SOUP

(PICTURED ON P. 80)

Years ago, I found the idea for tortellini with peas and carrots in a magazine and added my own touches to it. Even my meat-lover husband and son enjoy this. If I'm pressed for time, I'll skip the basil.
—Kari George, Ellicott City, MD

Takes: 25 min. • **Makes:** 4 servings

- 2 cartons (32 oz. each) reduced-sodium chicken broth
- 1 pkg. (10 oz.) julienned carrots
- 1 pkg. (9 oz.) refrigerated cheese tortellini
- 1 cup frozen peas (about 4 oz.)
- ¼ tsp. pepper
  Thinly sliced fresh basil leaves

In a large saucepan, bring broth to a boil. Add carrots, tortellini, peas and pepper; return to a boil. Cook, uncovered, 7-9 minutes or until the pasta is tender. Top individual servings with basil.
Freeze option: Freeze cooled soup in freezer containers. To use, partially thaw in refrigerator overnight. Heat through in a saucepan, stirring occasionally.
2¼ cups: 282 cal., 6g fat (3g sat. fat), 28mg chol., 1461mg sod., 43g carb. (9g sugars, 5g fiber), 17g pro.

ITALIAN SAUSAGE & BEAN SOUP

The combo of sausage, beans and coleslaw may sound unusual, but it is so comforting and delicious!
—Stacey Bennett, Locust Grove, VA

Takes: 30 min. • **Makes:** 6 servings

- 1 lb. bulk hot Italian sausage
- 2 cans (15½ oz. each) great northern beans, rinsed and drained
- 1 pkg. (16 oz.) coleslaw mix
- 1 jar (24 oz.) garlic and herb spaghetti sauce
- 3 cups water

In a Dutch oven, cook sausage over medium heat until no longer pink; drain. Stir in the remaining ingredients. Bring to a boil. Reduce heat; simmer until flavors are blended, 16-20 minutes.

1⅓ cups: 416 cal., 21g fat (8g sat. fat), 53mg chol., 1411mg sod., 35g carb. (9g sugars, 12g fiber), 23g pro.

ITALIAN SAUSAGE & BEAN SOUP

SPINACH & WHITE BEAN SOUP

For me, soup is love, comfort and memories. This one appeals to my kitchen-sink style of cooking.
—Annette Palermo, Beach Haven, NJ

Takes: 30 min. • **Makes:** 6 servings

- 2   tsp. olive oil
- 3   garlic cloves, minced
- 3   cans (15 oz. each) cannellini beans, rinsed and drained, divided
- ¼   tsp. pepper
- 1   carton (32 oz.) vegetable or reduced-sodium chicken broth
- 4   cups chopped fresh spinach (about 3 oz.)
- ¼   cup thinly sliced fresh basil Shredded Parmesan cheese, optional

1. In a large saucepan, heat oil over medium heat. Add garlic; cook and stir 30-45 seconds or until tender. Stir in two cans of the beans, the pepper and broth.
2. Puree the mixture with an immersion blender. Or, puree in a blender and return to the pan. Stir in the remaining can of beans; bring to a boil. Reduce heat; simmer, covered, 15 minutes, stirring occasionally.
3. Stir in spinach and basil; cook, uncovered, 2-4 minutes or until the spinach is wilted. If desired, serve with cheese.

1¼ cups: 192 cal., 2g fat (0 sat. fat), 0 chol., 886mg sod., 33g carb. (1g sugars, 9g fiber), 9g pro.

SPINACH & WHITE BEAN SOUP

SLOW-COOKER MEATBALL SANDWICHES

Our approach to meatball subs is simple: Cook the meatballs low and slow, load them into hoagie buns and top with provolone and pepperoncini. Presto!
—Stacie Nicholls, Spring Creek, NV

Prep: 5 min. • **Cook:** 3 hours
Makes: 8 servings

- 2   pkg. (12 oz. each) frozen fully cooked Italian meatballs, thawed
- 2   jars (24 oz. each) marinara sauce
- 8   hoagie buns, split
- 8   slices provolone cheese Sliced pepperoncini, optional

1. Place meatballs and sauce in a 3- or 4-qt. slow cooker. Cook, covered, on low for 3-4 hours until the meatballs are heated through.
2. On the bottom half of each bun, layer cheese, meatballs and, if desired, pepperoncini; replace tops.

1 sandwich: 611 cal., 33g fat (14g sat. fat), 59mg chol., 1929mg sod., 53g carb. (13g sugars, 5g fiber), 30g pro.

SLOW-COOKER MEATBALL SANDWICHES

**APPLE-WHITE CHEDDAR
GRILLED CHEESE**

APPLE-WHITE CHEDDAR GRILLED CHEESE

On rainy days when we need comfort food in a hurry, I toast sandwiches of cinnamon raisin bread with white cheddar, apple and red onion.
—Kathy Patalsky, New York, NY

Takes: 20 min. • **Makes:** 2 servings

- 4 slices whole wheat cinnamon-raisin bread
- 4 slices sharp white cheddar cheese (3 oz.)
- 1 small apple, thinly sliced
- 1 thin slice red onion, separated into rings
- ¼ tsp. crushed red pepper flakes, optional
- 1 Tbsp. butter, softened

1. Layer each of two bread slices with one slice cheese. Top with apple and onion. If desired, sprinkle with pepper flakes. Top with the remaining cheese and bread. Spread the outsides of the sandwiches with butter.
2. In a large skillet, toast the sandwiches over medium-low heat for 3-5 minutes on each side or until bread is golden brown and the cheese is melted.

1 sandwich: 456 cal., 27g fat (14g sat. fat), 75mg chol., 616mg sod., 37g carb. (13g sugars, 5g fiber), 20g pro.

TEST KITCHEN TIP
For a healthier spin on these sandwiches, you can use olive oil instead of butter to toast them.

PEA SOUP WITH QUINOA

This soup is low in fat, high in fiber, and has a fantastically fresh flavor and wonderful texture. Best of all, it's so simple to make.
—Jane Hacker, Milwaukee, WI

Prep: 10 min. • **Cook:** 25 min.
Makes: 6 servings

- 1 cup water
- ½ cup quinoa, rinsed
- 2 tsp. canola oil
- 1 medium onion, chopped
- 2½ cups frozen peas (about 10 oz.)
- 2 cans (14½ oz. each) reduced-sodium chicken broth or vegetable broth
- ½ tsp. salt
- ¼ tsp. pepper
  Optional toppings: Plain yogurt, croutons, shaved Parmesan cheese and cracked pepper

1. In a small saucepan, bring water to a boil. Add quinoa. Reduce heat; simmer, covered, until water is absorbed, 12-15 minutes.
2. Meanwhile, in a large saucepan, heat oil over medium-high heat; saute onion until tender. Stir in peas and broth; bring to a boil. Reduce heat; simmer, uncovered, until the peas are tender, about 5 minutes.
3. Puree soup using an immersion blender, or cool slightly and puree the soup in a blender and return to pan. Stir in the quinoa, salt and pepper; heat through. Serve with toppings as desired.

1 cup: 126 cal., 3g fat (0 sat. fat), 0 chol., 504mg sod., 19g carb. (4g sugars, 4g fiber), 7g pro.
Diabetic exchanges: 1 starch, ½ fat.

TROPICAL BEEF WRAPS

For my finicky little ones, I create fast, tasty recipes like this tropical sandwich wrap. I usually use roast beef I buy from the deli, but it's a great way to use up leftover roast beef, too.
—Amy Tong, Anaheim, CA

Takes: 15 min. • **Makes:** 4 servings

- 1 carton (8 oz.) spreadable pineapple cream cheese
- 4 flour tortillas (10 in.)
- 4 cups fresh baby spinach (about 4 oz.)
- ¾ lb. thinly sliced deli roast beef
- 1 medium mango, peeled and sliced

Spread cream cheese over the tortillas to within 1 in. of edges. Layer with spinach, roast beef and sliced mango. Roll up tightly and serve.

1 wrap: 522 cal., 20g fat (10g sat. fat), 100mg chol., 1211mg sod., 58g carb. (21g sugars, 4g fiber), 26g pro.

PEA SOUP WITH QUINOA

BACON-POTATO CORN CHOWDER

BACON-POTATO CORN CHOWDER

I was raised on a farm, and a warm soup with homey ingredients, like this one, was always a treat after a chilly day outside.
—Katie Lillo, Big Lake, MN

Takes: 30 min. • **Makes:** 6 servings

½ lb. bacon strips, chopped
¼ cup chopped onion
1½ lbs. Yukon Gold potatoes (about 5 medium), peeled and cubed
1 can (14¾ oz.) cream-style corn
1 can (12 oz.) evaporated milk
¼ tsp. salt
¼ tsp. pepper

1. In a large skillet, cook bacon over medium heat until crisp, stirring occasionally. Remove with a slotted spoon; drain on paper towels. Discard the drippings, reserving 1½ tsp. in pan. Add onion to pan; cook and stir over medium-high heat until tender.
2. Meanwhile, place potatoes in a large saucepan; add water to cover. Bring to a boil over high heat. Reduce heat to medium; cook, uncovered, 10-15 minutes or until tender. Drain, reserving 1 cup of the potato water.
3. Add corn, milk, salt, pepper and the reserved potato water to saucepan; heat through. Stir in the bacon and onion.
1 cup: 271 cal., 11g fat (5g sat. fat), 30mg chol., 555mg sod., 34g carb. (9g sugars, 2g fiber), 10g pro.

PEPPERONI ROLL-UPS

PEPPERONI ROLL-UPS

Each bite of these crescents has gooey melted cheese and real pizza flavor. One makes a great appetizer; two are lunch!
—Debra Purcell, Safford, AZ

Takes: 20 min.
Makes: 8 appetizers

1 tube (8 oz.) refrigerated crescent rolls
16 slices pepperoni, cut into quarters
2 pieces string cheese (1 oz. each), cut into quarters
¾ tsp. Italian seasoning, divided
¼ tsp. garlic salt

1. Preheat oven to 375°. Unroll the crescent dough; separate into eight triangles. Place eight pepperoni slices on each. Place a piece of cheese on the short side of each triangle; sprinkle with ½ tsp. of the Italian seasoning. Roll up each triangle, starting with the short side; pinch the seam to seal. Sprinkle with garlic salt and the remaining Italian seasoning.
2. Place 2 in. apart on a greased baking sheet. Bake 10-12 minutes or until golden brown. Serve warm, with pizza sauce on the side if desired.
2 roll-ups: 282 cal., 17g fat (5g sat. fat), 12mg chol., 766mg sod., 22g carb. (4g sugars, 0 fiber), 7g pro.

PEPPERED PORK PITAS

COLORFUL CHICKEN & SQUASH SOUP

When I turned 40, I decided to live a healthier lifestyle, which included cooking smarter for my family. I make this soup every week, and everyone loves it.
—Trina Bigham, Fairhaven, MA

Prep: 25 min. • **Cook:** 1½ hours
Makes: 14 servings (5¼ qt.)

- 1 broiler/fryer chicken (4 lbs.), cut up
- 13 cups water
- 5 lbs. butternut squash, peeled and cubed (about 10 cups)
- 1 bunch kale, trimmed and chopped
- 6 medium carrots, chopped
- 2 large onions, chopped
- 3 tsp. salt

1. Place chicken and water in a stockpot. Bring to a boil. Reduce heat; cover and simmer for 1 hour or until chicken is tender.
2. Remove chicken from broth. Strain broth and skim fat. Return broth to the pot; add the squash, kale, carrots and onions. Bring to a boil. Reduce heat; cover and simmer for 25-30 minutes or until vegetables are tender.
3. Remove meat from bones; cut into bite-size pieces. Discard bones and skin. Add chicken and salt to soup; heat through.
1½ cups: 228 cal., 8g fat (2g sat. fat), 50mg chol., 579mg sod., 22g carb. (6g sugars, 6g fiber), 18g pro. **Diabetic exchanges:** 2 lean meat, 1 starch, 1 vegetable, ½ fat.

PEPPERED PORK PITAS

Cracked black pepper is all it takes to give my pork pitas some pop.
—Katherine White, Henderson, NV

Takes: 20 min. • **Makes:** 4 servings

- 1 lb. boneless pork loin chops, cut into thin strips
- 1 Tbsp. olive oil
- 2 tsp. coarsely ground pepper
- 2 garlic cloves, minced
- 1 jar (12 oz.) roasted sweet red peppers, drained and julienned
- 4 whole pita breads, warmed Garlic mayonnaise and torn leaf lettuce, optional

Combine the pork, oil, pepper and garlic; toss to coat. In a large skillet over medium-high heat, cook and stir the pork mixture until the pork is no longer pink. Stir in red peppers; heat through. Serve mixture on pita breads. Top with mayonnaise and lettuce if desired.
1 sandwich: 380 cal., 11g fat (3g sat. fat), 55mg chol., 665mg sod., 37g carb. (4g sugars, 2g fiber), 27g pro. **Diabetic exchanges:** 3 lean meat, 2 starch, 1 fat.

COCONUT CURRY CAULIFLOWER SOUP

When I'm in need of comfort food, I stir up a batch of this velvety, Asian-spiced soup. I finish it with a sprinkle of cilantro.
—Elizabeth DeHart,
West Jordan, UT

Prep: 10 min. • **Cook:** 25 min.
Makes: 10 servings (2½ qt.)

- 2 Tbsp. olive oil
- 1 medium onion, finely chopped
- 3 Tbsp. yellow curry paste
- 2 medium heads cauliflower, broken into florets
- 1 carton (32 oz.) vegetable broth
- 1 cup coconut milk
  Minced fresh cilantro, optional

1. In a large saucepan, heat oil over medium heat. Add onion; cook and stir until softened, 2-3 minutes. Add curry paste; cook until fragrant, 1-2 minutes. Add the cauliflower and broth.

Increase heat to high; bring to a boil. Reduce heat to medium-low; cook, covered, about 20 minutes.
2. Stir in the coconut milk; cook an additional minute. Remove from heat; cool slightly. Puree soup in batches in a blender or food processor, or use an immersion blender to puree the soup in the pot. If desired, top individual servings with minced fresh cilantro.

1 cup: 111 cal., 8g fat (5g sat. fat), 0 chol., 532mg sod., 10g carb. (4g sugars, 3g fiber), 3g pro.

COCONUT CURRY CAULIFLOWER SOUP

HAM & BRIE MELTS

GREEK TOMATO SOUP WITH ORZO

My recipe for manestra, *which means orzo in Greek, is so easy and straightforward. In only a few steps, you can transform a few simple ingredients into a creamy one-pot wonder.*
—Kiki Vagianos, Melrose, MA

Prep: 10 min. • **Cook:** 25 min.
Makes: 4 servings

- 2 Tbsp. olive oil
- 1 medium onion, chopped
- 1¼ cups uncooked whole wheat orzo pasta
- 2 cans (14½ oz. each) whole tomatoes, undrained, coarsely chopped
- 3 cups reduced-sodium chicken broth
- 2 tsp. dried oregano
- ¼ tsp. salt
- ¼ tsp. pepper
  Crumbled feta cheese and minced fresh basil, optional

1. In large saucepan, heat oil over medium heat; saute onion until tender, 3-5 minutes. Add orzo; cook and stir until lightly toasted.
2. Stir in tomatoes, broth and seasonings; bring to a boil. Reduce heat; simmer, covered, until orzo is tender, 15-20 minutes, stirring occasionally. If desired, top with feta and basil.
1 cup: 299 cal., 8g fat (1g sat. fat), 0 chol., 882mg sod., 47g carb. (7g sugars, 12g fiber), 11g pro.

HAM & BRIE MELTS

Deli ham and apricot preserves pair up with melty special-occasion cheese in these crispy sandwiches that remind me of baked Brie.
—Bonnie Bahler, Ellington, CT

Takes: 20 min. • **Makes:** 4 servings

- 8 slices multigrain bread
- ¼ cup apricot preserves
- ½ lb. sliced deli ham
- 1 round (8 oz.) Brie cheese, rind removed, sliced
- 3 Tbsp. butter, softened

1. Spread four bread slices with half of the preserves. Layer with ham and cheese. Spread the remaining bread with remaining preserves; place over cheese, preserves side down. Spread the outside of each sandwich with butter.
2. In a large skillet, toast the sandwiches over medium heat for 2-3 minutes on each side or until bread is golden brown and the cheese is melted.
1 sandwich: 500 cal., 27g fat (16g sat. fat), 104mg chol., 1208mg sod., 39g carb. (14g sugars, 3g fiber), 27g pro.

**GREEK TOMATO
SOUP WITH ORZO**

BEEF
MACARONI
SOUP

BEEF MACARONI SOUP

You'll love my quick version of classic beef macaroni soup. Loaded with veggies and pasta, it's just as good as the original but with much less fuss.
—Debra Baker, Greenville, NC

Takes: 25 min. • **Makes:** 5 servings

1 lb. ground beef
2 cups frozen mixed vegetables
1 can (14½ oz.) diced tomatoes, undrained
1 can (14½ oz.) beef broth
¼ tsp. pepper
½ cup uncooked elbow macaroni

In a large saucepan, cook beef over medium heat until no longer pink; drain. Stir in the mixed vegetables, tomatoes, broth and pepper. Bring to a boil; add the macaroni. Reduce heat; cover and simmer for 8-10 minutes or until the macaroni and vegetables are tender.

1 cup: 260 cal., 11g fat (4g sat. fat), 58mg chol., 357mg sod., 19g carb. (5g sugars, 5g fiber), 21g pro.

TEST KITCHEN TIP
This versatile recipe is great for picky eaters (especially those who don't like garlic and onions), but also easy to spice up. Chili powder, paprika, onion powder and garlic powder are tasty additions. Start with ¼ tsp. of any or all, and increase to taste. You can also substitute any short pasta for the elbow macaroni. Shells and wagon wheels are fun shapes for this kid-friendly soup.

MINI CHICKEN & BISCUIT SANDWICHES

My son, Jake, invented these sliders at dinner one night when he plunked his chicken on a biscuit. The rest of us tried it his way, and a family favorite was born!
—Jodie Kolsan, Palm Coast, FL

Takes: 30 min. • **Makes:** 5 servings

- 1 tube (12 oz.) refrigerated buttermilk biscuits
- 5 boneless skinless chicken breasts (4 oz. each)
- ½ tsp. salt
- ½ tsp. dried thyme
- ¼ tsp. pepper
- 1 Tbsp. canola oil
- 1 Tbsp. butter
  Optional toppings: Cranberry chutney, lettuce leaves, sliced tomato and red onion

1. Bake biscuits according to package directions. Meanwhile, cut chicken crosswise in half. Pound with a meat mallet to ¼-in. thickness. Sprinkle with salt, thyme and pepper.
2. In a large skillet, heat oil and butter over medium-high heat. Add chicken in batches; cook until no longer pink, 2-3 minutes on each side. Split biscuits; top with chicken and toppings as desired. Replace tops.

2 mini sandwiches: 367 cal., 16g fat (4g sat. fat), 69mg chol., 1029mg sod., 28g carb. (4g sugars, 0 fiber), 27g pro.

CUCUMBER SANDWICHES

I was introduced to a similar sandwich by a friend many years ago, and made my own version. For a change of pace, I sometimes add thinly sliced onions on top.
—Karen Schriefer, Stevensville, MD

Takes: 15 min. • **Makes:** 6 servings

- 1 carton (8 oz.) spreadable cream cheese
- 2 tsp. ranch salad dressing mix
- 12 slices pumpernickel or rye bread
- 2 to 3 medium cucumbers, peeled (if desired) and thinly sliced

In a large bowl, combine cream cheese and dressing mix. Spread on one side of each slice of bread. Place cucumber slices on six of the bread slices. Top with the remaining bread slices. Serve immediately.
1 sandwich: 244 cal., 10g fat (6g sat. fat), 24mg chol., 672mg sod., 31g carb. (3g sugars, 4g fiber), 8g pro.

MINI CHICKEN & BISCUIT SANDWICHES

**EASY CHILI
VERDE**

EASY CHILI VERDE

I love chili verde and I order it at restaurants whenever I can. A few years ago, I figured out how to make an easy, tasty version of my own. There are never leftovers when I make it for my family!
—Julie Rowland, Salt Lake City, UT

Prep: 10 min. • **Cook:** 5 hours
Makes: 12 servings (3 qt.)

- 1 boneless pork shoulder roast (4 to 5 lbs.), cut into 1-in. pieces
- 3 cans (10 oz. each) green enchilada sauce
- 1 cup salsa verde
- 1 can (4 oz.) chopped green chiles
- ½ tsp. salt
  Hot cooked rice
  Sour cream, optional

In a 5-qt. slow cooker, combine the pork, enchilada sauce, salsa verde, green chiles and salt. Cook, covered, on low until the pork is tender, 5-6 hours. Serve with rice. If desired, top individual servings with sour cream.
1 cup: 287 cal., 17g fat (5g sat. fat), 90mg chol., 729mg sod., 5g carb. (1g sugars, 0 fiber), 27g pro.

TEX-MEX SHREDDED BEEF SANDWICHES

TEX-MEX SHREDDED BEEF SANDWICHES

You need only a few ingredients to make my delicious shredded beef. While the meat simmers to tender perfection, you will have plenty of time to do other things.
—Katherine White, Henderson, NV

Prep: 5 min. • **Cook:** 8 hours
Makes: 8 servings

- 1 boneless beef chuck roast (3 lbs.)
- 1 envelope chili seasoning
- ½ cup barbecue sauce
- 8 onion rolls, split
- 8 slices cheddar cheese

1. Cut roast in half; place in a 3-qt. slow cooker. Sprinkle with chili seasoning. Pour barbecue sauce over top. Cover and cook on low for 8-10 hours or until the meat is tender.
2. Remove roast; cool slightly. Shred meat with two forks. Skim fat from cooking juices. Return meat to the slow cooker; heat through. Using a slotted spoon, place ½ cup of the meat mixture on each roll bottom; top with cheese. Replace roll tops.
1 sandwich: 573 cal., 29g fat (13g sat. fat), 140mg chol., 955mg sod., 29g carb. (6g sugars, 2g fiber), 47g pro.

STUFFED SPINACH LOAF

My mom made this recipe years ago and I always remembered how good it tasted. So I made it myself from memory, and it was a big hit! Folks who think they don't like spinach are in for a surprise when they try it.

—Anita Harmala, Howell, MI

Prep: 15 min. • **Bake:** 25 min.
Makes: 10 servings

- 1   lb. bulk Italian sausage
- ½   tsp. salt
- ½   tsp. dried basil
- 1   loaf (1 lb.) frozen bread dough, thawed
- 1   pkg. (10 oz.) frozen spinach, thawed and well-drained
- 2   cups shredded mozzarella cheese

1. Preheat oven to 350°. In a large skillet, cook sausage over medium heat until no longer pink; drain. Sprinkle with salt and basil. Roll out bread dough to a 13x10-in. rectangle. Sprinkle with the meat mixture. Top with thawed spinach; sprinkle with mozzarella cheese. Roll up jelly-roll style, starting with a long side; pinch seams to seal and tuck ends under.
2. Place seam side down on a greased baking sheet. Bake for until the crust is golden brown, 25-30 minutes. Serve warm. Refrigerate any leftovers.
1 slice: 270 cal., 13g fat (5g sat. fat), 36mg chol., 688mg sod., 25g carb. (2g sugars, 2g fiber), 15g pro.

SPICY POTATO SOUP

My sister-in-law, who is from Mexico, shared this wonderful recipe. Since she prefers her foods spicier than we do, I've cut back on the heat by reducing the amount of pepper sauce. You can add more if you prefer a bigger kick!

—Audrey Wall, Industry, PA

Prep: 20 min. • **Cook:** 70 min.
Makes: 8 servings (2 qt.)

- 1   lb. ground beef
- 4   cups cubed peeled potatoes (½-in. cubes)
- 1   small onion, chopped
- 3   cans (8 oz. each) tomato sauce
- 4   cups water
- 2   tsp. salt
- 1½ tsp. pepper
- ½   to 1 tsp. hot pepper sauce

In a Dutch oven, brown the ground beef over medium heat until no longer pink; drain. Add the potatoes, onion and tomato sauce. Stir in the water, salt, pepper and hot pepper sauce; bring to a boil. Reduce heat and simmer for 1 hour or until the potatoes are tender and the soup has thickened.
1 cup: 159 cal., 5g fat (2g sat. fat), 28mg chol., 764mg sod., 16g carb. (2g sugars, 2g fiber), 12g pro.

CHEESY CHICKEN WAFFLEWICHES

I've had lots of fun experimenting with my waffle maker, and used shredded meat, cheese and vegetables for a savory twist. Be sure the griddle is hot before adding the sandwiches.
—Marietta Slater, Justin, TX

Prep: 25 min. • **Cook:** 5 min./batch
Makes: 8 servings

- 1 Tbsp. olive oil
- ½ cup chopped onion
- ½ cup chopped fresh mushrooms
- 1 cup shredded rotisserie chicken
- 1 cup shredded Swiss cheese
- 1 pkg. (17.3 oz., 2 sheets) frozen puff pastry, thawed

1. In a large skillet, heat oil over medium heat; saute onion until softened, 3-4 minutes. Reduce heat to medium-low; cook until caramelized, 6-8 minutes, stirring occasionally. Add mushrooms; cook and stir until tender, 2-3 minutes. Cool slightly. Stir in chicken and cheese.
2. Preheat a four-square waffle maker. Unfold one puff pastry sheet onto a lightly floured surface; cut into four squares. Top each square with ¼ cup of the filling; bring up the corners of the pastry over the filling and pinch firmly to seal. Refrigerate until ready to cook. Repeat with the remaining pastry sheet and filling.
3. Place one pastry bundle in each section of the waffle maker. Bake until golden brown and crisp, 5-7 minutes. Repeat to bake the remaining pastry bundlles.

1 wafflewich: 405 cal., 24g fat (7g sat. fat), 28mg chol., 243mg sod., 36g carb. (1g sugars, 5g fiber), 13g pro.

CHEESY CHICKEN WAFFLEWICHES

SIMPLE CHICKEN SOUP

BROCCOLI-CHEDDAR BEEF ROLLS

My grandma's recipe for beef rolls is a much-loved classic as it is, and is also easy to change up with different fillings. Load them with ham, veggies, even olives.
—Kent Call, Riverside, UT

Takes: 30 min. • **Makes:** 6 servings

- ½ lb. lean ground beef (90% lean)
- 2 cups chopped fresh broccoli
- 1 small onion, chopped
- ½ tsp. salt
- ¼ tsp. pepper
- 6 hard rolls
- 2 cups shredded cheddar cheese, divided

1. Preheat oven to 325°. In a large skillet, cook and crumble the beef with the broccoli and onion over medium heat until meat is no longer pink, 4-6 minutes. Season with salt and pepper.
2. Cut one-third off the top of each roll; discard or save tops for a future use. Hollow out the bottoms, leaving ½-in.-thick shells; place shells on a baking sheet.
3. Tear the bread removed from the shells into ½-in. pieces; place in a bowl. Stir in 1½ cups of cheese and the beef mixture. Spoon into bread shells. Sprinkle with the remaining cheese. Bake until heated through and the cheese is melted, 10-15 minutes.
1 roll: 394 cal., 18g fat (9g sat. fat), 61mg chol., 783mg sod., 34g carb. (2g sugars, 2g fiber), 23g pro.

SIMPLE CHICKEN SOUP

I revised a recipe that my family loved so it would be lighter and easier to make. It's a hearty and healthy meal served with a green salad and fresh bread.
—Sue West, Alvord, TX

Takes: 20 min. • **Makes:** 6 servings

- 2 cans (14½ oz. each) reduced-sodium chicken broth
- 1 Tbsp. dried minced onion
- 1 pkg. (16 oz.) frozen mixed vegetables
- 2 cups cubed cooked chicken breast
- 2 cans (10¾ oz. each) reduced-fat reduced-sodium condensed cream of chicken soup, undiluted

In a large saucepan, bring the broth and onion to a boil. Reduce heat. Add the vegetables; cover and cook for 6-8 minutes or until crisp-tender. Stir in the chicken and soup; heat through.
1⅓ cups: 195 cal., 3g fat (1g sat. fat), 44mg chol., 820mg sod., 21g carb. (3g sugars, 3g fiber), 19g pro.

**BROCCOLI-CHEDDAR
BEEF ROLLS**

HAM & SWISS
STROMBOLI

HAM & SWISS STROMBOLI

This is the perfect choice to take to someone for dinner. It's also easy to change up the recipe with your favorite meats or cheeses.
—Tricia Bibb, Hartselle, AL

Takes: 30 min. • **Makes:** 6 servings

- 1 **tube (11 oz.) refrigerated crusty French loaf**
- 6 **oz. sliced deli ham**
- ¼ **cup finely chopped onion**
- 8 **bacon strips, cooked and crumbled**
- 6 **oz. sliced Swiss cheese Honey mustard, optional**

1. Preheat oven to 375°. Unroll dough on a baking sheet. Place ham down the center third of dough to within 1 in. of the ends; top with onion, bacon and cheese. Fold long sides of dough over the filling, pinching seam and ends to seal; tuck ends under. Cut several slits in the top.

2. Bake until loaf is golden brown, 20-25 minutes. Cut into slices. If desired, serve stromboli with honey mustard.

Freeze option: Securely wrap and freeze cooled unsliced stromboli in heavy-duty foil. Reheat on an ungreased baking sheet at 375° until stromboli is heated through and a thermometer inserted in the center reads 165°.

1 slice: 272 cal., 11g fat (5g sat. fat), 40mg chol., 795mg sod., 26g carb. (3g sugars, 1g fiber), 18g pro.

★★★★★ **READER REVIEW**

"We love this recipe! I made this recently for my husband— it did not last long in our house. Not a crumb to be found!"
XXCSKIER TASTEOFHOME.COM

BARBECUE SLIDERS

When company dropped in by surprise, all I had defrosted was sausage and ground beef. We combined the two for juicy burgers on the grill.
—B.J. Larsen, Erie, CO

Takes: 25 min. • **Makes:** 8 servings

- 1 lb. ground beef
- 1 lb. bulk pork sausage
- 1 cup barbecue sauce, divided
- 16 Hawaiian sweet rolls, split
  Optional toppings: Lettuce leaves, sliced plum tomatoes and red onion

1. Mix the beef and sausage lightly but thoroughly. Shape into sixteen ½-in.-thick patties.

2. Grill beef patties, covered, over medium heat or broil 4-5 in. from heat until a thermometer reads 160°, 3-4 minutes on each side. Brush with ¼ cup of the barbecue sauce during the last 2 minutes of cooking. Serve on rolls with the remaining barbecue sauce; top as desired.

Freeze option: Place uncooked patties on a waxed paper-lined baking sheet; cover and freeze until firm. Remove from pan and transfer to an airtight container; return to freezer. Grill the frozen patties as directed, increasing time as necessary.

2 sliders: 499 cal., 24g fat (9g sat. fat), 96mg chol., 885mg sod., 47g carb. (23g sugars, 2g fiber), 24g pro.

CREAMY CAULIFLOWER & BACON SOUP

This is such a rich dish, you don't need to serve a lot with it. For a simple garnish, I add a drop of hot sauce to the top and drag a butter knife through it.
—Lynn Caruso, Gilroy, CA

Prep: 15 min. • **Cook:** 30 min.
Makes: 4 servings

- 1 medium head cauliflower (2 lbs.), cut into florets
- 2 cups half-and-half cream, divided
- ½ cup shredded Asiago cheese
- ½ tsp. salt
- ½ tsp. ground nutmeg
- ⅛ tsp. pepper
- ½ to 1 cup water
- 4 bacon strips, cooked and crumbled

1. Place cauliflower in a steamer basket; place in a large saucepan over 1 in. of water. Bring to a boil; cover and steam for 8-10 minutes or until tender. Cool slightly.
2. Place cauliflower and ½ cup cream in a food processor; cover and process until pureed. Transfer to a large saucepan.
3. Stir in the cheese, salt, nutmeg, pepper and remaining cream. Add enough water to reach desired consistency; heat through. Sprinkle each serving with bacon.
1 cup: 303 cal., 19g fat (11g sat. fat), 79mg chol., 605mg sod., 17g carb. (10g sugars, 6g fiber), 15g pro.

BARBECUE SLIDERS

POTATO
CHOWDER

POTATO CHOWDER

One of the ladies in our church quilting group brought this savory potato soup to a meeting, and everyone loved how the cream cheese and bacon made it so rich. Take a few minutes to assemble the ingredients in the morning, and then let the soup simmer on its own all day.

—Anna Mayer, Fort Branch, IN

Prep: 15 min. • **Cook:** 8 hours
Makes: 12 servings (3 qt.)

- 8 cups diced potatoes
- 3 cans (14½ oz. each) chicken broth
- 1 can (10¾ oz.) condensed cream of chicken soup, undiluted
- ⅓ cup chopped onion
- ¼ tsp. pepper
- 1 pkg. (8 oz.) cream cheese, cubed
- ½ lb. sliced bacon, cooked and crumbled, optional
  Minced chives, optional

1. In a 5-qt. slow cooker, combine the first five ingredients. Cover and cook on low for 8-10 hours or until the potatoes are tender.
2. Add cream cheese; stir until blended. Garnish with bacon and chives if desired.
1 cup: 179 cal., 9g fat (5g sat. fat), 25mg chol., 690mg sod., 21g carb. (2g sugars, 2g fiber), 4g pro.

ITALIAN BEEF HOAGIES

ITALIAN BEEF HOAGIES

This recipe makes enough tender, tangy sandwiches to feed a crowd. On weekends, I start the roast the night before, so I can shred it in the morning.

—Lori Piatt, Danville, IL

Prep: 25 min. • **Cook:** 8 hours
Makes: 18 servings

- 1 beef sirloin tip roast (4 lbs.), halved
- 2 envelopes Italian salad dressing mix
- 2 cups water
- 1 jar (16 oz.) mild pickled pepper rings, undrained
- 18 hoagie buns, split

1. Place beef roast in a 5-qt. slow cooker. Combine Italian salad dressing mix and water; pour over the roast. Cover and cook on low for 8-10 hours or until the meat is tender.
2. Remove the roast; shred with two forks and return the meat to the slow cooker. Add the pickled pepper rings and heat through. Spoon ½ cup of the meat mixture onto each bun.
1 sandwich: 346 cal., 9g fat (4g sat. fat), 53mg chol., 674mg sod., 39g carb. (8g sugars, 2g fiber), 26g pro.

ORANGE TURKEY CROISSANTS

OPEN-FACED GRILLED SALMON SANDWICHES

My family loves to fish. And what better reward from a day of fishing than eating your catch? We have several ways we like to cook our salmon. This is the family favorite.
—Stephanie Hanisak,
Port Murray, NJ

Takes: 30 min. • **Makes:** 4 servings

- 4 **salmon fillets (1 in. thick and 5 oz. each), skin removed**
- ¾ **cup mesquite marinade**
- ¼ **tsp. pepper**
- 4 **slices sourdough bread (½ in. thick)**
- ¼ **cup tartar sauce**
- 4 **iceberg lettuce leaves**
- 4 **lemon wedges, optional**

1. Place fillets in an 8-in. square dish. Pour marinade over fillets; turn fish to coat. Let salmon stand 15 minutes.
2. Drain salmon, discarding marinade. Sprinkle with pepper.
3. Grill salmon, covered, on an oiled rack over medium heat or broil 4 in. from heat until fish just begins to flake easily with a fork, 4-6 minutes on each side.
4. Grill sourdough bread, covered, over medium heat until lightly toasted, 1-2 minutes on each side. Spread with tartar sauce; top with lettuce and salmon. If desired, serve with lemon wedges.
1 open-faced sandwich: 436 cal., 17g fat (3g sat. fat), 74mg chol., 1226mg sod., 37g carb. (5g sugars, 1g fiber), 31g pro.

ORANGE TURKEY CROISSANTS

Here's an easy, amazing sandwich that feels special. Sweet and tangy orange and crunchy pecans make it truly delicious.
—Jennifer Moore, Centerville, IA

Takes: 10 min. • **Makes:** 6 servings

- 6 **Tbsp. spreadable cream cheese**
- 6 **Tbsp. orange marmalade**
- 6 **croissants, split**
- ½ **cup chopped pecans**
- 1 **lb. thinly sliced deli turkey**

1. Spread cream cheese and orange marmalade onto bottom half of croissants. Sprinkle witah pecans. Top with turkey; replace tops.
1 sandwich: 479 cal., 25g fat (11g sat. fat), 80mg chol., 1165mg sod., 43g carb. (19g sugars, 3g fiber), 21g pro.

TOMATO STEAK SANDWICHES

One day when we were light on groceries, I came up with steak and tomatoes over bagels. They have been a favorite in our house ever since, particularly when we need a quick dinner.

—Tessa Edwards, Provo, UT

Takes: 20 min. • **Makes:** 6 servings

- 2 tsp. canola oil
- 1 lb. beef top sirloin steak, cut into thin strips
- ⅛ tsp. salt
- Dash pepper
- 3 plain bagels, split
- ⅓ cup cream cheese, softened
- 6 thick slices tomato
- 6 slices part-skim mozzarella cheese

1. Preheat broiler. In a large skillet, heat oil over medium heat. Add beef; cook and stir for 3-5 minutes or until browned; drain. Stir in salt and pepper.

2. Spread cut sides of the bagels with cream cheese. Transfer to an ungreased baking sheet; spoon the beef over the bagels. Top with tomato and mozzarella cheese. Broil 4-6 in. from heat 3-5 minutes or until cheese is melted and lightly browned.

1 open-faced sandwich: 381 cal., 15g fat (7g sat. fat), 63mg chol., 544mg sod., 31g carb. (6g sugars, 1g fiber), 30g pro.

★ ★ ★ ★ ★ **READER REVIEW**

"My grown son always objects to sirloin beef. But by golly, he loved this sandwich!!"

DUCKYD TASTEOFHOME.COM

TOMATO STEAK SANDWICHES

REUBEN CALZONES

wilted. Stir in ½ cup part-skim ricotta cheese and ¼ tsp. each salt and pepper. Proceed as directed. Serve with marinara sauce if desired.

SLOW-COOKED BEEF VEGETABLE SOUP

Convenient frozen veggies and hash browns make this meaty soup a snap to mix up. It's wonderful served with bread and a salad.
—Carol Calhoun, Sioux Falls, SD

Prep: 10 min. • **Cook:** 8 hours
Makes: 10 servings (2½ qt.)

- 1 lb. ground beef
- 1 can (46 oz.) tomato juice
- 1 pkg. (16 oz.) frozen mixed vegetables, thawed
- 2 cups frozen cubed hash brown potatoes, thawed
- 1 envelope onion soup mix

In a large skillet, cook beef over medium heat until no longer pink; drain. Transfer to a 5-qt. slow cooker. Stir in the tomato juice, mixed vegetables, potatoes and soup mix. Cover and cook on low for 8-10 hours.

1 cup: 139 cal., 4g fat (2g sat. fat), 22mg chol., 766mg sod., 16g carb. (6g sugars, 3g fiber), 11g pro.

REUBEN CALZONES

I love a good Reuben, so I tried the fillings in a pizza pocket instead of on bread. This hand-held dinner is a big winner at our house.
—Nickie Frye, Evansville, IN

Takes: 30 min. • **Makes:** 4 servings

- 1 tube (13.8 oz.) refrigerated pizza crust
- 4 slices Swiss cheese
- 1 cup sauerkraut, rinsed and well drained
- ½ lb. sliced cooked corned beef
  Thousand Island salad dressing

1. Preheat oven to 400°. On a lightly floured surface, unroll the pizza crust dough and pat into a 12-in. square. Cut into four squares. Layer a fourth of the cheese, sauerkraut and corned beef diagonally over half of each square to within ½ in. of edges. Fold a corner over the filling to the opposite corner, forming a triangle; press edges with a fork to seal. Place calzones on greased baking sheets.

2. Bake until calzones are golden brown, 15-18 minutes. Serve with salad dressing.

1 calzone: 430 cal., 17g fat (6g sat. fat), 66mg chol., 1607mg sod., 49g carb. (7g sugars, 2g fiber), 21g pro.

Sausage & Spinach Calzones: Substitute mozzarella for Swiss cheese. Cook and drain ½ pound bulk Italian sausage; add 3 cups fresh baby spinach and cook until

**SLOW-COOKED BEEF
VEGETABLE SOUP**

JALAPENO-SWISS TURKEY BURGERS

JALAPENO-SWISS TURKEY BURGERS

These easy turkey burgers are extra juicy and loaded with flavor. I think the spicy jalapenos give it just the right level of heat, but feel free to adjust the amount to amp it up or tone it down.
—Wanda Allende, Orlando, FL

Takes: 25 min. • **Makes:** 4 servings

- 1 lb. ground turkey
- 1 small onion, finely chopped
- ¾ tsp. salt
- ¼ tsp. pepper
- 8 slices Swiss cheese
- 1 jalapeno pepper, sliced
- 4 pretzel hamburger buns, split and toasted
  Optional toppings: Sliced jalapenos, salsa and sour cream

1. Combine the turkey, onion, salt and pepper; mix lightly but thoroughly. Shape into four ½-in.-thick patties.
2. Place burgers on an oiled grill rack or in a greased 15x10x1-in. pan. Grilln burgers, covered, over medium heat or broil 4 in. from heat until a thermometer reads 165°, 4-6 minutes per side.
3. On each burger, layer 1 slice of cheese, jalapeno slices and a second slice of cheese. Grill or broil 1-2 minutes to melt cheese. Serve on buns; top as desired.
Note: Wear disposable gloves when cutting hot peppers; the oils can burn your skin. Avoid touching your face.
1 burger: 375 cal., 16g fat (6g sat. fat), 95mg chol., 767mg sod., 25g carb. (4g sugars, 1g fiber), 33g pro.

TEST KITCHEN TIPS
For tender burgers, handle the turkey mixture gently. And before topping the burgers with jalapenos, bear in mind that some pack more heat than others. Sample a slice first.

ROASTED TOMATO SOUP WITH FRESH BASIL

Roasting brings out the tomatoes' rich, sweet flavor for this soup. It has a slightly chunky texture that indicates it's fresh and homemade. Fresh summertime basil is the classic companion.
—Marie Forte, Raritan, NJ

Prep: 20 min. • **Bake:** 25 min.
Makes: 6 servings (1½ qt.)

- 3½ lbs. tomatoes (about 11 medium), halved
- 1 small onion, quartered
- 2 garlic cloves, peeled and halved
- 2 Tbsp. olive oil
- 2 Tbsp. fresh thyme leaves
- 1 tsp. salt
- ¼ tsp. pepper
- 12 fresh basil leaves
  Salad croutons and thinly sliced fresh basil, optional

1. Preheat oven to 400°. Place the tomatoes, onion and garlic in a greased 15x10x1-in. baking pan; drizzle with oil. Sprinkle with thyme, salt and pepper; toss to coat. Roast until vegetables are tender, 25-30 minutes, stirring once. Cool slightly.
2. Process the tomato mixture and basil leaves in batches in a blender until smooth. Transfer to a large saucepan; heat through. If desired, top individual servings with croutons and sliced basil.

1 cup: 107 cal., 5g fat (1g sat. fat), 0 chol., 411mg sod., 15g carb. (9g sugars, 4g fiber), 3g pro. **Diabetic exchanges:** 1 starch, 1 fat.

PRESTO CHILI

Canned soup and beans are the secrets to my chili's quick preparation. For even faster meals, I sometimes cook and freeze the ground beef in advance. Just combine frozen cooked beef with the other ingredients and simmer as directed.
—Jean Ward, Montogomery, TX

Takes: 30 min. • **Makes:** 4 servings

- 1 lb. lean ground beef (90% lean)
- 1 can (10¾ oz.) condensed tomato soup, undiluted
- 1 can (16 oz.) chili beans, undrained
- 2 to 3 tsp. chili powder
- ½ cup water, optional

In a saucepan, brown the ground beef until no longer pink; drain. Add soup, beans and chili powder. Reduce heat. Cover and simmer for 20 minutes. Add water if a thinner soup is desired.

1 serving: 337 cal., 10g fat (4g sat. fat), 71mg chol., 840mg sod., 35g carb. (9g sugars, 7g fiber), 30g pro. **Diabetic exchanges:** 3 meat, 1½ starch.

ROASTED TOMATO SOUP WITH FRESH BASIL

ENTREES

FETTUCCINE WITH SAUSAGE AND FRESH TOMATO SAUCE
P. 114

1

2

3

4

5

THESE GREAT MAIN COURSES
TAKE YOU FROM FAMILY MEALS TO
DATE NIGHTS TO HOLIDAY FEASTS—
ALL WITH JUST A FEW INGREDIENTS!

SMOTHERED BURRITOS

SMOTHERED BURRITOS

My brother-in-law thought I knew how to make only five things using ground beef. To prove him wrong, I came back with these burritos. Now it's his turn to cook!
—Kim Kenyon, Greenwood, MO

Takes: 30 min. • **Makes:** 4 servings

- 1 can (10 oz.) green enchilada sauce
- ¾ cup salsa verde
- 1 lb. ground beef
- 4 flour tortillas (10 in.)
- 1½ cups shredded cheddar cheese, divided

1. In a small bowl, mix enchilada sauce and salsa verde.
2. In a large skillet, cook beef over medium heat until no longer pink, for 8-10 minutes, breaking into crumbles; drain. Stir in ½ cup of the sauce mixture.
3. Spoon ⅔ cup of the beef mixture across the center of each tortilla; top each with 3 Tbsp. cheese. Fold bottom and sides of tortilla over filling and roll up.
4. Place the burritos in a greased 11x7-in. baking dish. Pour the remaining sauce over top; sprinkle with the remaining cheese. Bake, uncovered, at 375° until cheese is melted, 10-15 minutes.

1 burrito: 624 cal., 33g fat (15g sat. fat), 115mg chol., 1470mg sod., 44g carb. (6g sugars, 2g fiber), 36g pro.

FETTUCCINE WITH SAUSAGE & FRESH TOMATO SAUCE

(PICTURED ON P. 112)

Fresh sauce doesn't take much more time than using jarred— and the results are so good!
—*Taste of Home* Test Kitchen

Prep: 15 min. • **Cook:** 30 min.
Makes: 4 servings

- 2 Tbsp. olive oil, divided
- 1 pkg. (12 oz.) fully cooked Italian chicken sausage links, cut into ½-in. slices
- 1 large onion, finely chopped
- 2 lbs. plum tomatoes, chopped (about 5 cups)
- ½ tsp. salt
- ¼ tsp. pepper
- 8 oz. uncooked fettuccine
- ¼ cup thinly sliced fresh basil
- 1 tsp. sugar, optional
  Optional toppings: Grated Romano cheese and additional basil

1. In a 6-qt. stockpot, heat 1 Tbsp. oil over medium heat. Brown the sausage; remove. Add remaining oil and saute onion until tender, 3-5 minutes. Stir in the sausage, tomatoes, salt and pepper; bring to a boil. Reduce heat; simmer the sauce, uncovered, until thickened, 20-25 minutes.
2. Meanwhile, cook fettuccine according to package directions; drain pasta.
3. Stir basil and, if desired, sugar into sauce. Serve over fettuccine. If desired, top with cheese and additional basil.

1 cup fettuccine with 1 cup sauce: 457 cal., 15g fat (3g sat. fat), 65mg chol., 792mg sod., 56g carb. (9g sugars, 5g fiber), 25g pro.

JAVA ROAST BEEF

Coffee adds a lovely richness to this roast's gravy, which is perfect for sopping up with crusty bread or spooning over rice or potatoes.
—Charla Sackmann, Orange City, IA

Prep: 10 min. • **Cook:** 8 hours
Makes: 12 servings

- 5 garlic cloves, minced
- 1½ tsp. salt
- ¾ tsp. pepper
- 1 boneless beef chuck roast (3 to 3½ lbs.)
- 1½ cups strong brewed coffee
- 2 Tbsp. cornstarch
- ¼ cup cold water

1. Mix garlic, salt and pepper; rub over beef. Transfer to a 4-qt. slow cooker. Pour coffee around meat. Cook, covered, on low until the meat is tender, 8-10 hours.
2. Remove roast to a serving plate; keep warm. Transfer the cooking juices to a small saucepan; skim off fat. Bring to a boil. In a small bowl, mix cornstarch and water until smooth; gradually stir into the cooking juices. Bring to a boil; cook and stir 1-2 minutes or until thickened. Serve with roast.

3 oz. cooked beef with 2 Tbsp. gravy: 199 cal., 11g fat (4g sat. fat), 74mg chol., 342mg sod., 2g carb. (0 sugars, 0 fiber), 22g pro.
Diabetic exchanges: 3 lean meat.

JAVA ROAST BEEF

HONEY-PECAN PORK CHOPS

Sweet and nutty chops are delicious with a side of green beans, rice or sweet potatoes.
—Linda Bounds, Cedar Hill, TX

Takes: 25 min. • **Makes:** 2 servings

- 2 boneless pork loin chops (about ½ in. thick and 4 oz. each)
- 3 Tbsp. all-purpose flour
- ¼ tsp. salt
- ¼ tsp. pepper
- 2 Tbsp. light butter
- 2 Tbsp. honey
- 1 Tbsp. coarsely chopped pecans

1. Pound pork chops with a meat mallet to flatten slightly. In a shallow bowl, mix flour, salt and pepper. Add chops and turn to coat; shake off excess.
2. In a large skillet, heat butter over medium heat. Add chops; cook until a thermometer reads 145°, 3-4 minutes on each side. Remove from pan; keep warm.
3. Add honey and pecans to the same skillet; heat through, stirring to loosen browned bits from pan. Serve with pork.

1 pork chop with 2 Tbsp. sauce: 335 cal., 15g fat (7g sat. fat), 75mg chol., 398mg sod., 27g carb. (17g sugars, 1g fiber), 24g pro.

SUPER QUICK CHICKEN FRIED RICE

After my first child was born, I needed meals that were satisfying and fast. This fried rice was a great discovery, and it's now part of our routine dinner rotation.
—Alicia Gower, Auburn, NY

Takes: 30 min. • **Makes:** 6 servings

- 1 pkg. (12 oz.) frozen mixed vegetables
- 2 Tbsp. olive oil, divided
- 2 large eggs, lightly beaten
- 4 Tbsp. sesame oil, divided
- 3 pkg. (8.8 oz. each) ready-to-serve garden vegetable rice
- 1 rotisserie chicken, skin removed, shredded
- ¼ tsp. salt
- ¼ tsp. pepper

1. Prepare the frozen vegetables according to package directions. In a large skillet, heat 1 Tbsp. olive oil over medium-high heat. Pour in eggs; cook and stir until the eggs are thickened and no liquid egg remains. Remove from pan.
2. In the same skillet, heat 2 Tbsp. sesame oil and remaining olive oil over medium-high heat. Add rice; cook and stir until rice begins to brown, 10-12 minutes.
3. Stir in chicken, salt and pepper. Add eggs and vegetables; heat through, breaking eggs into small pieces and stirring to combine. Drizzle with remaining sesame oil.
1½ cups: 548 cal., 25 g fat (5 g sat. fat), 163 mg chol., 934 mg sod., 43 g carb. (3 g sugars, 3 g fiber), 38 g pro.

HONEY-PECAN PORK CHOPS

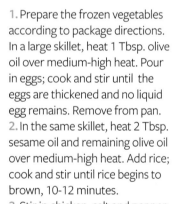

**SUPER QUICK
CHICKEN
FRIED RICE**

BUCATINI WITH SAUSAGE & KALE

I was short on time, but wanted to make an elegant dinner for my husband and me. That night, we happily ate this simple pasta starring spicy sausage and our homegrown kale.
—Angela Lemoine, Howell, NJ

Takes: 30 min. • **Makes:** 6 servings

- 1 pkg. (12 oz.) bucatini pasta or fettuccine
- 2 tsp. plus 3 Tbsp. olive oil, divided
- 1 lb. regular or spicy bulk Italian sausage
- 5 garlic cloves, thinly sliced
- 8 cups chopped fresh kale (about 5 oz.)
- ¾ tsp. salt
- ¼ tsp. pepper
  Shredded Romano cheese

1. Cook pasta according to the package directions, decreasing time by 3 minutes. Drain pasta, reserving 2 cups of pasta water. Toss pasta with 2 tsp. oil.
2. In a 6-qt. stockpot, cook sausage over medium heat until no longer pink, 5-7 minutes, breaking into large crumbles. Add garlic and remaining oil; cook and stir 2 minutes. Stir in the kale, salt and pepper; cook, covered, over medium-low until the kale is tender, about 10 minutes, stirring mixture occasionally.
3. Add pasta and reserved water; bring to a boil. Reduce the heat; simmer, uncovered, until pasta is al dente and liquid is absorbed, about 3 minutes, tossing to combine. Sprinkle with cheese.
1⅓ cups: 512 cal., 30g fat (8g sat. fat), 51mg chol., 898mg sod., 43g carb. (2g sugars, 3g fiber), 19g pro.

COD WITH BACON & BALSAMIC TOMATOES

Let's face it, everything really is better with bacon. I fry it, add cod fillets to the pan and finish it up with a big, tomato-y pop.
—Maureen McClanahan, Saint Louis, MO

Takes: 30 min. • **Makes:** 4 servings

- 4   center-cut bacon strips, chopped
- 4   cod fillets (5 oz. each)
- ½   tsp. salt
- ¼   tsp. pepper
- 2   cups grape tomatoes, halved
- 2   Tbsp. balsamic vinegar

1. In a large skillet, cook the bacon over medium heat until crisp, stirring occasionally. Remove with a slotted spoon, leaving drippings in the pan. Drain on paper towels.
2. Sprinkle fish fillets with salt and pepper. Add fillets to the pan; cook over medium-high heat until fish just begins to flake easily with a fork, 4-6 minutes on each side or. Remove and keep warm.
3. Add tomatoes to skillet; cook and stir until the tomatoes are softened, for 2-4 minutes. Stir in vinegar; reduce heat to medium-low. Cook until the sauce is thickened, 1-2 minutes longer. Serve cod topped with tomato mixture and bacon.

1 fillet with ¼ cup tomato mixture and 1 Tbsp. bacon: 178 cal., 6g fat (2g sat. fat), 64mg chol., 485mg sod., 5g carb. (4g sugars, 1g fiber), 26g pro. **Diabetic exchanges:** 4 lean meat, 1 vegetable.

GARLIC HERBED BEEF TENDERLOIN

You don't need much seasoning to add flavor to this tender beef roast. The mild blend of rosemary, basil and garlic does the trick in this recipe.
—Ruth Andrewson, Leavenworth, WA

Prep: 5 min.
Bake: 40 min. + standing
Makes: 12 servings

- 1   beef tenderloin roast (3 lbs.)
- 2   tsp. olive oil
- 2   garlic cloves, minced
- 1½ tsp. dried basil
- 1½ tsp. dried rosemary, crushed
- 1   tsp. salt
- 1   tsp. pepper

1. Preheat the oven to 45°. Tie tenderloin at 2-in. intervals with kitchen string. Combine oil and garlic; brush over meat. Combine the basil, rosemary, salt and pepper; sprinkle evenly over meat. Place on a rack in a shallow roasting pan.
2. Bake, uncovered, until the meat reaches desired doneness (for medium-rare, a thermometer should read 135°; medium, 140°; medium-well, 145°), for 40-50 minutes. Let stand 10 minutes before slicing.

3 oz. cooked beef: 198 cal., 10g fat (4g sat. fat), 78mg chol., 249mg sod., 1g carb. (0 sugars, 0 fiber), 25g pro. **Diabetic exchanges:** 3 lean meat.

COD WITH BACON & BALSAMIC TOMATOES

ROSEMARY
TURKEY BREAST

ROSEMARY TURKEY BREAST

I season turkey with a blend of rosemary, garlic and paprika. Because I rub it directly on the meat under the skin, I can remove the skin before serving and not lose any of the flavor. The result is a lower fat, yet delicious, entree.
—Dorothy Pritchett, Wills Point, TX

Prep: 10 min.
Bake: 1½ hours + standing
Makes: 15 servings

- 2 Tbsp. olive oil
- 8 to 10 garlic cloves, peeled
- 3 Tbsp. chopped fresh rosemary or 3 tsp. dried rosemary, crushed
- 1 tsp. salt
- 1 tsp. paprika
- ½ tsp. coarsely ground pepper
- 1 bone-in turkey breast (5 lbs.)

1. Preheat oven to 325°. In a food processor, combine the oil, garlic, rosemary, salt, paprika and pepper; cover and process until the garlic is coarsely chopped.
2. With your fingers, carefully loosen the skin from both sides of turkey breast. Spread half the garlic mixture over the meat under the skin. Smooth skin over meat and secure to underside of breast with toothpicks. Spread remaining garlic mixture over turkey skin.
3. Place turkey breast on a rack in a shallow roasting pan. Bake, uncovered, until a thermometer reads 170°, 1½ to 2 hours. Let the breast stand for 15 minutes before slicing. Discard toothpicks.

CHICKEN & VEGETABLE KABOBS

4 oz. cooked turkey: 148 cal., 3g fat (0 sat. fat), 78mg chol., 207mg sod., 1g carb. (0 sugars, 0 fiber), 29g pro. **Diabetic exchanges:** 4 lean meat.

CHICKEN & VEGETABLE KABOBS

In the summer, my husband and I love to cook out, especially fresh vegetables. These kabobs not only taste wonderful but they look great, too!
—Tina Oles, Nashwauk, MN

Takes: 30 min. • **Makes:** 4 servings

- 1 lb. boneless skinless chicken breasts, cut into 1½-in. cubes
- 1 medium sweet red pepper, cut into 1½-in. pieces
- 1 medium zucchini, cut into 1½-in. pieces
- 1 medium red onion, cut into thick wedges
- ⅔ cup sun-dried tomato salad dressing, divided

1. In a large bowl, combine the chicken and vegetables. Drizzle with ⅓ cup of the salad dressing; toss to coat. Alternately thread the chicken and vegetables onto 4 metal or soaked wood skewers.
2. Grill the kabobs, covered, over medium heat or broil 4 in. from heat until the chicken is no longer pink, 8-10 minutes, turning the skewers occasionally and basting with remaining dressing during the last 3 minutes.

1 kabob: 228 cal., 10g fat (1g sat. fat), 63mg chol., 515mg sod., 11g carb. (7g sugars, 2g fiber), 24g pro. **Diabetic exchanges:** 3 lean meat, 1 vegetable, 1 fat.

RAVIOLI LASAGNA

to 4 cups. Assemble and bake as directed, layering with 2 cups mozzarella each time. Sprinkle ¼ cup grated Parmesan over the top. Bake as directed, uncovering during the last 10 minutes.

Spinach Ravioli Lasagna: Replace beef with 3 cups fresh baby spinach (do not cook); use meatless spaghetti sauce. Assemble and bake as directed.

SAVORY PORK ROAST

I love this herbed roast so much that I make it as often as I can. It's wonderful for special occasions, particularly when served with sweet potatoes and corn muffins.
—Edie DeSpain, Logan, UT

Prep: 5 min.
Bake: 80 min. + standing
Makes: 12 servings

- 1 garlic clove, minced
- 2 tsp. dried marjoram
- 1 tsp. salt
- 1 tsp. rubbed sage
- 1 boneless whole pork loin roast (4 lbs.)

1. Preheat oven to 350°. Combine the seasonings; rub over roast. Place roast on a rack in a shallow roasting pan.
2. Bake roast, uncovered, until a thermometer reads 145°, about 80 minutes. Let stand for 10-15 minutes before slicing.

4 oz. cooked pork: 188 cal., 7g fat (3g sat. fat), 75mg chol., 240mg sod., 0 carb. (0 sugars, 0 fiber), 29g pro. **Diabetic exchanges:** 4 lean meat.

RAVIOLI LASAGNA

When you taste this casserole, you might think that it came from a complicated, from-scratch recipe. Really, though, it starts with frozen ravioli and has only three other ingredients.
—Patricia Smith, Asheboro, NC

Prep: 25 min. • **Bake:** 40 min.
Makes: 8 servings

- 1 lb. ground beef
- 1 jar (28 oz.) spaghetti sauce
- 1 pkg. (25 oz.) frozen sausage or cheese ravioli
- 1½ cups shredded part-skim mozzarella cheese
  Minced fresh basil, optional

1. Preheat oven to 400°. In a large skillet, cook beef over medium heat until no longer pink; drain. In a greased 2½-qt. baking dish, layer a third of the spaghetti sauce, half of the ravioli and beef, and ½ cup cheese; repeat layers. Top with remaining sauce and cheese.
2. Cover and bake until heated through, about 40-45 minutes. If desired, top with basil to serve.

1 cup: 438 cal., 18g fat (7g sat. fat), 77mg chol., 1178mg sod., 42g carb. (7g sugars, 5g fiber), 26g pro.

Ultimate Cheese Ravioli: Replace beef with 2 cups small-curd 4% cottage cheese; use cheese ravioli. Increase mozzarella

ASIAN BEEF & NOODLES

The ingredients for this yummy dish are easy to keep on hand. Serve with a dash of soy sauce and a side of fresh pineapple slices. You can also try it with ground turkey instead of beef.

—Laura Stenberg, Wyoming, MN

Takes: 20 min. • **Makes:** 4 servings

- 1 **lb. lean ground beef (90% lean)**
- 2 **pkg. (3 oz. each) ramen noodles, crumbled**
- 2½ **cups water**
- 2 **cups frozen broccoli stir-fry vegetable blend**
- ¼ **tsp. ground ginger**
- 2 **Tbsp. thinly sliced green onion**

1. In a large skillet, cook beef over medium heat until no longer pink; drain. Add the contents of one ramen noodle flavoring packet; stir until dissolved. Remove beef and set aside.

2. In the same skillet, combine the water, vegetables, ginger, noodles and the contents of the remaining flavoring packet. Bring to a boil. Reduce heat; cover and simmer until the noodles are tender, for 3-4 minutes, stirring occasionally. Return beef to the pan and heat through. Stir in the onion.

1½ cups: 383 cal., 16g fat (7g sat. fat), 71mg chol., 546mg sod., 29g carb. (2g sugars, 2g fiber), 27g pro.

ASIAN BEEF & NOODLES

**WEEKDAY
BEEF STEW**

Add tomatoes, vegetables and pepper; bring to a boil. In a small bowl, mix cornstarch and water until smooth; stir into the beef mixture. Return to a boil, stirring constantly; cook and stir until thickened, 1-2 minutes.

3. Ladle stew into four bowls; top each with a pastry round.

1½ cups with 1 pastry round: 604 cal., 25g fat (8g sat. fat), 73mg chol., 960mg sod., 65g carb. (10g sugars, 9g fiber), 32g pro.

BASIL PORK CHOPS

These tender glazed chops get a kick from basil, chili powder and a little brown sugar. Served with roasted veggies, they're a meal.
—Lisa Gilliland, Fort Collins, CO

Takes: 25 min. • **Makes:** 4 servings

- ¼ cup packed brown sugar
- 1½ tsp. dried basil
- ½ tsp. salt
- ½ tsp. chili powder
- 2 Tbsp. canola oil, divided
- 4 boneless pork loin chops (½ in. thick and 4 oz. each)

1. Mix the first 4 ingredients; gradually stir in 1 Tbsp. of the oil (mixture will be crumbly). Rub over both sides of pork chops.
2. In a large skillet, heat remaining oil over medium heat; cook chops until a thermometer reads 145°, 4-6 minutes per side. Let stand 5 minutes before serving.

1 pork chop: 152 cal., 8g fat (1g sat. fat), 14mg chol., 312mg sod., 14g carb. (13g sugars, 0 fiber), 6g pro.

WEEKDAY BEEF STEW

Beef stew capped with flaky puff pastry adds comfort to the weeknight menu. Make a salad and call your crowd to the table.
—Daniel Anderson, Kenosha, WI

Takes: 30 min. • **Makes:** 4 servings

- 1 sheet frozen puff pastry, thawed
- 1 pkg. (15 oz.) refrigerated beef roast au jus
- 2 cans (14½ oz. each) diced tomatoes, undrained
- 1 pkg. (16 oz.) frozen vegetables for stew
- ¾ tsp. pepper
- 2 Tbsp. cornstarch
- 1¼ cups water

1. Preheat oven to 400°. Unfold puff pastry. Using a 4-in. round cookie cutter, cut out four circles. Place 2 in. apart on a greased baking sheet. Bake until golden brown, 14-16 minutes.
2. Meanwhile, shred beef with two forks; transfer to a large saucepan.

BASIL PORK CHOPS

MOIST & TENDER TURKEY BREAST

The first time I slow-cooked turkey I was on vacation. It simmered while we were out, and we came back to a spectacularly juicy bird.
—Heidi Vawdrey, Riverton, UT

Prep: 10 min. • **Cook:** 4 hours
Makes: 12 servings

- 1 **bone-in turkey breast (6 to 7 lbs.)**
- 4 **fresh rosemary sprigs**
- 4 **garlic cloves, peeled**
- ½ **cup water**
- 1 **Tbsp. brown sugar**
- ½ **tsp. coarsely ground pepper**
- ¼ **tsp. salt**

Place the turkey breast, rosemary, garlic and water in a 6-qt. slow cooker. Mix the brown sugar, pepper and salt; sprinkle over the turkey. Cook, covered, on low until tender and a thermometer inserted in the turkey reads at least 170°, 4-6 hours.

5 oz. cooked turkey: 318 cal., 12g fat (3g sat. fat), 122mg chol., 154mg sod., 2g carb. (1g sugars, 0 fiber), 47g pro.

★ ★ ★ ★ ★ **READER REVIEW**

"This was easy, convenient, and my family loved the flavors of rosemary and garlic ever so slightly flavoring the moist turkey."

SHAUCKOGS92
TASTEOFHOME.COM

CRISPY BUFFALO CHICKEN ROLL-UPS FOR TWO

These winning chicken rolls with a crispy crust are both impressive and easy to make. My family and friends absolutely love them!
—Lisa Keys, Kennett Square, PA

Prep: 15 min. • **Bake:** 30 min.
Makes: 2 servings

- 2 boneless skinless chicken breast halves (6 oz. each)
- ¼ tsp. salt
- ¼ tsp. pepper
- 2 Tbsp. crumbled blue cheese
- 2 Tbsp. hot pepper sauce
- 1 Tbsp. mayonnaise
- ½ cup crushed cornflakes

1. Preheat oven to 400°. Flatten chicken breasts to ¼-in. thickness. Season with salt and pepper; sprinkle with blue cheese. Roll up each from a short side and secure with toothpicks.

2. In a shallow bowl, combine pepper sauce and mayonnaise. Place cornflakes in a separate shallow bowl. Dip the chicken in the pepper sauce mixture, then coat with cornflakes. Place seam side down in a greased 11x7-in. baking dish.

3. Bake, uncovered, until chicken is no longer pink, 30-35 minutes. Discard toothpicks.

1 serving: 270 cal., 8g fat (3g sat. fat), 101mg chol., 617mg sod., 10g carb. (1g sugars, 0 fiber), 37g pro

Diabetic exchanges: 5 lean meat, ½ starch, ½ fat.

GINGER-CHUTNEY SHRIMP STIR-FRY

I made this recipe a lot when I was juggling college, work and a growing family. It tastes like you spent a lot of time making it, yet takes less than half an hour to toss together.
—Sally Sibthorpe, Shelby Township, MI

Takes: 25 min. • **Makes:** 4 servings

- 2 Tbsp. peanut or canola oil
- 1 lb. uncooked medium shrimp, peeled and deveined, tails removed
- 1 Tbsp. minced fresh gingerroot
- 3 cups frozen pepper and onion stir-fry blend, thawed
- ¾ cup mango chutney
- 2 Tbsp. water
- ¾ tsp. salt
  Hot cooked rice, optional

In a large skillet, heat oil over medium-high heat. Add shrimp and ginger; stir-fry until shrimp turn pink, 4-5 minutes. Stir in the remaining ingredients; cook until the vegetables are crisp-tender, stirring occasionally. If desired, serve with rice.

1 cup: 356 cal., 8g fat (1g sat. fat), 138mg chol., 1102mg sod., 47g carb. (30g sugars, 1g fiber), 19g pro.

CRISPY BUFFALO CHICKEN ROLL-UPS FOR TWO

BACON & SPINACH PIZZA

Our go-to pizza is a snap to make using packaged pizza crust and ready-to-serve bacon. The kids don't even mind the spinach on top!
—Annette Riva, Naperville, IL

Takes: 20 min. • **Makes:** 6 servings

- 1   prebaked 12-in. pizza crust
- ⅓ cup pizza sauce
- 1   cup shaved Parmesan cheese
- 2   cups fresh baby spinach, thinly sliced
- 8   ready-to-serve fully cooked bacon strips, cut into 1-in. pieces

Preheat oven to 450°. Place crust on an ungreased baking sheet. Spread with sauce; top with ½ cup of the cheese, the spinach and bacon. Sprinkle with the remaining cheese. Bake until the cheese is melted, 8-10 minutes.

1 slice: 269 cal., 10g fat (4g sat. fat), 10mg chol., 726mg sod., 31g carb. (2g sugars, 2g fiber), 15g pro. **Diabetic exchanges:** 2 starch, 2 medium-fat meat.

✳
TEST KITCHEN TIP
Shaving Parmesan gives wider, flat pieces of cheese, not shreds. You can buy it already shaved, or shave your own from a block of Parmesan using a special cheese shaver, a vegetable peeler or the shaving face of a grater.

CAESAR SALMON WITH ROASTED TOMATOES & ARTICHOKES

CAESAR SALMON WITH ROASTED TOMATOES & ARTICHOKES

This is my go-to recipe for quick dinners for family or guests. It's colorful, healthy, easy to prepare and absolutely delicious.
—Mary Hawkes, Prescott, AZ

Takes: 25 min. • **Makes:** 4 servings

- 4   salmon fillets (5 oz. each)
- 5   Tbsp. reduced-fat Caesar vinaigrette, divided
- ¼ tsp. pepper, divided
- 2   cups grape tomatoes
- 1   can (14 oz.) water-packed artichoke hearts, drained and quartered
- 1   medium sweet orange or yellow pepper, cut into 1-in. pieces

1. Preheat oven to 425°. Place salmon fillets on one half of a 15x10x1-in. baking pan coated with cooking spray. Brush with 2 Tbsp. vinaigrette; sprinkle with ⅛ tsp. pepper.

2. In a large bowl, combine the tomatoes, artichoke hearts and sweet pepper. Add the remaining vinaigrette and pepper; toss to coat. Place the tomato mixture on the remaining half of pan. Roast until fish just begins to flake easily with a fork and the vegetables are tender, 12-15 minutes.

1 fillet with ¾ cup tomato mixture: 318 cal., 16g fat (3g sat. fat), 73mg chol., 674mg sod., 12g carb. (4g sugars, 2g fiber), 28g pro. **Diabetic exchanges:** 4 lean meat, 1 vegetable, 1 fat.

EASY STUFFED SHELLS

HAMBURGER CASSEROLE

This recipe is such a hit it's traveled all over the country. My mother began making it in Pennsylvania, I took it to Texas when I married and I'm still making it in California, and my daughter treats her friends to it in Colorado.

—Helen Carmichall, Santee, CA

Prep: 20 min. • **Cook:** 45 min.
Makes: 10 servings

- 2 lbs. lean ground beef (90% lean)
- 4 lbs. potatoes, peeled and sliced ¼ in. thick
- 1 large onion, sliced
- 1 tsp. salt
- ½ tsp. pepper
- 1 tsp. beef bouillon granules
- 1 cup boiling water
- 1 can (28 oz.) diced tomatoes, undrained
   Minced fresh parsley, optional

In a Dutch oven, layer half of each of the meat, potatoes and onion. Sprinkle with half the salt and pepper. Repeat layers. Dissolve the bouillon in water; pour over all. Top with the tomatoes. Cover and cook over medium heat until the potatoes are tender, about 45-50 minutes. If desired, garnish with parsley.

1 cup: 270 cal., 8g fat (3g sat. fat), 57mg chol., 493mg sod., 30g carb. (5g sugars, 3g fiber), 21g pro.
Diabetic exchanges: 3 lean meat, 2 starch.

EASY STUFFED SHELLS

I created a super easy way to fill pasta shells—just use meatballs! Putting the kids on stuffing duty is a great way to get them involved.
—Dolores Betchner, Cudahy, WI

Prep: 20 min. • **Bake:** 40 min.
Makes: 12 servings

- 36 uncooked jumbo pasta shells
- 1 jar (24 oz.) spaghetti sauce
- 36 frozen fully cooked Italian meatballs (½ oz. each), thawed
- 2 cups shredded part-skim mozzarella cheese

1. Preheat oven to 350°. Cook pasta shells according to the package directions; drain and rinse in cold water.
2. Spread ½ cup of the sauce into a greased 13x9-in. baking dish. Fill each shell with a meatball; place shells over sauce. Top with the remaining sauce and the cheese.
3. Bake, covered, for 35 minutes. Uncover; bake until mixture is bubbly and the cheese is melted, 3-5 minutes longer.

3 stuffed shells: 334 cal., 17g fat (8g sat. fat), 45mg chol., 711mg sod., 30g carb. (6g sugars, 3g fiber), 16g pro.

BLUE CHEESE-CRUSTED SIRLOIN STEAKS

This smothered steak is my specialty. I like to make it for my wife on Friday evenings to say goodbye to a long week.
—Michael Rouse, Minot, ND

Takes: 30 min. • **Makes:** 4 servings

- 2 Tbsp. butter, divided
- 1 medium onion, chopped
- ⅓ cup crumbled blue cheese
- 2 Tbsp. soft bread crumbs
- 1 beef top sirloin steak (1 in. thick and 1½ lbs.)
- ¾ tsp. salt
- ½ tsp. pepper

1. Preheat the broiler. In a large broiler-safe skillet, heat 1 Tbsp. butter over medium heat; saute onion until tender. Transfer to a bowl; stir in the cheese and bread crumbs.
2. Cut the steak into four pieces; sprinkle with salt and pepper. In the same pan, heat the remaining butter over medium heat; cook steaks until desired doneness (for medium-rare, a thermometer should read 135°; medium, 140°), 4-5 minutes per side.
3. Spread the onion mixture over steaks. Broil 4-6 in. from heat until lightly browned, 2-3 minutes.

Note: To make soft bread crumbs, tear bread into pieces and place in a food processor or blender. Cover and pulse until crumbs form. One slice of bread yields ½ to ¾ cup crumbs.

1 serving: 326 cal., 16g fat (8g sat. fat), 92mg chol., 726mg sod., 5g carb. (2g sugars, 1g fiber), 39g pro.

BLUE CHEESE-CRUSTED SIRLOIN STEAKS

TORTELLINI CARBONARA

Bacon, cream and Parmesan cheese make a classic pasta sauce that's absolutely heavenly. It's a great option for company.
—Cathy Croyle, Davidsville, PA

Takes: 20 min. • **Makes:** 4 servings

- 1 pkg. (9 oz.) refrigerated cheese tortellini
- 8 bacon strips, chopped
- 1 cup heavy whipping cream
- ½ cup grated Parmesan cheese
- ½ cup chopped fresh parsley

1. Cook tortellini according to package directions; drain.

2. Meanwhile, in a large skillet, cook bacon over medium heat until crisp, stirring occasionally. Remove with a slotted spoon; drain on paper towels. Pour off the drippings.

3. In the same pan, combine the cream, cheese, parsley and bacon; heat through over medium heat. Stir in the tortellini. Serve tortellini carbonara immediately.

1 cup: 527 cal., 36g fat (20g sat. fat), 121mg chol., 728mg sod., 33g carb. (3g sugars, 2g fiber), 19g pro.

SAUSAGE & FETA STUFFED TOMATOES

As a pro weight-loss coach, I'm all about eating healthy. My clients and friends absolutely love these healthy and tasty tomatoes.
—Shana Conradt, Greenville, WI

Takes: 25 min. • **Makes:** 4 servings

- 3 Italian turkey sausage links (4 oz. each), casings removed
- 1 cup (4 oz.) crumbled feta cheese, divided
- 8 plum tomatoes
- ¼ tsp. salt
- ¼ tsp. pepper
- 3 Tbsp. balsamic vinegar
  Minced fresh parsley

1. In a large skillet, cook sausage over medium heat for 4-6 minutes or until no longer pink, breaking into crumbles. Transfer to a small bowl; stir in ½ cup of the cheese.

2. Cut tomatoes in half lengthwise. Scoop out the pulp, leaving a ½-in. shell; discard pulp. Sprinkle tomatoes with salt and pepper; transfer to an ungreased 13x9-in. baking dish. Spoon the sausage mixture into the tomato shells; drizzle with vinegar. Sprinkle with the remaining cheese.

3. Bake, uncovered, at 350° until heated through, 10-12 minutes. Sprinkle with parsley.

4 stuffed tomato halves: 200 cal., 10g fat (4g sat. fat), 46mg chol., 777mg sod., 12g carb. (8g sugars, 3g fiber), 16g pro. **Diabetic exchanges:** 2 medium-fat meat, 1 vegetable, ½ starch.

TORTELLINI CARBONARA

SAUSAGE & FETA STUFFED TOMATOES

SCALLOPS WITH WILTED SPINACH

SCALLOPS WITH WILTED SPINACH

In this dish, I bring together two of my favorite foods—bacon and seafood—in an elegant mix with white wine, shallots and baby spinach. If you like, serve with bread to soak up the tasty broth.
—Deborah Williams, Peoria, AZ

Takes: 25 min. • **Makes:** 4 servings

- 4 bacon strips, chopped
- 12 sea scallops (about 1½ lbs.), side muscles removed
- 2 shallots, finely chopped
- ½ cup white wine or chicken broth
- 8 cups fresh baby spinach (about 8 oz.)

1. In a large nonstick skillet, cook bacon over medium heat until crisp, stirring occasionally. Remove with a slotted spoon; drain on paper towels. Discard drippings, reserving 2 Tbsp. Wipe skillet clean if necessary.
2. Pat the scallops dry with paper towels. In the same skillet, heat 1 Tbsp. drippings over medium-high heat. Add scallops; cook until golden brown and firm, 2-3 minutes on each side. Remove from pan; keep warm.
3. Heat the remaining drippings in the same pan over medium-high heat. Add the shallots; cook and stir until tender, 2-3 minutes. Add the wine; bring to a boil, stirring to loosen browned bits from pan. Add the spinach; cook and stir until wilted, 1-2 minutes. Stir in the bacon. Serve with scallops.

3 scallops with ½ cup spinach mixture: 247 cal., 11g fat (4g sat. fat), 56mg chol., 964mg sod., 12g carb. (1g sugars, 1g fiber), 26g pro.

LUNCH BOX PIZZAS

It's a challenge to find lunches the kids will eat. These pack nicely in sandwich bags and travel well, so there's no mess.
—Rhonda Cliett, Belton, TX

Takes: 20 min.
Makes: 10 servings

- 1 tube (7½ oz.) refrigerated buttermilk biscuits (10 biscuits)
- ¼ cup tomato sauce
- 1 tsp. Italian seasoning
- 10 slices pepperoni
- ¾ cup shredded Monterey Jack cheese

1. Preheat oven to 425°. Flatten each biscuit into a 3-in. circle and press into a greased muffin cup. Combine the tomato sauce and Italian seasoning; spoon 1 teaspoonful into each cup. Top each with a slice of pepperoni and about 1 Tbsp. of the cheese.
2. Bake until golden brown, for 10-15 minutes. Serve immediately or store in the refrigerator.
1 serving: 94 cal., 4g fat (2g sat. fat), 9mg chol., 292mg sod., 11g carb. (0 sugars, 0 fiber), 4g pro.

MEXICAN RICE WITH CHICKEN

This skillet supper comes together quickly with leftover chicken and packaged mix. If you don't eat it all, serve it the next day on tortillas with cheese and sour cream. It's just as good both ways.
—Debra Rzodkiewicz, Erie, PA

Prep: 5 min. • **Cook:** 30 min.
Makes: 4 servings

- 1 pkg. (6.4 oz.) Mexican-style rice and pasta mix
- 2 Tbsp. butter
- 1¾ cups water
- 1 can (14½ oz.) diced tomatoes with onions, undrained
- 2 cups cubed cooked chicken
- 1 jalapeno pepper, seeded and chopped

In a large skillet, cook and stir rice and pasta mix in butter until lightly browned, about 5 minutes. Add water, tomatoes and the contents of rice seasoning packet. Bring to a boil. Reduce heat; cover and cook for 10 minutes. Add chicken and jalapeno. Cover and cook until the rice is tender and the liquid is absorbed, 8-10 minutes .
Note: Wear disposable gloves when cutting hot peppers; the oils can burn skin. Avoid touching your face. • This recipe was tested with Rice-a-Roni rice and pasta mix.
1½ cups: 385 cal., 12g fat (5g sat. fat), 79mg chol., 1217mg sod., 42g carb. (9g sugars, 2g fiber), 25g pro.

LUNCH BOX PIZZAS

**SHRIMP
FRIED RICE**

SHRIMP FRIED RICE

This colorful, delectable dish vanishes quickly—our family of four can't get enough of it. Bacon adds crispness and heartiness. Consider it when you need a different entree or brunch item.
—Sandra Thompson, White Hall, AR

Takes: 20 min. • **Makes:** 6 servings

- 4 Tbsp. butter, divided
- 4 large eggs, lightly beaten
- 3 cups cold cooked rice
- 1 pkg. (16 oz.) frozen mixed vegetables
- 1 lb. uncooked medium shrimp, peeled and deveined
- ½ tsp. salt
- ¼ tsp. pepper
- 8 bacon strips, cooked and crumbled, optional

1. In a large skillet, melt 1 Tbsp. butter over medium-high heat. Pour eggs into skillet. As eggs set, lift edges, letting the uncooked portion flow underneath. Remove eggs and keep warm.
2. Melt remaining butter in the skillet. Add rice, vegetables and shrimp; cook and stir 5 minutes or until shrimp turn pink. Chop eggs into small pieces; return to pan and sprinkle with salt and pepper. Cook until heated through, stirring occasionally. Sprinkle with bacon if desired.

1 serving: 332 cal., 12g fat (6g sat. fat), 236mg chol., 422mg sod., 33g carb. (3g sugars, 4g fiber), 21g pro.

CHICKEN PROVOLONE

CHICKEN PROVOLONE

Though it's one of my simplest dishes, this version of an Italian favorite is one of my husband's favorites. It looks fancy served on a dark plate with a garnish of fresh parsley or basil.
—Dawn Bryant, Thedford, NE

Takes: 25 min. • **Makes:** 4 servings

- 4 boneless skinless chicken breast halves (4 oz. each)
- ¼ tsp. pepper
  Butter-flavored cooking spray
- 8 fresh basil leaves
- 4 thin slices prosciutto or deli ham
- 4 slices provolone cheese

1. Sprinkle chicken with pepper. In a large skillet coated with butter-flavored cooking spray, cook chicken over medium heat for 4-5 minutes on each side or until a thermometer reads 170°.
2. Transfer to an ungreased baking sheet; top with basil, prosciutto and cheese. Broil 6-8 in. from the heat until cheese is melted, 1-2 minutes.

1 serving: 236 cal., 11g fat (6g sat. fat), 89mg chol., 435mg sod., 1g carb. (0 sugars, 0 fiber), 33g pro.
Diabetic exchanges: 4 lean meat.

MEDITERRANEAN CHICKEN

PECAN-COCONUT CRUSTED TILAPIA

When I have guests with dietary restrictions, tilapia coated in pecans and coconut makes everyone happy. Gluten-free, it's loaded with flavor.
—Caitlin Roth, Chicago, IL

Takes: 25 min. • **Makes:** 4 servings

- 2 large eggs
- ½ cup unsweetened finely shredded coconut
- ½ cup finely chopped pecans
- ½ tsp. salt
- ¼ tsp. crushed red pepper flakes
- 4 tilapia fillets (6 oz. each)
- 2 Tbsp. canola oil

1. In a shallow bowl, whisk eggs. In a separate shallow bowl, combine coconut, pecans, salt and pepper flakes. Dip fillets in eggs, then in coconut mixture, patting to help coating adhere.
2. In a large skillet, heat oil over medium heat. In batches, add the tilapia and cook until lightly browned and the fish just begins to flake easily with a fork, for 2-3 minutes on each side.
Note: Look for unsweetened coconut in the baking or health food section.
1 fillet: 380 cal., 26g fat (8g sat. fat), 129mg chol., 377mg sod., 4g carb. (1g sugars, 3g fiber), 35g pro.

MEDITERRANEAN CHICKEN

Chicken goes Mediterranean with tomatoes, olives and capers in this skillet creation, a warm welcome to the table. It's as special as it is simple to prepare.
—Mary Relyea, Canastota, NY

Takes: 25 min. • **Makes:** 4 servings

- 4 boneless skinless chicken breast halves (6 oz. each)
- ¼ tsp. salt
- ¼ tsp. pepper
- 3 Tbsp. olive oil
- 1 pint grape tomatoes
- 16 pitted Greek or ripe olives, sliced
- 3 Tbsp. capers, drained

1. Sprinkle chicken with salt and pepper. In a large ovenproof skillet, cook chicken in oil over medium heat 2-3 minutes on each side or until golden brown. Add the tomatoes, olives and capers.
2. Bake, uncovered, at 475° for 10-14 minutes or until a thermometer reads 170°.
1 serving: 336 cal., 18g fat (3g sat. fat), 94mg chol., 631mg sod., 6g carb. (3g sugars, 2g fiber), 36g pro. **Diabetic exchanges:** 5 lean meat, 3 fat, 1 vegetable.

CHORIZO PUMPKIN PASTA

I'm a busy student, and I'm always looking for a perfect quick dinner like this spicy-sweet pasta. Even better, it works when scaled up to feed a bunch of friends.
—Christine Yang, Syracuse, NY

Takes: 30 min. • **Makes:** 6 servings

- 3 cups uncooked gemelli or spiral pasta (about 12 oz.)
- 1 pkg. (12 oz.) fully cooked chorizo chicken sausage links or flavor of choice, sliced
- 1 cup canned pumpkin
- 1 cup half-and-half cream
- ¾ tsp. salt
- ¼ tsp. pepper
- 1½ cups shredded Manchego or Monterey Jack cheese
  Minced fresh cilantro, optional

Cook pasta according to package directions. Drain, reserving ¾ cup pasta water. Meanwhile, in a large skillet, saute sausage over medium heat until lightly browned; reduce heat to medium-low. Add the pumpkin, cream, salt and pepper; cook and stir mixture until heated through. Toss with the pasta and enough pasta water to moisten; stir in cheese. If desired, sprinkle with cilantro.

1⅓ cups: 471 cal., 20g fat (11g sat. fat), 92mg chol., 847mg sod., 48g carb. (7g sugars, 3g fiber), 26g pro.

CHORIZO PUMPKIN PASTA

SOUTHWEST KIELBASA BOWLS

Here's our own at-home take on restaurant burrito bowls. We start with rice, kielbasa and black beans, then top 'em with salsa, red onion and cilantro. Use a spicier sausage if you want more heat.

—Abby Williamson, Dunedin, FL

Takes: 20 min. • **Makes:** 4 servings

- 2 cups uncooked instant brown rice
- 2 Tbsp. olive oil
- 1 pkg. (14 oz.) smoked turkey kielbasa, cut into ¼-in. slices
- 1 can (15 oz.) black beans, rinsed and drained
- 1½ cups fresh salsa
- ¼ cup finely chopped red onion Fresh cilantro leaves, optional

1. Cook the rice according to package directions.
2. Meanwhile, in a large skillet, heat oil over medium-high heat. Add kielbasa; cook and stir for 4-6 minutes or until browned. Stir in the beans and salsa.
3. Divide rice among four bowls. Top with kielbasa mixture, onion and, if desired, cilantro.

1 serving: 454 cal., 14g fat (3g sat. fat), 62mg chol., 1192mg sod., 54g carb. (4g sugars, 7g fiber), 26g pro.

SOUTHWEST KIELBASA BOWLS

CHEESY BOW TIE CHICKEN

Here's a super simple dish that tastes like it's straight from a nice Italian restaurant. You can find spinach and artichoke dip in the freezer section, and usually it's also available fresh not far from the rotisserie chicken at the deli.

—Sally Sibthorpe, Shelby Township, MI

Takes: 30 min. • **Makes:** 4 servings

- 2 pkg. (8 oz. each) frozen spinach and artichoke cheese dip
- 3 cups uncooked bow tie pasta
- 3 cups cubed rotisserie chicken
- 1 cup chopped roasted sweet red peppers
- ⅓ cup pitted Greek olives, halved
- ½ tsp. salt
- ¼ tsp. pepper

1. Heat the dip according to the package directions. Meanwhile, in a Dutch oven, cook the pasta according to package directions; drain, reserving ½ cup of the pasta water. Return to pan.
2. Stir in chicken, dip, peppers, olives, salt and pepper, adding enough reserved pasta water to reach a creamy consistency; heat through.

1½ cups: 453 cal., 12g fat (3g sat. fat), 93mg chol., 795mg sod., 44g carb. (4g sugars, 2g fiber), 38g pro.

CHEESY BOW TIE CHICKEN

SPINACH STEAK PINWHEELS

SPINACH STEAK PINWHEELS

Bacon and spinach bring plenty of flavor to these sirloin steak spirals. It looks impressive but it's easy to make for a backyard cookout.
—Helen Vail, Glenside, PA

Takes: 25 min. • **Makes:** 6 servings

1½ lbs. beef top sirloin steak
 8 bacon strips, cooked
 1 pkg. (10 oz.) frozen chopped spinach, thawed and squeezed dry
 ¼ cup grated Parmesan cheese
 ½ tsp. salt
 ⅛ tsp. cayenne pepper

1. Lightly score steak by making shallow diagonal cuts at 1-in. intervals into top of steak; repeat cuts in the opposite direction. Cover steak with plastic wrap; pound with a meat mallet to ½-in. thickness. Remove plastic.

2. Place bacon widthwise at the center of the steak. In a bowl, mix remaining ingredients; spoon over the bacon. Starting at a short side, roll up steak jelly-roll style; secure with toothpicks. Cut into 6 slices.

3. On a lightly oiled grill rack, grill pinwheels, covered, over medium heat 5-6 minutes on each side or until beef reaches desired doneness (for medium-rare, a thermometer should read 135°; medium, 140°). Discard toothpicks before serving.

1 pinwheel: 227 cal., 10g fat (4g sat. fat), 60mg chol., 536mg sod., 3g carb. (0 sugars, 1g fiber), 31g pro. **Diabetic exchanges:** 4 lean meat, 1 fat.

CHICKEN PESTO WITH PASTA

If you keep pesto in the freezer, it's easy to whip up this simple pasta when you have leftover chicken.
—*Taste of Home* Test Kitchen

Takes: 20 min. • **Makes:** 8 servings

- 1 pkg. (16 oz.) cellentani or spiral pasta
- 2 cups cubed rotisserie chicken
- 2 medium tomatoes, chopped
- 1 container (7 oz.) prepared pesto
- ¼ cup pine nuts, toasted

In a Dutch oven, cook pasta according to package directions; drain and return to pan. Stir in chicken, tomatoes and pesto; heat through. Sprinkle mixture with pine nuts.

Note: To toast nuts, bake in a shallow pan in a 350° oven for 5-10 minutes or cook in a skillet over low heat until lightly browned, stirring occasionally.

1¼ cups: 433 cal., 18g fat (5g sat. fat), 40mg chol., 239mg sod., 45g carb. (3g sugars, 3g fiber), 24g pro.

OVEN-BAKED BURGERS

A crispy coating mix is the secret ingredient that dresses up burgers that you bake in the oven instead of grill or fry. For the best flavor, I use a sweet and spicy steak sauce.
—Mike Goldman, Arden Hills, MN

Takes: 30 min. • **Makes:** 4 servings

- ¼ cup steak sauce
- 2 Tbsp. plus ⅓ cup seasoned coating mix, divided
- 1 lb. ground beef
- 4 hamburger buns, split
- 4 lettuce leaves

1. Preheat the oven to 350°. In a bowl, combine the steak sauce and 2 Tbsp. of the coating mix. Crumble beef over the sauce mixture and mix well. Shape into four 3½-in. patties. Dip both sides of the patties in the remaining coating. Place on an ungreased baking sheet.

2. Bake until a thermometer reads 160°, about 20 minutes, turning once. Serve on buns with lettuce.

1 burger: 403 cal., 17g fat (6g sat. fat), 70mg chol., 889mg sod., 35g carb. (6g sugars, 1g fiber), 26g pro.

CHICKEN PESTO WITH PASTA

PEACHY PORK WITH RICE

PEACHY PORK WITH RICE

Pork tenderloin does an awesome job of showing off my homemade peach preserves. Tweak your preferred heat level using mild or spicy salsa and seasonings.
—Melissa Molaison, Hawkinsville, GA

Takes: 30 min. • **Makes:** 4 servings

- 1½ cups uncooked instant brown rice
- 1 lb. pork tenderloin, cut into 1-in. cubes
- 2 Tbsp. olive oil
- 2 Tbsp. reduced-sodium taco seasoning
- 1 cup salsa
- 3 Tbsp. peach preserves

1. Cook the rice according to package directions. Meanwhile, place the pork in a large bowl; drizzle with oil. Sprinkle with taco seasoning; toss to coat.
2. Place a large nonstick skillet over medium heat. Add the pork; cook and stir until no longer pink, 8-10 minutes. Stir in salsa and preserves; heat through. Serve with rice.

1 cup pork mixture with ½ cup rice: 387 cal., 12g fat (2g sat. fat), 63mg chol., 540mg sod., 42g carb. (13g sugars, 2g fiber), 25g pro.
Diabetic exchanges: 3 lean meat, 2½ starch, 1½ fat.

RAVIOLI WITH APPLE CHICKEN SAUSAGE

RAVIOLI WITH APPLE CHICKEN SAUSAGE

I love butternut squash ravioli but was never quite sure what flavors would best complement the squash. Turns out that creamy spinach, chicken sausage and a hint of sweet spice are the perfect go-alongs.
—Mary Brodeur, Millbury, MA

Takes: 30 min. • **Makes:** 4 servings

- 1 pkg. (18 oz.) frozen butternut squash ravioli
- 2 pkg. (10 oz. each) frozen creamed spinach
- 1 Tbsp. olive oil
- 1 pkg. (12 oz.) fully cooked apple chicken sausage links, cut into ½-in. slices
- 1 tsp. maple syrup
- ¼ tsp. pumpkin pie spice

1. Cook ravioli according to the package directions. Prepare spinach according to package directions. Meanwhile, in a large skillet, heat oil over medium heat. Add sausage; cook and stir until browned, 2-4 minutes.
2. Drain the ravioli. Add ravioli, spinach, maple syrup and pie spice to sausage; heat through.
1½ cups: 532 cal., 16g fat (4g sat. fat), 64mg chol., 1409mg sod., 69g carb. (19g sugars, 4g fiber), 26g pro.

MEXICAN STUFFED PEPPERS

PESTO GRILLED SALMON

Buttery, colorful and flaky, this rich and impressive salmon will be a family favorite. Toss the leftovers with pasta for another delicious dish!
—Sonya Labbe,
West Hollywood, CA

Takes: 30 min.
Makes: 12 servings

- 1 salmon fillet (3 lbs.)
- ½ cup prepared pesto
- 2 green onions, finely chopped
- ¼ cup lemon juice
- 2 garlic cloves, minced

1. Place salmon skin side down on a lightly oiled grill rack. Grill, covered, over medium heat or broil 4 in. from the heat for 5 minutes.
2. In a small bowl, combine the pesto, onions, lemon juice and garlic. Carefully spoon some of the pesto mixture over salmon. Grill until the fish flakes easily with a fork, for 15-20 minutes longer, basting occasionally with the remaining pesto mixture.
3 oz. cooked salmon: 262 cal., 17g fat (4g sat. fat), 70mg chol., 147mg sod., 1g carb. (0 sugars, 0 fiber), 25g pro. **Diabetic exchanges:** 3 lean meat, 3 fat.

MEXICAN STUFFED PEPPERS

This tasty summer meal makes the most of homegrown peppers. Dab sour cream on top and serve tortilla chips and salsa alongside.
—Kim Coleman, Columbia, SC

Prep: 25 min. • **Bake:** 30 min.
Makes: 8 servings

- 1 lb. lean ground beef (90% lean)
- 1 can (14½ oz.) diced tomatoes and green chilies, undrained
- 1 envelope (5.4 oz.) Mexican-style rice and pasta mix
- 1½ cups water
- 8 medium sweet peppers
- 2 cups shredded Mexican cheese blend, divided

1. Preheat oven to 375°. In a large skillet, cook and crumble beef over medium heat until no longer pink, 5-7 minutes; drain. Stir in tomatoes, rice mix and water; bring to a boil. Reduce the heat; simmer, covered, until liquid is absorbed, 6-8 minutes.
2. Cut and discard tops from peppers; remove seeds. Place peppers in a greased 13x9-in. baking dish. Place ⅓ cup of the beef mixture in each pepper; sprinkle each with 2 Tbsp. cheese. Top with remaining rice mixture. Bake, covered, for 25 minutes.
3. Sprinkle with remaining cheese. Bake peppers, uncovered, until the cheese is melted and peppers are crisp-tender, 5-10 minutes.
1 stuffed pepper: 301 cal., 14g fat (8g sat. fat), 61mg chol., 797mg sod., 23g carb. (4g sugars, 3g fiber), 20g pro.

SKILLET BEEF & POTATOES

Even if you're not all about meat and potatoes, sirloin strips with red potatoes and fresh rosemary are seriously amazing and ready in a flash. The key is precooking the potatoes in a microwave.
—*Taste of Home* Test Kitchen

Takes: 25 min. • **Makes:** 4 servings

- 1½ lbs. red potatoes (about 5 medium), halved and cut into ¼-in. slices
- ⅓ cup water
- ½ tsp. salt
- 1 lb. beef top sirloin steak, cut into thin strips
- ½ cup chopped onion
- 3 Tbsp. olive oil, divided
- 2 tsp. garlic pepper blend
- 1½ tsp. minced fresh rosemary

1. Place the potatoes, water and salt in a microwave-safe dish; microwave, covered, on high until the potatoes are tender, 7-9 minutes. Drain.

2. Meanwhile, toss the beef with the onion, 2 Tbsp. of oil and the pepper blend. Place a large skillet over medium-high heat. Add half of the beef mixture; cook and stir until the beef is browned, 1-2 minutes. Remove from pan; repeat browning with remaining beef mixture.

3. In a clean skillet, heat remaining oil over medium-high heat. Add the potatoes; cook until lightly browned, 4-5 minutes, turning occasionally. Stir in beef mixture; heat through. Sprinkle beef and potatoes with rosemary.

1½ cups: 320 cal., 16g fat (4g sat. fat), 63mg chol., 487mg sod., 20g carb. (2g sugars, 2g fiber), 23g pro. **Diabetic exchanges:** 3 lean meat, 2 fat, 1 starch.

SKILLET BEEF & POTATOES

PLUM-GLAZED COUNTRY RIBS

QUICK CHICKEN PICCATA

Laced with lemon and simmered in white wine, this stovetop entree is super easy and elegant. Most any side—noodles or veggies or bread—tastes better next to this lovely chicken.
—Cynthia Heil, Augusta, GA

Takes: 30 min. • **Makes:** 4 servings

¼ cup all-purpose flour
½ tsp. salt
½ tsp. pepper
4 boneless skinless chicken breast halves (4 oz. each)
¼ cup butter, cubed
¼ cup white wine or chicken broth
1 Tbsp. lemon juice
   Minced fresh parsley, optional

1. In a shallow bowl, mix flour, salt and pepper. Pound chicken breasts with a meat mallet to ½-in. thickness. Dip chicken in the flour mixture to coat both sides; shake off excess.
2. In a large skillet, heat butter over medium heat. Brown the chicken on both sides. Add wine; bring to a boil. Reduce heat; simmer, uncovered, until the chicken is no longer pink, for 12-15 minutes. Drizzle with the lemon juice. If desired, sprinkle chicken with parsley.

1 chicken breast half with about 1 Tbsp. sauce: 265 cal., 14g fat (8g sat. fat), 93mg chol., 442mg sod., 7g carb. (0 sugars, 0 fiber), 24g pro.

PLUM-GLAZED COUNTRY RIBS

When planning to make ribs one day, I remembered that a friend had given me homemade plum jelly. I stirred some into the sauce for a pleasant fruity accent.
—Ila Mae Alderman, Galax, VA

Prep: 5 min. • **Bake:** 1¼ hours
Makes: 8 servings

4 to 4½ lbs. bone-in country-style pork ribs
1 bottle (12 oz.) chili sauce
1 jar (12 to 13 oz.) plum preserves (or preserves of your choice)
¼ cup soy sauce
¼ tsp. hot pepper sauce

1. Preheat oven to 350°. Place ribs in two ungreased 13x9-in. baking dishes. Bake, uncovered, for 45 minutes; drain.
2. In a small saucepan, combine the remaining ingredients. Bring to a boil, stirring occasionally. Remove from the heat. Set aside ¾ cup of the sauce for serving.
3. Brush the ribs with some of the remaining sauce. Bake ribs, uncovered, until ribs are tender, for 30-45 minutes, turning and basting frequently with remaining sauce. Serve with reserved sauce.
8 oz. cooked ribs: 391 cal., 14g fat (5g sat. fat), 86mg chol., 1214mg sod., 40g carb. (35g sugars, 0 fiber), 27g pro.

QUICK
CHICKEN
PICCATA

**GRILLED
LEMON-DILL
SHRIMP**

GRILLED LEMON-DILL SHRIMP

This grilled shrimp is one of my go-to recipes whenever I stare at the freezer and draw a blank. Add veggies if desired, but grill them separately.

—Jane Whittaker, Pensacola, FL

Takes: 30 min. • **Makes:** 4 servings

- ¼ cup olive oil
- 1 Tbsp. lemon juice
- 2 tsp. dill weed
- 2 garlic cloves, minced
- ¾ tsp. salt
- ½ tsp. pepper
- 1 lb. uncooked shrimp (31-40 per lb.), peeled and deveined

1. In a large bowl, whisk the first 6 ingredients until blended. Reserve 3 Tbsp. of the marinade for basting. Add shrimp to the remaining marinade; toss to coat. Refrigerate, covered, 15 minutes.
2. Drain shrimp, discarding any marinade remaining in the bowl.

Thread shrimp onto 4 or 8 metal or soaked wooden skewers. Grill shrimp, covered, over medium heat or broil 4 in. from heat for 2-4 minutes on each side, basting with reserved marinade during the last minute of cooking.

1 serving: 221 cal., 15g fat (2g sat. fat), 138mg chol., 578mg sod., 2g carb. (0 sugars, 0 fiber), 19g pro. **Diabetic exchanges:** 3 lean meat, 3 fat.

BARBECUED CHICKEN PIZZA

I often cut this easy pizza into little squares and serve it as an appetizer at parties.

—Patricia Richardson, Verona, ON

Takes: 20 min. • **Makes:** 4 servings

1 prebaked 12-in. pizza crust
⅔ cup honey garlic barbecue sauce
1 small red onion, chopped
1 cup cubed cooked chicken
2 cups shredded part-skim mozzarella cheese

Place the crust on a 14-in. pizza pan. Spread barbecue sauce to within ½ in. of edges. Sprinkle with the onion, chicken and cheese. Bake at 350° until the cheese is melted, 10 minutes.

1 slice: 510 cal., 18g fat (7g sat. fat), 64mg chol., 1158mg sod., 52g carb. (7g sugars, 1g fiber), 35g pro.

PECAN-CRUSTED CATFISH

Mustard and dill give this catfish its savory flavor, and the pecan crust lends a delightful crunch. You'll have dinner on the table in no time with this dish.

—*Taste of Home* Test Kitchen

Takes: 20 min. • **Makes:** 2 servings

2 Tbsp. Dijon mustard
1 Tbsp. 2% milk
¼ tsp. dill weed
½ cup ground pecans
2 catfish fillets (6 oz. each)

1. Preheat oven to 425°. In a shallow bowl, combine mustard, milk and dill. Place the pecans in another shallow bowl. Dip fillets in the mustard mixture and then the pecans. Place on a baking sheet coated with cooking spray.
2. Bake until the fish flakes easily with a fork, 10-12 minutes.

1 serving: 341 cal., 23g fat (4g sat. fat), 80mg chol., 333mg sod., 4g carb. (1g sugars, 1g fiber), 29g pro.

BARBECUED CHICKEN PIZZA

BACON-WRAPPED PESTO PORK TENDERLOIN

TEX-MEX PASTA

BACON-WRAPPED PESTO PORK TENDERLOIN

I love to serve this family-favorite tenderloin—maybe because of the compliments that come with it! When the weather warms up, we grill it instead.
—Megan Riofski, Frankfort, IL

Prep: 30 min. • **Bake:** 20 min.
Makes: 4 servings

- 10 bacon strips
- 1 pork tenderloin (1 lb.)
- ¼ tsp. pepper
- ⅓ cup prepared pesto
- 1 cup shredded Italian cheese blend
- 1 cup fresh baby spinach

1. Preheat oven to 425°. Arrange the bacon strips lengthwise in a foil-lined 15x10x1-in. baking pan, overlapping slightly.
2. Cut the tenderloin lengthwise through the center to within ½ in. of bottom. Open tenderloin flat; cover with plastic wrap. Pound with a meat mallet to ½-in. thickness. Remove plastic; place tenderloin on center of bacon, perpendicular to strips.
3. Sprinkle pepper over the pork. Spread with pesto; layer with cheese and spinach. Close the tenderloin; wrap with the bacon strips, overlapping ends. Tie with kitchen string at 3-in. intervals. Secure ends with toothpicks.
4. In a 12-in. skillet, brown roast on all sides, about 8 minutes. Return to baking pan; roast in oven until a thermometer inserted in pork reads 145°, about 17-20 minutes.

Remove string and toothpicks; let stand 5 minutes before slicing.
1 serving: 402 cal., 25g fat (9g sat. fat), 104mg chol., 864mg sod., 4g carb. (1g sugars, 1g fiber), 37g pro.

TEX-MEX PASTA

After a recent surgery, I wasn't able to stock up on groceries. But I still had to make dinner. One night, I looked in my pantry and created this from what was there. The results were fabulous!
—Michele Orthner, Lethbridge, AB

Takes: 30 min. • **Makes:** 4 servings

- 2 cups uncooked spiral pasta
- 1 lb. ground beef
- 1 jar (16 oz.) salsa
- 1 can (10¾ oz.) condensed cream of chicken soup, undiluted
- 1 cup shredded Mexican cheese blend, divided

1. Preheat the oven to 350°. Cook the pasta according to package directions.
2. Cook beef in a Dutch oven over medium heat until no longer pink; drain. Stir in the salsa, soup and ½ cup of cheese; heat through.
3. Drain pasta; stir into the meat mixture. Transfer to a greased 11x7-in. baking dish. Sprinkle with the remaining cheese. Cover and bake until cheese is melted, about 15-20 minutes.
1½ cups: 585 cal., 28g fat (11g sat. fat), 101mg chol., 1241mg sod., 46g carb. (6g sugars, 3g fiber), 33g pro.

CHICKEN & WAFFLES

ROASTED TURKEY WITH MAPLE CRANBERRY GLAZE

The sweet maple flavor comes through even in the breast meat. After about two hours of roasting, you may start to see a caramelized color. That's when I cover the bird loosely with foil while it finishes cooking. The meat will stay tender and juicy.
—Suzanne Anctil, Aldergrove, BC

Prep: 10 min.
Bake: 3 hours + standing
Makes: 24 servings

- 1 turkey (12 to 14 lbs.)
- 1 cup maple syrup
- ¾ cup whole-berry cranberry sauce
- ¼ cup finely chopped walnuts

1. Preheat oven to 325°. Place turkey on a rack in a shallow roasting pan, breast side up. Tuck wings under turkey; tie drumsticks together. In a small bowl, combine the maple syrup, cranberry sauce and walnuts. Pour over turkey.
2. Bake, uncovered, until a thermometer inserted in thickest part of thigh reads 170° to 175°, basting occasionally with pan drippings, 3 to 3½ hours. Cover loosely with foil if turkey browns too quickly. Cover and let stand for 20 minutes before carving.

5 oz. cooked turkey: 320 cal., 13g fat (4g sat. fat), 123mg chol., 93mg sod., 12g carb. (10g sugars, 0 fiber), 36g pro.

CHICKEN & WAFFLES

My first experience with chicken and waffles sent my taste buds into orbit. It's a great breakfast-for-dinner option!
—Lisa Renshaw, Kansas City, MO

Takes: 25 min. • **Makes:** 4 servings

- 12 frozen crispy chicken strips (about 18 oz.)
- ½ cup honey
- 2 tsp. hot pepper sauce
- 8 frozen waffles, toasted

1. Bake chicken strips according to package directions. Meanwhile, in a small bowl, mix the honey and pepper sauce.
2. Cut chicken into bite-sized pieces; serve on waffles. Drizzle with the honey mixture.

1 serving: 643 cal., 22g fat (3g sat. fat), 32mg chol., 958mg sod., 93g carb. (39g sugars, 6g fiber), 21g pro.

TEST KITCHEN TIP
For a spicy southern twist, substitute peach preserves for the honey.

CREAMY BEEF & POTATOES

One of my husband's favorite childhood memories was eating his Grandma Barney's Tater Tot casserole. Once, when I didn't have tots, I prepared it using O'Brien potatoes instead. Now I always make it this way.
—Heather Matthews, Keller, TX

Takes: 20 min. • **Makes:** 4 servings

- 4 cups frozen O'Brien potatoes
- 1 Tbsp. water
- 1 lb. ground beef
- ½ tsp. salt
- ¼ tsp. pepper
- 2 cans (10¾ oz. each) condensed cream of mushroom soup, undiluted
- ⅔ cup 2% milk
- 2 cups shredded Colby-Monterey Jack cheese

1. Place potatoes and water in a microwave-safe bowl. Microwave, covered, on high for 8-10 minutes or until tender, stirring twice.
2. Meanwhile, in a Dutch oven, cook the beef over medium heat until no longer pink, 6-8 minutes, breaking into crumbles; drain. Stir in salt and pepper. In a small bowl, whisk soup and milk until blended; add to beef. Stir in the potatoes. Sprinkle with cheese. Reduce heat to low; cook, covered, until the cheese is melted.

1¾ cups: 664 cal., 38g fat (19g sat. fat), 130mg chol., 1851mg sod., 40g carb. (5g sugars, 6g fiber), 37g pro.

CREAMY BEEF & POTATOES

**ARTICHOKE
BLUE CHEESE
FETTUCCINE**

CONTEST-WINNING BROCCOLI CHICKEN CASSEROLE

This delicious twist on chicken divan came from an old boss, who gave me the recipe when I got married. It's quick, satisfying comfort food.
—Jennifer Schlachter, Big Rock, IL

Prep: 15 min. • **Bake:** 30 min
Makes: 6 servings

- 1 **pkg. (6 oz.) chicken stuffing mix**
- 2 **cups cubed cooked chicken**
- 1 **cup frozen broccoli florets, thawed**
- 1 **can (10¾ oz.) condensed broccoli cheese soup, undiluted**
- 1 **cup shredded cheddar cheese**

1. Preheat oven to 350°. Prepare stuffing mix according to package directions, using 1½ cups water.
2. In large bowl, combine chicken, broccoli and soup; transfer to a greased 11x7-in. baking dish. Top with stuffing; sprinkle with cheese. Bake, covered, for 20 minutes. Uncover dish; bake until heated through, 10-15 minutes longer.
1⅓ cups: 315 cal., 13g fat (6g sat. fat), 66mg chol., 1025mg sod., 25g carb. (4g sugars, 2g fiber), 23g pro.

ARTICHOKE BLUE CHEESE FETTUCCINE

Store-bought Alfredo sauce speeds along my blue-cheesy noodles with mushrooms. Fresh refrigerated fettuccine gets it done even faster.
—Jolanthe Erb, Harrisonburg, VA

Takes: 20 min. • **Makes:** 4 servings

- 1 **pkg. (12 oz.) fettuccine**
- 1 **cup sliced fresh mushrooms**
- 1 **can (14 oz.) water-packed artichoke hearts, drained and chopped**
- 1½ **cups Alfredo sauce**
- ¼ **cup crumbled blue cheese**

1. Cook fettuccine according to package directions.
2. Meanwhile, place a large nonstick skillet over medium-high heat. Add the mushrooms and artichoke hearts; cook and stir until mushrooms are tender. Stir in Alfredo sauce; bring to a boil over medium heat. Reduce heat; simmer, uncovered, 5 minutes, stirring occasionally.
3. Drain the fettuccine, reserving ⅓ cup of the pasta water. Add the fettuccine to the artichoke mixture; toss to combine, adding reserved pasta water if desired. Sprinkle with blue cheese.
1 cup: 499 cal., 14g fat (9g sat. fat), 33mg chol., 770mg sod., 74g carb. (6g sugars, 4g fiber), 21g pro.

CONTEST-WINNING
BROCCOLI CHICKEN
CASSEROLE

LOADED FLANK STEAK

LOADED FLANK STEAK

I wanted to do something a little different with flank steak, so I stuffed it with bacon, green onions and ranch dressing. The recipe is fast, but it's a little bit fancy, too.
—Tammy Thomas, Mustang, OK

Takes: 25 min. • **Makes:** 6 servings

½ cup butter, softened
6 bacon strips, cooked and crumbled
3 green onions, chopped
2 Tbsp. ranch salad dressing mix
½ tsp. pepper
1 beef flank steak (1½ to 2 lbs.)

1. In a small bowl, beat the first 5 ingredients. Cut a pocket horizontally in steak; fill with the butter mixture.
2. Grill steak, covered, over medium heat or broil 4 in. from heat 5-7 minutes on each side or until meat reaches desired doneness (for medium-rare, a thermometer should read 135°; medium, 140°; medium-well, 145°). Let stand 5 minutes before serving. To serve, slice across the grain.

4 oz. cooked beef: 267 cal., 20g fat (10g sat. fat), 76mg chol., 714mg sod., 4g carb. (0 sugars, 0 fiber), 18g pro.

BACON-WRAPPED SCALLOPS WITH PINEAPPLE QUINOA

This is the first recipe I developed using quinoa. My husband thoroughly enjoyed helping me test it! We both loved that it can be prepared in under 30 minutes.
—Laura Greenberg, Lake Balboa, CA

Takes: 30 min. • **Makes:** 4 servings

- 1 can (14½ oz.) vegetable broth
- 1 cup quinoa, rinsed
- ¼ tsp. salt
- ⅛ tsp. plus ¼ tsp. pepper, divided
- 10 bacon strips
- 16 sea scallops (about 2 lbs.), side muscles removed
- 1 cup drained canned pineapple tidbits

1. In a small saucepan, bring broth to a boil. Add the quinoa, salt and ⅛ tsp. of the pepper. Reduce heat; simmer, covered, until the liquid is absorbed, 12-15 minutes.

2. Meanwhile, place bacon in a large nonstick skillet. Cook over medium heat, removing eight of the strips when partially cooked but not crisp. Continue cooking the remaining strips until crisp. Remove to paper towels to drain. Finely chop crisp bacon strips. Cut the remaining bacon strips in half lengthwise.

3. Wrap a halved bacon strip around each scallop; secure with a toothpick. Sprinkle with the remaining pepper.

4. Wipe pan clean, if necessary; heat over medium-high heat. Add the scallops; cook until firm and opaque, 3-4 minutes on each side.

5. Remove quinoa from heat; fluff with a fork. Stir in pineapple and the chopped bacon. Serve with scallops.

Note: Look for quinoa in the cereal, rice or organic food aisle.

4 scallops with ¾ cup quinoa: 468 cal., 11g fat (3g sat. fat), 89mg chol., 1364mg sod., 43g carb. (7g sugars, 3g fiber), 48g pro.

BACON-WRAPPED SCALLOPS WITH PINEAPPLE QUINOA

★ ★ ★ ★ ★ READER REVIEW

"Very good and easy to make. The pineapple really helps the quinoa. The quinoa I use requires a longer cooking time (25 minutes), but I really enjoyed it. Nice presentation as well!"

RENEEMURBY
TASTEOFHOME.COM

SPAGHETTI WITH BACON

SPAGHETTI WITH BACON

As children, we always requested this dish for our birthday dinners. Our mother got the recipe from her grandmother. Now I pass on our tasty tradition.
—Ruth Keogh, North St. Paul, MN

Prep: 20 min. • **Bake:** 40 min.
Makes: 4 servings

- 8 oz. uncooked spaghetti
- ½ lb. bacon strips, chopped
- 1 medium onion, chopped
- 1 can (14½ oz.) diced tomatoes, undrained
- 1 can (8 oz.) tomato sauce

1. Preheat oven to 350°. Cook the spaghetti according to package directions for al dente.
2. In a large skillet, cook bacon and onion over medium heat until the bacon is crisp, stirring occasionally; drain. Stir in the tomatoes and tomato sauce; bring to a boil.
3. Drain spaghetti; transfer to a greased 11x7-in. baking dish. Spread the sauce over top. Bake spaghetti, covered, until bubbly, 40-45 minutes.

1 serving: 159 cal., 6g fat (2g sat. fat), 11mg chol., 498mg sod., 18g carb. (4g sugars, 2g fiber), 7g pro.

MANGO CHUTNEY CHICKEN CURRY

MANGO CHUTNEY CHICKEN CURRY

My father invented this recipe while we were traveling together. Adjust the amount of curry according to your taste and the level of heat you desire.
—Dina Moreno, Seattle, WA

Takes: 25 min. • **Makes:** 4 servings

- 1 Tbsp. canola oil
- 1 lb. boneless skinless chicken breasts, cubed
- 1 Tbsp. curry powder
- 2 garlic cloves, minced
- ¼ tsp. salt
- ¼ tsp. pepper
- ½ cup mango chutney
- ½ cup half-and-half cream

1. In a large skillet, heat oil over medium-high heat; brown the chicken. Stir in curry powder, garlic, salt and pepper; cook until aromatic, 1-2 minutes longer.
2. Stir in chutney and cream. Bring to boil. Reduce the heat; simmer, uncovered, until the chicken is no longer pink, 4-6 minutes, stirring occasionally.

½ cup: 320 cal., 9g fat (3g sat. fat), 78mg chol., 558mg sod., 30g carb. (19g sugars, 1g fiber), 24g pro.

SHRIMP TORTELLINI PASTA TOSS

garlic; cook until the shrimp turn pink, 1-2 minutes longer.

3. Drain the tortellini mixture; add to pan. Stir in salt, thyme, pepper and remaining oil; toss to coat.

1¼ cups: 413 cal., 17g fat (4g sat. fat), 165mg chol., 559mg sod., 36g carb. (4g sugars, 3g fiber), 29g pro. **Diabetic exchanges:** 4 lean meat, 2 starch, 2 fat.

Shrimp Asparagus Fettuccine: Bring 4 qt. water to a boil. Add 9 oz. refrigerated fettuccine in place of the tortellini and 1 cup cut fresh asparagus instead of the peas. Boil for 2-3 minutes or until pasta is tender. Proceed with the recipe as written but replace thyme with ¾ tsp. dried basil.

Soy Shrimp with Rice Noodles: Cook 8.8 oz. thin rice noodles according to package directions instead of the tortellini, adding 1 cup frozen shelled edamame instead of peas during the last 4 minutes of cooking. Proceed with the recipe as written but replace the thyme with ¼ cup reduced-sodium soy sauce and omit salt.

SHRIMP TORTELLINI PASTA TOSS

No matter how you toss 'em up, shrimp and thyme play nicely with spring-fresh vegetables. Using the same basic method, you can use different pastas as well!
—*Taste of Home* Test Kitchen

Takes: 20 min. • **Makes:** 4 servings

- 1 pkg. (9 oz.) refrigerated cheese tortellini
- 1 cup frozen peas
- 3 Tbsp. olive oil, divided
- 1 lb. uncooked shrimp (31-40 per lb.), peeled and deveined
- 2 garlic cloves, minced
- ¼ tsp. salt
- ¼ tsp. dried thyme
- ¼ tsp. pepper

1. Cook the tortellini according to package directions, adding the peas during the last 5 minutes of cooking.

2. Meanwhile, in a large nonstick skillet, heat 2 Tbsp. of oil over medium-high heat. Add shrimp; cook and stir 2 minutes. Add

SLOW-COOKER TURKEY BREAST

Try this tender, wonderful flavored slow-cooker entree when you're craving turkey. It's so easy to make, there's no reason to save turkey for Thanksgiving.
—Maria Juco, Milwaukee, WI

Prep: 10 min. • **Cook:** 5 hours
Makes: 14 servings

- 1 **bone-in turkey breast (6 to 7 lbs.), skin removed**
- 1 **Tbsp. olive oil**
- 1 **tsp. dried minced garlic**
- 1 **tsp. seasoned salt**
- 1 **tsp. paprika**
- 1 **tsp. Italian seasoning**
- 1 **tsp. pepper**
- ½ **cup water**

Brush turkey with oil. Combine the garlic, seasoned salt, paprika, Italian seasoning and pepper; rub over turkey. Transfer to a 6-qt. slow cooker; add water. Cover and cook on low for 5-6 hours or until tender.

4 oz. cooked turkey: 174 cal., 2g fat (0 sat. fat), 101mg chol., 172mg sod., 0 carb. (0 sugars, 0 fiber), 37g pro. **Diabetic exchanges:** 4 lean meat.
Lemon-Garlic Turkey Breast: Combine ¼ cup minced fresh parsley, 8 minced garlic cloves, 4 tsp. grated lemon zest, 2 tsp. salt-free lemon-pepper seasoning and 1½ tsp. salt; rub over turkey breast. Add water and cook as directed.

SLOW COOKER TURKEY BREAST

ADS & MORE

CHEESY CHEDDAR BROCCOLI
CASSEROLE
P. 166

1

2

3

4

5

YOUR ENTREE DOESN'T HAVE TO
STAND ALONE! WITH A HANDFUL OF
INGREDIENTS, CREATE A STUNNING
SIDE TO COMPLETE YOUR MEAL.

NO-FUSS
ROLLS

CHEESY CHEDDAR BROCCOLI CASSEROLE

(PICTURED ON P. 164)

Even people who don't really like broccoli ask me to make this comforting recipe. It's similar to the classic green bean casserole, but the melted cheese just puts it over the top.

—Elaine Hubbard, Pocono Lake, PA

Prep: 15 min. • **Bake:** 35 min.
Makes: 8 servings

- 1   can (10¾ oz.) condensed cream of mushroom soup, undiluted
- 1   cup sour cream
- 1½ cups shredded sharp cheddar cheese, divided
- 1   can (6 oz.) french-fried onions, divided
- 2   pkg. (16 oz. each) frozen broccoli florets, thawed

1. Preheat oven to 325°. In a large saucepan, combine soup, sour cream, 1 cup of the cheese and 1¼ cups onions; heat through over medium heat, stirring until blended, 4-5 minutes. Stir in the broccoli. Transfer to a greased 2-qt. baking dish.
2. Bake, uncovered, until bubbly, 25-30 minutes. Sprinkle with the remaining cheese and onions. Bake until the cheese is melted, 10-15 minutes.
¾ cup: 359 cal., 26g fat (11g sat. fat), 30mg chol., 641mg sod., 19g carb. (4g sugars, 3g fiber), 8g pro.

Ⓛ NO-FUSS ROLLS

These four-ingredient rolls are ready in no time. And they taste great with herb butter or jam.

—Glenda Trail, Manchester, TN

Takes: 25 min. • **Makes:** 6 rolls

- 1   cup self-rising flour
- ½   cup 2% milk
- 2   Tbsp. mayonnaise
- ½   tsp. sugar

Preheat oven to 450°. In a small bowl, combine all ingredients. Spoon into 6 muffin cups coated with cooking spray. Bake until a toothpick comes out clean, for 12-14 minutes. Cool 5 minutes before removing from the pan to a wire rack. Serve warm.
Note: As a substitute for 1 cup of self-rising flour, place 1½ tsp. baking powder and ½ tsp. salt in a measuring cup. Add all-purpose flour to measure 1 cup.
1 serving: 111 cal., 4g fat (1g sat. fat), 3mg chol., 275mg sod., 16g carb. (1g sugars, 0 fiber), 3g pro.
Diabetic exchanges: 1 starch, 1 fat.

CONFETTI CORN

This easy corn dish is sure to dress up almost any entree. The tender corn is paired with some crunchy veggies—water chestnuts, red pepper and chopped carrot.
—Glenda Watts, Charleston, IL

Takes: 15 min. • **Makes:** 4 servings

- ¼ cup chopped carrot
- 1 Tbsp. olive oil
- 2¾ cups fresh or frozen corn, thawed
- ¼ cup chopped water chestnuts
- ¼ cup chopped sweet red pepper

In a large cast-iron or other heavy skillet, saute carrot in oil until crisp-tender. Stir in corn, water chestnuts, and red pepper; heat mixture through.

¾ cup: 140 cal., 4g fat (1g sat. fat), 0 chol., 7mg sod., 26g carb. (3g sugars, 3g fiber), 4g pro.
Diabetic exchanges: 1½ starch, ½ fat.

TEST KITCHEN TIP
Water chestnuts aren't actually nuts—they're vegetables that grow underwater. You can find them among the Asian foods in your grocery. To add a similar crunch, you can use chopped celery hearts instead.

CONFETTI CORN

SPINACH RICE

I like to serve this Greek-style rice dish alongside steaks with mushrooms. It makes an elegant meal that can be doubled easily when we have guests.
—Jeanette Cakouros, Brunswick, ME

Takes: 20 min. • **Makes:** 2 servings

- 2 Tbsp. olive oil
- ½ cup chopped onion
- ¾ cup water
- 1 Tbsp. dried parsley flakes
- ¼ to ½ tsp. salt
- ⅛ tsp. pepper
- ½ cup uncooked instant rice
- 2 cups fresh baby spinach

1. In a saucepan, heat oil over medium-high heat; saute onion until tender. Stir in water, parsley, salt and pepper; bring to a boil. Stir in rice; top with spinach.
2. Cover; remove from heat. Let stand until the rice is tender, 7-10 minutes. Stir to combine.
¾ cup: 235 cal., 14g fat (2g sat. fat), 0 chol., 326mg sod., 25g carb. (2g sugars, 2g fiber), 3g pro.
Diabetic exchanges: 3 fat, 1½ starch, 1 vegetable.

SPINACH RICE

PULL-APART BACON BREAD

I stumbled across this recipe while looking for something different to take to a brunch. Boy, am I glad I did! Everyone who asked for the recipe was surprised it called for only five ingredients. If you're planning an informal get-together, it's the perfect treat to bake.
—Traci Collins, Cheyenne, WY

Prep: 20 min. + rising
Bake: 55 min. • **Makes:** 16 servings

- 12 bacon strips, diced
- 1 loaf (1 lb.) frozen bread dough, thawed
- 2 Tbsp. olive oil, divided
- 1 cup shredded part-skim mozzarella cheese
- 1 envelope (1 oz.) ranch salad dressing mix

1. In a large skillet, cook bacon over medium heat for 5 minutes or until partially cooked; drain on paper towels. Roll out dough to ½-in. thickness; brush with 1 Tbsp. of oil. Cut into 1-in. pieces; place in a large bowl. Add the bacon, cheese, dressing mix and remaining oil; toss to coat.
2. Arrange pieces in a 9x5-in. oval on a parchment-lined baking sheet, layering as needed. Cover and let dough rise in a warm place for 30 minutes or until doubled.
3. Bake at 350° for 40 minutes. Cover with foil; bake 15 minutes longer or until golden brown.
1 serving: 149 cal., 6g fat (2g sat. fat), 8mg chol., 621mg sod., 17g carb. (1g sugars, 1g fiber), 6g pro.

**PULL-APART
BACON BREAD**

CREAMY HASH BROWN POTATOES

CREAMY HASH BROWN POTATOES

I like to fix a batch of these cheesy slow-cooker potatoes for potlucks and other big gatherings. Frozen hash browns, canned soup and flavored cream cheese make this wildly popular dish quick to put together.
—Julianne Henson, Streamwood, IL

Prep: 5 min. • **Cook:** 3½ hours • **Makes:** 14 servings

1 pkg. (32 oz.) frozen cubed hash brown potatoes
1 can (10¾ oz.) condensed cream of potato soup, undiluted
2 cups shredded Colby-Monterey Jack cheese
1 cup sour cream
¼ tsp. pepper
⅛ tsp. salt
1 carton (8 oz.) spreadable chive and onion cream cheese

1. Place potatoes in a lightly greased 4-qt. slow cooker. In a large bowl, combine the soup, cheese, sour cream, pepper and salt. Pour over potatoes and mix well.
2. Cover and cook on low for 3½ to 4 hours or until potatoes are tender. Stir in cream cheese.

¾ cup: 214 cal., 13g fat (9g sat. fat), 42mg chol., 387mg sod., 17g carb. (2g sugars, 2g fiber), 6g pro

GREEN OLIVE FOCACCIA

Green olives complement this speedy version of a beloved Italian bread. Try serving focaccia with minestrone, Italian wedding soup or an antipasto tray.

—Ivy Laffoon, Ceres, CA

Takes: 30 min. • **Makes:** 8 servings

- 1 loaf (1 lb.) frozen bread dough, thawed
- ½ cup sliced pimiento-stuffed olives
- ½ cup shredded Colby-Monterey Jack cheese
- ½ cup shredded Parmesan cheese
- 1 tsp. Italian seasoning
- 2 Tbsp. olive oil

1. Preheat oven to 350°. On an ungreased baking sheet, pat dough into a 12x6-in. rectangle. Build up the edges slightly. Top with olives, cheeses and Italian seasoning; press toppings gently into dough. Drizzle with oil.
2. Bake until cheese is melted and golden brown, 15-20 minutes. Let stand for 5 minutes before slicing.
1 slice: 249 cal., 11g fat (3g sat. fat), 10mg chol., 623mg sod., 31g carb. (2g sugars, 2g fiber), 9g pro.

MY MOTHER'S MAC & CHEESE

I remember my mother sending me to the store for 15 cents worth of cheese. The butcher would cut off a slice from a gigantic wheel covered with a wax-coated cloth. Mother would then blend that cheese into this tasty dish. Today, the memory of her cooking is like food for my soul.

—Phyllis Burkland, Portland, OR

Prep: 10 min. • **Bake:** 1 hour
Makes: 4 servings

- 2 cups elbow macaroni, cooked and drained
- 1 can (28 oz.) diced tomatoes, undrained
- ½ tsp. onion salt, optional
- ¼ tsp. pepper
- 2 cups shredded cheddar cheese, divided
- 2 Tbsp. butter

Preheat oven to 350°. In a bowl, combine macaroni, tomatoes, onion salt, pepper and 1½ cups of the cheese. Pour into a greased 2-qt. baking dish. Dot with butter. Bake, uncovered, for 45 minutes. Sprinkle with remaining cheese; bake 15 minutes longer.
1 cup: 373 cal., 22g fat (16g sat. fat), 75mg chol., 759mg sod., 27g carb. (6g sugars, 2g fiber), 16g pro.

GREEN OLIVE FOCACCIA

OAT DINNER
ROLLS

OAT DINNER ROLLS

These soft rolls are out of this world. The addition of oats makes them a little heartier than most other dinner rolls.
—Patricia Rutherford, Winchester, IL

Prep: 30 min. + rising
Bake: 20 min. • **Makes:** 2 dozen

- 2⅓ cups water, divided
- 1 cup quick-cooking oats
- ⅔ cup packed brown sugar
- 3 Tbsp. butter
- 1½ tsp. salt
- 2 pkg. (¼ oz. each) active dry yeast
- 5 to 5¾ cups all-purpose flour

1. In a large saucepan, bring 2 cups of water to a boil. Stir in the oats; reduce heat. Simmer, uncovered, for 1 minute. Stir in brown sugar, butter, salt and the remaining water.
2. Transfer to a large bowl; let stand until oat mixture reaches 110°-115°. Stir in the yeast. Add 3 cups of flour; beat well. Add enough of the remaining flour to form a soft dough.
3. Turn onto a floured surface; knead until smooth and elastic, about 6-8 minutes. Place in a greased bowl; turn once to grease top. Cover and let rise in a warm place until doubled, about 1 hour.
4. Punch dough down; shape into 24 rolls. Place on greased baking sheets. Cover rolls and let rise until doubled, about 30 minutes.
5. Bake at 350° for 20-25 minutes or until golden brown. Remove from pan and cool on wire racks.

CHERRY TOMATO MOZZARELLA SAUTE

1 roll: 132 cal., 1g fat (0 sat. fat), 0 chol., 150mg sod., 28g carb. (6g sugars, 1g fiber), 3g pro.

CHERRY TOMATO MOZZARELLA SAUTE

This dish is fast to fix and full of flavor. The mix of cherry tomatoes and mozzarella make it the perfect partner for almost any main dish.
—Summer Jones, Pleasant Grove, UT

Takes: 25 min. • **Makes:** 4 servings

- 2 tsp. olive oil
- ¼ cup chopped shallots
- 1 tsp. minced fresh thyme
- 1 garlic clove, minced
- 2½ cups cherry tomatoes, halved
- ¼ tsp. salt
- ¼ tsp. pepper
- 4 oz. fresh mozzarella cheese cut into ½-in. cubes

In a large skillet, heat the oil over medium-high heat; saute shallots with thyme until tender. Add the garlic; cook and stir 1 minute. Stir in the tomatoes, salt and pepper; heat through. Remove from heat; stir in cheese.
⅔ cup: 127 cal., 9g fat (4g sat. fat), 22mg chol., 194mg sod., 6g carb. (4g sugars, 2g fiber), 6g pro.

ROASTED BALSAMIC RED POTATOES

¾ **cup:** 159 cal., 5g fat (1g sat. fat), 0 chol., 143mg sod., 27g carb. (4g sugars, 3g fiber), 3g pro. **Diabetic exchanges:** 2 starch, 1 fat.

SOFT OATMEAL BREAD

My husband loves to make this bread. With its mild oat taste and soft texture, it's sure to be a hit with the whole family. Slices are a treat toasted for breakfast, too.
—Nancy Montgomery, Plainwell, MI

Prep: 10 min. • **Bake:** 3 hours
Makes: 1 loaf (20 slices)

1½ cups water (70° to 80°)
¼ cup canola oil
1 tsp. lemon juice
¼ cup sugar
2 tsp. salt
3 cups all-purpose flour
1½ cups quick-cooking oats
2½ tsp. active dry yeast

1. In bread machine pan, place all ingredients in order suggested by manufacturer. Select basic bread setting. Choose crust color and loaf size if available.
2. Bake according to the bread machine directions (check dough after 5 minutes of mixing; add 1-2 Tbsp. of water or flour if needed).
Freeze option: Securely wrap and freeze cooled loaf in foil and place in a freezer container. To use, thaw at room temperature.
1 slice: 127 cal., 3g fat (0 sat. fat), 0 chol., 237mg sod., 21g carb. (3g sugars, 1g fiber), 3g pro.

ROASTED BALSAMIC RED POTATOES

I was intrigued when I found a potato recipe that called for vinegar. Since I didn't have the seasonings on hand, I had to improvise. I gave the recipe a whirl using Italian seasoning and balsamic vinegar, and it turned out great!
—Lisa Varner, El Paso, TX

Prep: 10 min. • **Bake:** 30 min.
Makes: 6 servings

2 lbs. small red potatoes, cut into wedges
2 Tbsp. olive oil
¾ tsp. garlic pepper blend
½ tsp. Italian seasoning
¼ tsp. salt
¼ cup balsamic vinegar

1. Preheat oven to 425°. Toss potatoes with oil and seasonings; spread in a 15x10x1-in. pan.
2. Roast for 25 minutes, stirring halfway. Drizzle with vinegar; roast until potatoes are tender, about 5-10 minutes.

ZUCCHINI PANCAKES

For a tasty change of pace from ordinary potato pancakes, use zucchini instead. A little shredded onion gives them a savory kick.
—Charlotte Goldberg, Honey Grove, PA

Takes: 20 min. • **Makes:** 2 servings

- 1½ cups shredded zucchini
- 1 large egg, lightly beaten
- 3 Tbsp. grated Parmesan cheese
- 2 Tbsp. biscuit/baking mix
  Dash pepper
- 1 Tbsp. canola oil
  Sour cream, optional

1. Place zucchini in a colander over a plate; let stand to drain. Squeeze and blot dry with paper towels.

2. In a bowl, mix the egg, cheese, baking mix and pepper. Add the zucchini; toss to coat.

3. In a large skillet, heat oil over medium heat. Drop four pancakes into skillet; press lightly to flatten. Cook the pancakes until golden brown, 2 minutes per side. If desired, serve with sour cream.

2 pancakes: 177 cal., 13g fat (3g sat. fat), 99mg chol., 271mg sod., 10g carb. (2g sugars, 1g fiber), 7g pro.

ZUCCHINI PANCAKES

**MUSHROOM &
PEAS RICE PILAF**

SLOW-COOKER BAKED POTATOES

This baked potato recipe is so easy—just add your favorite toppings. Save any extra potatoes to make baked potato soup the next day.
—Teresa Emrick, Tipp City, OH

Prep: 10 min. • **Cook:** 8 hours
Makes: 6 potatoes

- 6   medium russet potatoes
- 3   Tbsp. butter, softened
- 3   garlic cloves, minced
- 1   cup water
     Salt and pepper to taste
     Optional toppings: Sour cream, butter, crumbled bacon, minced chives, guacamole, shredded cheddar cheese, minced fresh cilantro

1. Scrub potatoes; pierce several times with a fork. Mix butter and garlic. Rub potatoes with butter mixture. Wrap each tightly with a piece of foil.
2. Pour water into a 6-qt. slow cooker; add potatoes. Cook, covered, on low for 8-10 hours or until tender. Season and top as desired.

1 potato: 217 cal., 6g fat (4g sat. fat), 15mg chol., 59mg sod., 38g carb. (2g sugars, 5g fiber), 5g pro.

TEST KITCHEN TIP
Serve the potatoes right in the foil packets to get the most out of the garlic butter.

MUSHROOM & PEAS RICE PILAF

Anything goes in a rice pilaf, so I add peas and baby portobello mushrooms for extra color, texture and a touch of comfort.
—Stacy Mullens, Gresham, OR

Takes: 25 min. • **Makes:** 6 servings

- 1   pkg. (6.6 oz.) rice pilaf mix with toasted almonds
- 1   Tbsp. butter
- 1½ cups fresh or frozen peas
- 1   cup sliced baby portobello mushrooms

Prepare pilaf according to the package directions. In a large skillet, heat butter over medium heat. Add peas and mushrooms; cook and stir until tender, about 6-8 minutes. Stir in rice.
⅔ cup: 177 cal., 6g fat (2g sat. fat), 10mg chol., 352mg sod., 28g carb. (3g sugars, 3g fiber), 5g pro.
Diabetic exchanges: 2 starch, ½ fat.

SLOW-COOKER BAKED POTATOES

ONE-DISH
NO-KNEAD
BREAD

ONE-DISH NO-KNEAD BREAD

Here's a very easy way to have homemade bread for dinner tonight. Don't worry if you're new to baking. Anyone who can stir can make this a success!
—Heather Chambers, Largo, FL

Prep: 15 min. + rising
Bake: 40 min.
Makes: 1 loaf (12 slices)

1   tsp. active dry yeast
1½ cups warm water
     (110° to 115°)
2¾ cups all-purpose flour
2   Tbsp. sugar
2   Tbsp. olive oil
1½ tsp. salt

1. In a large bowl, dissolve yeast in warm water. Stir in the remaining ingredients to form a wet dough; transfer the dough to a greased 2½-qt. baking dish. Cover; let stand in a warm place for 1 hour.

2. Stir down the dough. Cover; let stand for 1 hour.

3. Bake at 425° for 20 minutes. Reduce oven setting to 350° and bake until top is golden brown and a thermometer reads 210°, about 20 minutes longer.

4. Remove bread from the baking dish to a wire rack to cool. Serve bread warm.

1 slice: 133 cal., 3g fat (0 sat. fat), 0 chol., 296mg sod., 24g carb. (2g sugars, 1g fiber), 3g pro. **Diabetic exchanges:** 1½ starch, ½ fat.

PARMESAN ROASTED BROCCOLI

Simple, healthy and delicious—the perfect combo! Cutting the stalks into tall trees turns this ordinary veggie into a standout side dish.
—Holly Sander, Lake Mary, FL

Takes: 30 min. • **Makes:** 4 servings

- 2 small broccoli crowns (about 8 oz. each)
- 3 Tbsp. olive oil
- ½ tsp. salt
- ½ tsp. pepper
- ¼ tsp. crushed red pepper flakes
- 4 garlic cloves, thinly sliced
- 2 Tbsp. grated Parmesan cheese
- 1 tsp. grated lemon zest

1. Preheat oven to 425°. Cut broccoli crowns into quarters from top to bottom. Drizzle with the oil; sprinkle with salt, pepper and pepper flakes. Place in a parchment-lined 15x10x1-in. pan.
2. Roast until crisp-tender, for 10-12 minutes. Sprinkle with garlic; roast 5 minutes longer. Sprinkle with cheese; roast until the cheese is melted and the broccoli stalks are tender, about 2-4 minutes more. Sprinkle with lemon zest.

2 broccoli pieces: 144 cal., 11g fat (2g sat. fat), 2mg chol., 378mg sod., 9g carb. (2g sugars, 3g fiber), 4g pro. **Diabetic exchanges:** 2 fat, 1 vegetable.

ONION-GARLIC BUBBLE BREAD

I've relied on this bread recipe often over the years. Frozen dough hurries along prep for the golden pull-apart loaf. It's wonderful with Italian dishes, especially spaghetti and lasagna.
—Charlene Bzdok, Little Falls, MN

Prep: 10 min. + rising
Bake: 20 min. • **Makes:** 12 servings

- ½ cup butter, melted
- ½ cup finely chopped sweet onion
- 2 garlic cloves, minced
- 1 tsp. dried parsley flakes
- ¼ tsp. salt
- 1 loaf (1 lb.) frozen bread dough, thawed
  Marinara sauce, warmed, optional

1. Preheat oven to 375°. In a small bowl, mix the first 5 ingredients.
2. Divide dough into 24 pieces. Dip each piece into the onion mixture; place in a 10-in. fluted tube pan coated with cooking spray. Cover; let rise in a warm place until doubled, about 1 hour.
3. Bake until golden brown, for 20-25 minutes. Cool bread in pan for 5 minutes before inverting onto a serving plate. If desired, serve with marinara sauce.

2 pieces: 177 cal., 9g fat (5g sat. fat), 20mg chol., 322mg sod., 19g carb. (2g sugars, 2g fiber), 4g pro.

PARMESAN ROASTED BROCCOLI

**CRISPY SMASHED
HERBED POTATOES**

CRISPY SMASHED HERBED POTATOES

Their name says it all—these potatoes are crispy, herbed and delightfully smashed. Try them as an alternative to traditional mashed potatoes.
—Althea Dye, Howard, OH

Prep: 25 min. • **Bake:** 20 min.
Makes: 4 servings

- 12 small red potatoes (about 1½ lbs.)
- 3 Tbsp. olive oil
- ¼ cup butter, melted
- ¾ tsp. salt
- ¼ tsp. pepper
- 3 Tbsp. minced fresh chives
- 1 Tbsp. minced fresh parsley

MINTY SUGAR SNAP PEAS

1. Preheat oven to 450°. Place the potatoes in a large saucepan; add water to cover. Bring to a boil. Reduce heat; cook, uncovered, 15-20 minutes or until potatoes are tender. Drain.
2. Drizzle oil over the bottom of a 15x10x1-in. baking pan; arrange potatoes over oil. Using a potato masher, flatten potatoes to ½-in. thickness. Brush the flattened potatoes with butter; sprinkle with salt and pepper.
3. Roast until golden brown, for 20-25 minutes. Sprinkle with the chives and parsley.
3 smashed potatoes: 292 cal., 22g fat (9g sat. fat), 31mg chol., 543mg sod., 22g carb. (1g sugars, 2g fiber), 3g pro.
Lemon-Rosemary Smashed Potatoes: Boil and flatten potatoes; add 1 small halved and sliced lemon and 1½ tsp. minced

fresh rosemary. Butter, season and roast. Omit herbs.
Dill Smashed Potatoes: Boil, flatten and season potatoes, adding ¼ tsp. garlic powder. Butter, season and roast. Sprinkle with 2 to 3 tsp. snipped fresh dill instead of the chives and parsley.

MINTY SUGAR SNAP PEAS

Fresh mint is bright touch on cooked sugar snap peas. It's also nice on green beans or carrots.
—Alice Kaldahl, Ray, ND

Takes: 10 min. • **Makes:** 4 servings

- 3 cups fresh sugar snap peas, trimmed
- ¼ tsp. sugar
- 2 to 3 Tbsp. minced fresh mint
- 2 Tbsp. butter

Place 1 in. of water in a large skillet. Add peas and sugar; bring to a boil. Reduce heat; simmer, covered, until peas are crisp-tender, 4-5 minutes; drain. Stir in mint and butter.
¾ cup: 102 cal., 6g fat (4g sat. fat), 15mg chol., 45mg sod., 9g carb. (4g sugars, 3g fiber), 4g pro.
Diabetic exchanges: 2 vegetable, 1½ fat.

SUPER SIMPLE SCALLOPED POTATOES

2. Bake, uncovered, until potatoes are tender and the top is lightly browned, 45-55 minutes. Let stand 10 minutes before serving.
¾ cup: 353 cal., 27g fat (17g sat. fat), 99mg chol., 390mg sod., 26g carb. (3g sugars, 3g fiber), 4g pro.

PARMESAN SWEET CREAM BISCUITS

Sweet cream biscuits were the first kind I mastered. Since the ingredients are so simple, I can scale the recipe up or down. But usually it's up, they're so good.
—Helen Nelander, Boulder Creek, CA

Takes: 25 min.
Makes: about 1 dozen

- 2 cups all-purpose flour
- ⅓ cup grated Parmesan cheese
- 2 tsp. baking powder
- ½ tsp. salt
- 1½ cups heavy whipping cream

1. Preheat oven to 400°. Whisk together first four ingredients. Add the cream; stir just until the mixture is moistened.
2. Turn the dough onto a lightly floured surface; knead gently 6-8 times. Roll or pat the dough to ½-in. thickness; cut with a floured 2¾-in. biscuit cutter. Place the biscuits 1 in. apart on ungreased baking sheet.
3. Bake until light golden brown, 12-15 minutes. Serve warm.
1 biscuit: 187 cal., 12g fat (7g sat. fat), 36mg chol., 227mg sod., 17g carb. (1g sugars, 1g fiber), 4g pro.

SUPER SIMPLE SCALLOPED POTATOES

I've made many types of scalloped potatoes but I always seem to come back to this rich, creamy, foolproof recipe. The dish gets scraped clean every time I make it.
—Kallee Krong-McCreery, Escondido, CA

Prep: 20 min.
Bake: 45 min. + standing
Makes: 10 servings

- 3 cups heavy whipping cream
- 1½ tsp. salt
- ½ tsp. pepper
- 1 tsp. minced fresh thyme, optional
- 3 lbs. russet potatoes, thinly sliced (about 10 cups)

1. Preheat oven to 350°. In a bowl, combine the cream, salt, pepper and, if desired, thyme. Arrange potatoes in a greased 13x9-in. baking dish. Pour cream mixture over top.

SALSA RICE

It's a snap to change the spice level in this rice dish by choosing milder or hotter salsa. And it's a delicious way to round out burritos or tacos when the clock is ticking.
—Molly Ingle, Canton, NC

Takes: 15 min. • **Makes:** 5 servings

1½ cups water
1½ cups chunky salsa
2 cups uncooked instant rice
1 to 1½ cups shredded Colby-Monterey Jack cheese

In a saucepan, bring water and salsa to a boil. Stir in rice. Remove from the heat; cover and let stand for 5 minutes. Stir in the cheese; cover and let stand for 30 seconds or until the cheese is melted.

1 serving: 232 cal., 4g fat (3g sat. fat), 12mg chol., 506mg sod., 35g carb. (3g sugars, 3g fiber), 9g pro. **Diabetic exchanges:** 2 starch, 1 lean meat.

SALSA RICE

EASY GRILLED SQUASH

This is one of my favorite ways to use butternut squash, which I love not just for its flavor but because it's full of vitamin A. I usually make it when I'm grilling steak or chicken.

—Esther Horst, Monterey, TN

Takes: 20 min. • **Makes:** 4 servings

- 3 Tbsp. olive oil
- 2 garlic cloves, minced
- ¼ tsp. salt
- ¼ tsp. pepper
- 1 small butternut squash, peeled and cut lengthwise into ½-in. slices

1. In a small bowl, combine the oil, garlic, salt and pepper. Brush over the squash slices.

2. Grill the squash, covered, over medium heat or broil 4 in. from the heat until tender, for about 4-5 minutes on each side.

2 slices: 178 cal., 10g fat (1g sat. fat), 0 chol., 156mg sod., 23g carb. (5g sugars, 7g fiber), 2g pro. **Diabetic exchanges:** 1½ starch, 1½ fat.

SWEET ONION SKILLET BREAD

Because there are just a few ingredients in this recipe, you'll get the best results if you use the finest-quality ingredients, like fresh Vidalia onions and aged Parmesan cheese.

—Lisa Speer, Palm Beach, FL

Prep: 25 min. • **Bake:** 10 min. **Makes:** 4 servings

- 1 large sweet onion, thinly sliced
- 2 Tbsp. butter
- 2 Tbsp. olive oil, divided
- 1 can (13.8 oz.) refrigerated pizza crust
- ¼ cup grated Parmesan cheese

1. Preheat oven to 450°. In a large cast-iron or other ovenproof skillet, saute onion in butter and 1 Tbsp. oil until softened. Reduce heat to medium-low; cook, stirring occasionally, until golden brown, 15-20 minutes. Set aside.

2. Brush the bottom and sides of skillet with remaining oil. Unroll dough into skillet; flatten and build up the edge slightly. Top the crust with the onion mixture and the cheese. Bake until golden brown, 10-12 minutes. Cut into wedges.

1 wedge: 415 cal., 17g fat (5g sat. fat), 19mg chol., 776mg sod., 53g carb. (9g sugars, 2g fiber), 11g pro.

EASY GRILLED SQUASH

**SWEET ONION
SKILLET BREAD**

PARMESAN-RANCH PAN ROLLS

My mother taught me this easy recipe, perfect for feeding a crowd. There is never a crumb left over. Mom used her own homemade bread dough, but I use frozen dough to save time.
—Trisha Kruse, Eagle, ID

Prep: 30 min. + rising
Bake: 20 min. • **Makes:** 1½ dozen

2   loaves (1 lb. each) frozen bread dough, thawed
1   cup grated Parmesan cheese
½   cup butter, melted
1   envelope buttermilk ranch salad dressing mix
1   small onion, finely chopped

1. On a lightly floured surface, divide dough into 18 portions; shape each into a ball. In a small bowl, combine the cheese, butter and ranch dressing mix.

2. Roll balls in cheese mixture; arrange in two greased 9-in. square baking pans. Sprinkle with onion. Cover and let rolls rise in a warm place until doubled, about 45 minutes.

3. Meanwhile, preheat oven to 350°. Bake until golden brown, 20-25 minutes. Remove from pans to wire racks.

1 roll: 210 cal., 8g fat (4g sat. fat), 17mg chol., 512mg sod., 26g carb. (2g sugars, 2g fiber), 7g pro.

WHITE BEANS & SPINACH

This skillet side dish is a variation of a recipe I received from my Italian mother. I've prepared spinach like this for years because it's easy and my children love it this way!
—Lucia Johnson, Massena, NY

Takes: 10 min. • **Makes:** 2 servings

- 2 Tbsp. water
- 2 garlic cloves, minced
- 8 cups fresh spinach (about 6 oz.)
- ¾ cup canned cannellini beans, rinsed and drained
- ⅛ tsp. salt
  Dash cayenne pepper
  Dash ground nutmeg

Place water, garlic and spinach in a large skillet. Cook, covered, over medium heat just until tender, 2-3 minutes, stirring occasionally. Stir in the remaining ingredients; heat through.

½ cup: 116 cal., 1g fat (0 sat. fat), 0 chol., 561mg sod., 21g carb. (1g sugars, 7g fiber), 7g pro. **Diabetic exchanges:** 1½ starch.

WHITE BEANS & SPINACH

LEEKS AU GRATIN

Leeks are just too delicious to stand only as an enhancement. Here, with a bit of French flair, they're the star of a side dish.
—Chuck Mallory, Chicago, IL

Prep: 35 min.
Bake: 15 min. + standing
Makes: 8 servings

- 6 medium leeks (white and pale green portion only)
- 1½ cups heavy whipping cream
- 1 tsp. kosher salt
- ½ tsp. pepper
- ½ cup grated Pecorino Romano cheese

1. Preheat oven to 375°. Cut the leeks lengthwise in half; cut halves crosswise into 3-in. pieces. Place cream, salt, pepper and leeks in a large cast-iron or other ovenproof skillet; bring mixture to a boil over medium-high heat. Reduce heat; simmer, covered, for 5 minutes. Uncover; simmer 15 minutes longer. Remove leeks from heat; sprinkle with cheese.
2. Bake, uncovered, until golden and the leeks are tender, about 15-20 minutes. Let leeks stand for 5-10 minutes before serving.

½ cup: 224 cal., 19g fat (12g sat. fat), 52mg chol., 378mg sod., 11g carb. (4g sugars, 1g fiber), 5g pro.

**MINI NUTELLA
DOUGHNUTS**

MINI NUTELLA DOUGHNUTS

These crispy bites can be made in advance and refrigerated before frying. Pop them into your mouth still warm from the fryer for the best results!
—Renee Murphy, Smithtown, NY

Prep: 30 min. • **Cook:** 5 min./batch
Makes: 32 doughnuts

- 1 large egg
- 1 Tbsp. water
- 1 tube (16.3 oz.) large refrigerated flaky biscuits (8 count)
- ⅔ cup Nutella
  Oil for deep-fat frying
  Confectioners' sugar

1. Whisk the egg with water. On a lightly floured surface, roll each biscuit into a 6-in. circle; cut each into 4 wedges. Brush lightly with egg mixture; top each wedge with 1 tsp. Nutella. Bring up corners over filling; pinch the edges firmly to seal.
2. In a large cast-iron or electric skillet, heat oil to 350°. In small batches, place doughnuts in the hot oil, seam side down; fry until golden brown, 1-2 minutes per side. Drain on paper towels. Dust with confectioners' sugar; serve warm.

1 doughnut: 99 cal., 6g fat (1g sat. fat), 6mg chol., 142mg sod., 10g carb. (5g sugars, 0 fiber), 2g pro.

JASMINE RICE WITH COCONUT & CHERRIES

JASMINE RICE WITH COCONUT & CHERRIES

Our favorite rice is even better with a bit of added color, crunch and sweetness: cherries, peanuts, orange zest and coconut.
—Joy Zacharia, Clearwater, FL

Prep: 10 min.
Cook: 20 min. + standing
Makes: 4 servings

- 2½ cups water
- 1 Tbsp. olive oil
- ¾ tsp. salt
- 1½ cups uncooked jasmine rice
- ⅓ cup dried cherries
- ¼ cup chopped salted peanuts
- 1 tsp. grated orange zest
- ¼ cup sweetened shredded coconut, toasted

1. In a large saucepan, bring water, oil and salt to a boil. Stir in rice; return to a boil, stirring once. Reduce heat; simmer, covered, until water is absorbed, for about 15-17 minutes.
2. Stir in the cherries, peanuts and zest; let stand, covered, for 10 minutes. Sprinkle with coconut.
Note: To toast coconut, bake in a shallow pan in a 350° oven for 5-10 minutes or cook in a skillet over low heat until golden brown, stirring occasionally.

1 cup: 411 cal., 10g fat (3g sat. fat), 0 chol., 498mg sod., 71g carb. (10g sugars, 3g fiber), 7g pro.

BUTTERMILK SMASHED POTATOES

MONKEY BREAD BISCUITS

Classic monkey bread is a sweetly spiced breakfast treat. I came up with a savory, individual-sized dinner version. With garlic and Italian seasoning, it's a hit.
—Dana Johnson, Scottsdale, AZ

Takes: 20 min. • **Makes:** 1 dozen

- 1   tube (16.3 oz.) large refrigerated flaky biscuits
- 3   Tbsp. butter, melted
- 1   garlic clove, minced
- ½   tsp. Italian seasoning
- ¼   cup grated Parmesan cheese
  Additional Italian seasoning

1. Preheat oven to 425°. Separate biscuits; cut each into 6 pieces. In a large bowl, combine the butter, garlic and Italian seasoning; add the biscuit pieces and toss to coat.
2. Place 4 biscuit pieces in each of 12 greased muffin cups. Sprinkle with cheese and additional Italian seasoning. Bake until the biscuits are golden brown, 8-10 minutes. Serve warm.
1 biscuit: 159 cal., 9g fat (3g sat. fat), 9mg chol., 418mg sod., 16g carb. (3g sugars, 1g fiber), 3g pro.

BUTTERMILK SMASHED POTATOES

Our family loves this luscious, buttery potato recipe that uses buttermilk to reduce the fat a little. Serve with your favorite toppings and indulge!
—Marla Clark, Albuquerque, NM

Takes: 30 min. • **Makes:** 8 servings

- 4   lbs. Yukon Gold potatoes, peeled and cubed (about 8 cups)
- ½   cup butter, softened
- 1¼   tsp. salt
- ¼   tsp. pepper
- ¾   to 1 cup buttermilk

Optional toppings: crumbled cooked bacon, sour cream and thinly sliced green onions

1. Place the potatoes in a 6-qt. stockpot; add water to cover. Bring to a boil. Reduce heat; cook, uncovered, until tender, 10-15 minutes.
2. Drain; return to the pan. Mash potatoes, gradually adding the butter, salt, pepper and enough buttermilk to reach the desired consistency. Serve with toppings as desired.
¾ cup: 313 cal., 12g fat (7g sat. fat), 31mg chol., 531mg sod., 46g carb. (4g sugars, 4g fiber), 6g pro.

BACON PEA SALAD

My husband loves peas. My middle son isn't the biggest fan, but he loves bacon. So I combined the two, and it was perfect. This side is especially great for barbecue.
—Angela Lively, Conroe, TX

Prep: 10 min. + chilling
Makes: 6 servings

4 cups frozen peas (about 16 oz.), thawed
½ cup shredded sharp cheddar cheese
½ cup ranch salad dressing
⅓ cup chopped red onion
¼ tsp. salt
¼ tsp. pepper
4 bacon strips, cooked and crumbled

Combine the first 6 ingredients; toss to coat. Refrigerate, covered, at least 30 minutes. Stir in bacon before serving.

¾ cup: 218 cal., 14g fat (4g sat. fat), 17mg chol., 547mg sod., 14g carb. (6g sugars, 4g fiber), 9g pro.

★ ★ ★ ★ ★ **READER REVIEW**

"This was very tasty. I think it was the easiest dish I have ever made."

DUBLINLAB
TASTEOFHOME.COM

BACON PEA SALAD

CILANTRO GINGER CARROTS

Peppery-sweet ginger and cooling cilantro have starring roles in this colorful side, and the flavors are a nice surprise. Crisp-tender carrots go from pan to plate in a twinkling.
—*Taste of Home* Test Kitchen

Takes: 15 min. • **Makes:** 4 servings

- 1   Tbsp. butter
- 1   lb. fresh carrots, sliced diagonally
- 1½ tsp. minced fresh gingerroot
- 2   Tbsp. chopped fresh cilantro
- ½   tsp. salt
- ¼   tsp. pepper

In a large skillet, heat butter over medium-high heat. Add carrots; cook and stir 4-6 minutes or until crisp-tender. Add the ginger; cook 1 minute longer. Stir in cilantro, salt and pepper.

½ cup: 73 cal., 3g fat (2g sat. fat), 8mg chol., 396mg sod., 11g carb. (5g sugars, 3g fiber), 1g pro.
Diabetic exchanges: 1 vegetable, ½ fat.

HERBED GRILLED CORN ON THE COB

I'd never grilled corn. Then one summer my sister-in-law served it for us. What a treat! So simple, yet so delicious, grilled sweet corn is now a summer menu regular.
—Angela Leinenbach, Mechanicsville, VA

Prep: 20 min. + soaking
Grill: 25 min. • **Makes:** 8 servings

- 8   medium ears sweet corn
- ½   cup butter, softened
- 2   Tbsp. minced fresh basil
- 2   Tbsp. minced fresh parsley
- ½   tsp. salt

1. Place corn in a stockpot; cover with cold water. Soak 20 minutes; drain. Carefully peel back corn husks to within 1 in. of bottoms; remove silk.
2. In a small bowl, mix remaining ingredients; spread over corn. Rewrap corn in husks; secure with kitchen string.
3. Grill the corn; covered, over medium heat until tender, for 25-30 minutes, turning often. Cut string and peel back husks.

1 ear of corn with 1 Tbsp. butter mixture: 178 cal., 12g fat (7g sat. fat), 31mg chol., 277mg sod., 17g carb. (5g sugars, 2g fiber), 3g pro.

CILANTRO GINGER CARROTS

HERBED GRILLED CORN ON THE COB

CHEESE SMASHED POTATOES

CHEESE SMASHED POTATOES

Know anyone who doesn't like mashed potatoes? This slimmed-down variation on the classic hits all the same comfort-food spots and goes with any entree.
—Janet Homes, Surprise, AZ

Prep: 10 min. • **Cook:** 25 min.
Makes: 4 servings

1 lb. small red potatoes, quartered
1 cup fresh cauliflowerets
⅔ cup shredded reduced-fat cheddar cheese
¼ cup reduced-fat sour cream
¼ tsp. salt

1. Place the potatoes in a large saucepan and cover with water. Bring to a boil. Reduce heat; cover and cook for 10 minutes.

Add the cauliflower; cook until the vegetables are tender, 10 minutes.
2. Drain; mash with cheese, sour cream and salt.

¾ cup: 161 cal., 5g fat (3g sat. fat), 18mg chol., 292mg sod., 21g carb. (3g sugars, 3g fiber), 8g pro.
Diabetic exchanges: 1 starch, 1 medium-fat meat.

ZUCCHINI MUSHROOM BAKE

This quick and easy recipe dresses up my garden-fresh zucchini with mushrooms, onion, cheddar and a sprinkle of basil. Only 10 minutes of prep time required!
—Jacquelyn Smith, Carmel, ME

Prep: 10 min. • **Bake:** 30 min.
Makes: 4 servings

- 3 cups sliced zucchini
- 2 cups sliced fresh mushrooms
- ⅓ cup sliced onion
- ½ tsp. dried basil
- ¼ tsp. salt
- ½ cup shredded cheddar cheese

Preheat the oven to 350°. Toss together first 5 ingredients; place in a shallow greased 2-qt. baking dish. Bake, covered, 30 minutes. Sprinkle with the cheese; bake, uncovered, until vegetables are tender, about 10 minutes.

⅔ cup: 83 cal., 5g fat (3g sat. fat), 14mg chol., 249mg sod., 5g carb. (3g sugars, 1g fiber), 5g pro.
Diabetic exchanges: 1 medium-fat meat, 1 vegetable.

EASY HOMEMADE CHUNKY APPLESAUCE

Here's a comforting homestyle treat that never loses its appeal. Dish up big bowlfuls and wait for the smiles!
—Marilee Cardinal, Burlington, NJ

Takes: 30 min. • **Makes:** 5 cups

- 7 medium McIntosh, Empire or other apples (about 3 lbs.)
- ½ cup sugar
- ½ cup water
- 1 Tbsp. lemon juice
- ¼ tsp. almond or vanilla extract

1. Peel, core and cut each apple into eight wedges. Cut each wedge crosswise in half; place in a large saucepan. Add sugar, water, lemon juice and extract.
2. Bring to a boil. Reduce heat; simmer, covered, until desired consistency is reached, 15-20 minutes, stirring occasionally.

¾ cup: 139 cal., 0 fat (0 sat. fat), 0 chol., 0 sod., 36g carb. (33g sugars, 2g fiber), 0 pro.

★ ★ ★ ★ ★ **READER REVIEW**

"This is so fast and easy to make that I won't be buying much applesauce at the grocery store anymore."
TEACHERSHIRL
TASTEOFHOME.COM

ZUCCHINI MUSHROOM BAKE

HURRY-UP BISCUITS

HURRY-UP BISCUITS

When I was young, my mom would make these biscuits with fresh cream she got from a local farmer. I don't go to those lengths anymore, but this family recipe is still a real treat.

—Beverly Sprague, Baltimore, MD

Takes: 30 min. • **Makes:** 1 dozen

- 3 cups all-purpose flour
- 4 tsp. baking powder
- 4 tsp. sugar
- 1 tsp. salt
- 2 cups heavy whipping cream

1. Preheat oven to 375°. In a large bowl, whisk together flour, baking powder, sugar and salt. Add the cream; stir just until moistened.
2. Drop by ¼ cupfuls 1 in. apart onto greased baking sheets. Bake until bottoms are golden brown, 17-20 minutes. Serve warm.
1 biscuit: 256 cal., 15g fat (9g sat. fat), 54mg chol., 346mg sod., 26g carb. (2g sugars, 1g fiber), 4g pro.

ROASTED ITALIAN GREEN BEANS & TOMATOES

When you roast green beans and tomatoes, their flavors really shine through. The vibrant colors light up our holiday table.

—Brittany Allyn, Mesa, AZ

Takes: 25 min. • **Makes:** 8 servings

- 1½ lbs. fresh green beans, trimmed and halved
- 1 Tbsp. olive oil

ROASTED ITALIAN GREEN BEANS & TOMATOES

- 1 tsp. Italian seasoning
- ½ tsp. salt
- 2 cups grape tomatoes, halved
- ½ cup grated Parmesan cheese

1. Preheat oven to 425°. Place green beans in a 15x10x1-in. baking pan coated with cooking spray. Mix oil, Italian seasoning and salt; drizzle over beans. Toss to coat. Roast for 10 minutes, stirring once.
2. Add tomatoes to pan. Roast until beans are crisp-tender and tomatoes are softened, about

4-6 minutes longer. Sprinkle with Parmesan cheese.
¾ cup: 70 cal., 3g fat (1g sat. fat), 4mg chol., 231mg sod., 8g carb. (3g sugars, 3g fiber), 4g pro.
Diabetic exchanges: 1 vegetable, ½ fat.

TEST KITCHEN TIP
If you don't have any Italian seasoning on your spice shelf, you can make your own: mix ¼ teaspoon each of basil, thyme, rosemary and oregano for each teaspoon of Italian seasoning called for in a recipe.

GERMAN RED CABBAGE

HAWAIIAN BARBECUE BEANS

Guests always wonder about the intriguing flavor in this recipe— fresh ginger is the hidden surprise. It's a hit at every barbecue.
—Helen Reynolds, Quincy, CA

Prep: 10 min. • **Cook:** 5 hours
Makes: 9 servings

- 4 cans (15 oz. each) black beans, rinsed and drained
- 1 can (20 oz.) crushed pineapple, drained
- 1 bottle (18 oz.) barbecue sauce
- 1½ tsp. minced fresh gingerroot
- ½ lb. bacon strips, cooked and crumbled

In a 4-qt. slow cooker, combine the beans, pineapple, barbecue sauce and ginger. Cover and cook on low for 5-6 hours. Stir in bacon before serving.

¾ cup: 286 cal., 5g fat (1g sat. fat), 9mg chol., 981mg sod., 47g carb. (20g sugars, 9g fiber), 13g pro.

GERMAN RED CABBAGE

Sunday afternoons were times for family gatherings when I was a kid. While the uncles played cards, the aunts made German treats such as this traditional red cabbage.
—Jeannette Heim, Dunlap, TN

Prep: 10 min. • **Cook:** 65 min.
Makes: 10 servings

- 1 medium onion, halved and sliced
- 1 medium apple, sliced
- 1 medium head red cabbage, shredded (about 8 cups)
- ⅓ cup sugar
- ⅓ cup white vinegar
- ¾ tsp. salt, optional
- ¼ tsp. pepper

In a large Dutch oven coated with cooking spray, cook and stir onion and apple over medium heat until onion is tender, about 5 minutes. Stir in the remaining ingredients; cook, covered, until the cabbage is tender, about 1 hour, stirring occasionally. Serve warm or cold.

1 cup: 64 cal., 0 fat (0 sat. fat), 0 chol., 23mg sod., 16g carb. (12g sugars, 2g fiber), 1g pro. **Diabetic exchanges:** 1 vegetable, ½ starch.

PASSOVER POPOVERS

Popovers have an important role at our table during Passover: They substitute for bread. When they are puffed and golden brown, you know they are ready to share.
—Gloria Mezikofsky, Wakefield, MA

Prep: 25 min.
Bake: 20 min. + standing
Makes: 1 dozen

  1 **cup water**
  ½ **cup safflower oil**
  ⅛ **to ¼ tsp. salt**
  1 **cup matzo cake meal**
  7 **large eggs**

1. Preheat the oven to 450°. Generously grease 12 muffin cups. In a large saucepan, bring water, oil and salt to a rolling boil. Add cake meal all at once and beat until blended. Remove from heat; let stand 5 minutes.

2. Transfer mixture to a blender. Add two eggs; process, covered, until blended. Continue adding eggs, one at a time, and process until incorporated. Process until the mixture is smooth, about 2 minutes longer.

3. Fill the prepared muffin cups three-fourths full. Bake until puffed, very firm and golden brown, 18-22 minutes. Turn off oven (do not open door); leave popovers in the oven 10 minutes. Remove from oven; immediately remove from the pan to a wire rack. Serve hot.

Note: This recipe was tested with Manischewitz cake meal. Look for it in the baking aisle or the kosher foods section.

1 popover: 174 cal., 12g fat (2g sat. fat), 109mg chol., 66mg sod., 11g carb. (0 sugars, 0 fiber), 5g pro.

PASSOVER POPOVERS

GRILLED CAJUN GREEN BEANS

I created this recipe by accident when the weather was very hot and I didn't want to cook in the house. I threw the green beans on the grill and forgot about them, and they turned out great!
—Shannon Lewis, Andover, MN

Takes: 30 min. • **Makes:** 4 servings

- 1 lb. fresh green beans, trimmed
- ½ tsp. Cajun seasoning
- 1 Tbsp. butter

1. Place green beans on a double thickness of heavy-duty foil (about 18 in. square). Sprinkle with Cajun seasoning and dot with butter. Fold foil around the beans, sealing tightly.

2. Grill, covered, over medium heat for 9-11 minutes on each side or until the beans are tender. Open foil carefully to allow steam to escape.

¾ cup: 56 cal., 3g fat (2g sat. fat), 8mg chol., 109mg sod., 7g carb. (3g sugars, 3g fiber), 2g pro.
Diabetic exchanges: 1 vegetable, ½ fat.

ORANGE POMEGRANATE SALAD WITH HONEY

I discovered this fragrant salad in a cooking class. If you can, try to find orange flower water (also called orange blossom water), which really perks up the orange segments. But orange juice adds a nice zip, too!
—Carol Richardson Marty, Lynwood, WA

Takes: 15 min. • **Makes:** 6 servings

- 5 medium oranges or 10 clementines
- ½ cup pomegranate seeds
- 2 Tbsp. honey
- 1 to 2 tsp. orange flower water or orange juice

1. Cut a thin slice from the top and bottom of each orange; stand orange upright on a cutting board. With a knife, remove the peel and outer membrane from oranges. Cut crosswise into ½-in. slices.

2. Arrange the orange slices on a serving platter; sprinkle with pomegranate seeds. In a small bowl, mix the honey and orange flower water; drizzle over fruit.

⅔ cup: 62 cal., 0 fat (0 sat. fat), 0 chol., 2mg sod., 15g carb. (14g sugars, 0 fiber), 1g pro.
Diabetic exchanges: 1 fruit.

GRILLED CAJUN GREEN BEANS

ORANGE POMEGRANATE SALAD WITH HONEY

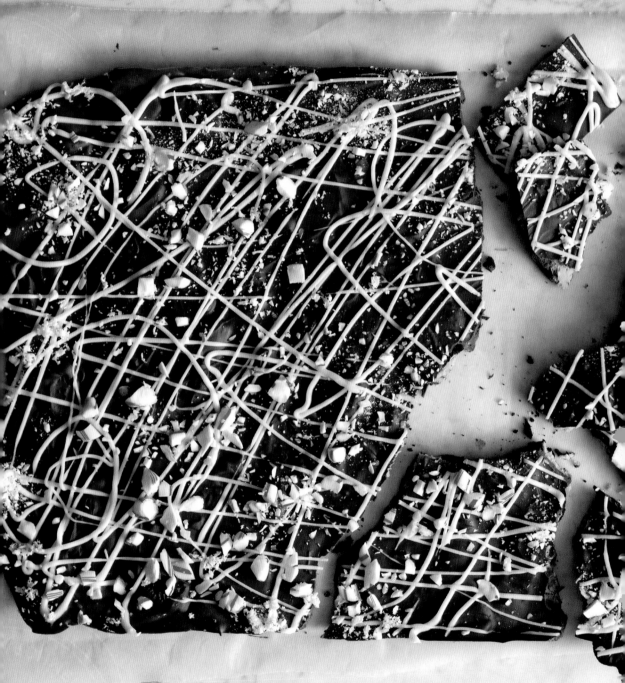

& CANDIES

OREOS & CANDY CANE CHOCOLATE BARK P. 204

1

2

3

4

5

FOR SWEET SNACKS, BAKE SALES,
POTLUCKS AND HOLIDAY PLATTERS,
THESE SCRUMPTIOUS TREATS
COME TOGETHER WITHOUT A FUSS!

CHOCOLATE TRUFFLES

CHOCOLATE TRUFFLES

You may be tempted to save this recipe for a special occasion since these smooth, creamy chocolates are divine. But they're so easy to make, why not indulge any time?
—Darlene Wiese-Appleby, Creston, OH

Prep: 20 min. + chilling
Makes: 4 dozen

- 3 cups (18 oz.) semisweet chocolate chips
- 1 can (14 oz.) sweetened condensed milk
- 1 Tbsp. vanilla extract

Optional coatings: chocolate sprinkles, Dutch-processed cocoa, espresso powder and cocoa nibs

1. In a microwave, melt chocolate chips and milk; stir until smooth. Stir in vanilla. Refrigerate mixture, covered, until firm enough to roll, about 2 hours.
2. Shape into 1-in. balls. Roll in coatings as desired.
1 truffle: 77 cal., 4g fat (2g sat. fat), 3mg chol., 12mg sod., 11g carb. (10g sugars, 1g fiber), 1g pro.

OREOS & CANDY CANE CHOCOLATE BARK

(PICTURED ON P. 202)

There are two super-duper treats in this brilliant bark confection— cream-filled cookies and candy canes. We keep a big supply ready for giving to teachers, neighbors and friends.
—Robin Turner, Lake Elsinore, CA

Prep: 15 min. + chilling
Makes: 27 pieces

- 2 pkg. (10 oz. each) dark chocolate chips
- 10 candy cane or chocolate mint creme Oreo cookies, split and chopped
- ⅓ cup white baking chips
- ⅛ tsp. peppermint extract
- 2 candy canes, crushed

1. Line a 15x10x1-in. baking pan with parchment. In the top of a double boiler or a metal bowl over hot water, melt dark chocolate; stir until smooth. Remove from heat. Stir in cookies; spread over prepared pan.
2. Microwave white baking chips on high until melted, stirring every 30 seconds. Stir in extract. Drizzle over the dark chocolate mixture; sprinkle with the crushed candy canes. Cool. Refrigerate until set, about 1 hour.
3. Break into pieces. Store in an airtight container.
1 piece: 141 cal., 8g fat (5g sat. fat), 0 chol., 32mg sod., 19g carb. (16g sugars, 2g fiber), 2g pro.

APPLE KUCHEN BARS

This homey recipe is about family, comfort and simplicity. My mom made these bars, and now I bake them in my own kitchen. I always make double batches to pass along the love!
—Elizabeth Monfort, Celina, OH

Prep: 35 min.
Bake: 1 hour + cooling
Makes: 2 dozen

- 3 cups all-purpose flour, divided
- ¼ tsp. salt
- 1½ cups cold butter, divided
- 4 to 5 Tbsp. ice water
- 8 cups thinly sliced peeled tart apples (about 8 medium)
- 2 cups sugar, divided
- 2 tsp. ground cinnamon

1. Preheat oven to 350°. Grease a 13x9-in. baking pan; set aside. Place 2 cups of flour and the salt in a food processor; pulse until blended. Add 1 cup butter; pulse until the butter is the size of peas. While pulsing, add just enough ice water to form moist crumbs. Press the dough mixture onto the bottom of the prepared pan. Bake until the crust edges are lightly browned, 20-25 minutes. Cool on a wire rack.

2. In a large bowl, combine apples, 1 cup sugar and the cinnamon; toss to coat. Spoon over crust. Place the remaining flour, butter and sugar in food processor; pulse until coarse crumbs form. Sprinkle over apples. Bake until golden brown and the apples are tender, for 60-70 minutes. Cool kuchen completely on a wire rack. Cut into bars.

1 bar: 240 cal., 12g fat (7g sat. fat), 30mg chol., 106mg sod., 33g carb. (21g sugars, 1g fiber), 2g pro.

APPLE KUCHEN BARS

FUDGY MINT COOKIES

Chocolate lovers get a double dose with this cakelike cookie and its mint-flavored middle.
—Renee Schwebach, Dumont, MN

Prep: 15 min. • **Bake:** 10 min./batch
Makes: 3 dozen

- 1 pkg. devil's food cake mix (regular size)
- ½ cup butter, softened
- 2 large eggs, room temperature
- 1 Tbsp. water
- 2 Tbsp. confectioners' sugar
- 2 pkg. (5 oz. each) chocolate-covered thin mints

1. Preheat oven to 375°. Mix cake mix, butter, eggs and water to form a soft dough. Shape into 1-in. balls; roll in confectioners' sugar. Place cookies 2 in. apart on ungreased baking sheets.
2. Bake until set, 8-10 minutes. Immediately press a mint into center of each cookie. Cool on pans 2 minutes. Remove from pans to wire racks to cool.
1 cookie: 102 cal., 4g fat (2g sat. fat), 17mg chol., 129mg sod., 16g carb. (11g sugars, 0 fiber), 1g pro.

AUNT ROSE'S FANTASTIC BUTTER TOFFEE

Every year, you'll find me at our county fair, entering a recipe contest. This toffee is a winner!
—Kathy Dorman, Snover, MI

Prep: 25 min. • **Cook:** 15 min.
Makes: 32 pieces

- 2 cups unblanched whole almonds
- 11 oz. milk chocolate, chopped
- 1 cup butter, cubed
- 1 cup sugar
- 3 Tbsp. cold water

1. Preheat the oven to 350°. In a shallow baking pan, toast almonds until golden brown, 5-10 minutes, stirring occasionally. Cool. Pulse chocolate in a food processor just until finely ground; transfer to a bowl. Pulse almonds in a food processor until coarsely chopped. Sprinkle 1 cup of almonds over bottom of a greased 15x10x1-in. pan. Sprinkle with 1 cup of the chopped chocolate.
2. In a heavy saucepan, combine butter, sugar and water. Cook over medium heat until a candy thermometer reads 290° (soft-crack stage), stirring the mixture occasionally.
3. Immediately pour mixture over almonds and chocolate in pan. Sprinkle with remaining chocolate and almonds. Refrigerate until set; break into pieces.
Note: Test candy thermometer before each use by bringing water to a boil; the thermometer should read 212°. Adjust your recipe temperature based on your test.
1 piece: 177 cal., 13g fat (6g sat. fat), 17mg chol., 51mg sod., 14g carb. (12g sugars, 1g fiber), 3g pro.

FUDGY MINT COOKIES

AUNT ROSE'S FANTASTIC BUTTER TOFFEE

PEANUT
BUTTER
FUDGE

PEANUT BUTTER FUDGE

*If you thought fudge was difficult
or time-consuming, think again.
This is a favorite never-fail recipe,
and the combination of peanuts
butter and walnuts is a delight.*
—Eleanore Peterson,
Fort Atkinson, WI

Prep: 10 min. + chilling
Makes: 64 pieces

1 lb. white candy coating
1 cup creamy peanut butter
1 cup coarsely
   chopped walnuts

Melt the coating in a saucepan
over medium-low heat, stirring
constantly until smooth. Remove
from the heat; stir in the peanut
butter and walnuts. Spread into
a greased 8-in. square pan. Chill
until firm. Cut into 1-in. squares.

2 squares: 147 cal., 10g fat (5g
sat. fat), 0 chol., 37mg sod., 12g
carb. (10g sugars, 1g fiber), 3g
pro.

TEST KITCHEN TIP
You'll generally find candy
coating in the cake-decorating
section of the baking aisle
of your market.

CHOCOLATE ALMOND DROPS

So much rich, chocolaty flavor, so little time. My unbaked cookies, almost truffles, are easy to make and elegant on a party tray.
—Elizabeth King, Duluth, MN

Prep: 30 min. + chilling
Makes: 4 dozen

- 2 cups (12 oz.) semisweet chocolate chips
- 1 can (14 oz.) sweetened condensed milk
- 1 cup granola without raisins
- ½ cup sliced almonds
- 3 cups (18 oz.) miniature semisweet chocolate chips

1. In a heavy saucepan over low heat, melt chocolate chips with milk, stirring occasionally. Remove from heat. Stir in the granola and almonds. Refrigerate until firm enough to roll, about 1 hour.
2. Shape mixture into 1-in. balls; roll in miniature chocolate chips. Refrigerate, covered, until firm, about 2 hours. Store cookies in the refrigerator.
1 cookie: 127 cal., 7g fat (4g sat. fat), 3mg chol., 13mg sod., 18g carb. (15g sugars, 2g fiber), 2g pro.

SCOTCH SHORTBREAD BARS

This simple three-ingredient recipe makes wonderfully rich, tender cookies. You'll get miles of smiles when you provide these for afternoon tea or at a bridal shower.
—Marlene Hellickson, Big Bear City, CA

Prep: 15 min. • **Bake:** 25 min.
Makes: 4 dozen

- 4 cups all-purpose flour
- 1 cup sugar
- 1 lb. cold butter, cubed

1. Preheat oven to 325°. In a bowl, combine flour and sugar. Cut in butter until the mixture resembles fine crumbs. Knead the dough until smooth, about 6-10 times. Pat dough into an ungreased 15x10x1-in. baking pan. Pierce with a fork.
2. Bake until lightly browned, 25-30 minutes. Cut into squares while warm. Cool on a wire rack.
Note: This recipe makes a dense, crisp bar, so it does not call for baking powder or soda.
2 bars: 244 cal., 16g fat (10g sat. fat), 41mg chol., 157mg sod., 24g carb. (8g sugars, 1g fiber), 2g pro.

CHOCOLATE ALMOND DROPS

**EASY
OATMEAL
CREAM PIES**

EASY OATMEAL CREAM PIES

Everything's better from your own kitchen than store-bought, but why not use some shortcuts like cake mix to make these big sandwich cookies? Try rolling out your dough between two sheets of lightly floured waxed paper to simplify that process, too.
—Crystal Schlueter, Babbitt, MN

Prep: 20 min. + chilling
Bake: 10 min./batch + cooling
Makes: 1½ dozen

- ¾ **cup butter, softened**
- 2 **large eggs, room temperature**
- 1 **pkg. spice cake mix (regular size)**
- 1 **cup quick-cooking oats**
- 1 **can (16 oz.) vanilla frosting**

1. Beat the butter and eggs until blended. Beat in cake mix and oats. Refrigerate, covered, 2 hours or until firm enough to roll; dough will remain fairly soft.
2. Preheat oven to 350°. On a well-floured surface, roll half of the dough to ¼-in. thickness. Cut with a floured 2½-in. round cookie cutter. Place cookies 1 in. apart on parchment-lined baking sheets. Bake until set, for 8-10 minutes. Remove from pans to wire racks to cool completely. Repeat with the remaining dough.
3. Spread frosting on bottoms of half of the cookies; cover with remaining cookies.

1 cookie: 296 cal., 13g fat (8g sat. fat), 41mg chol., 316mg sod., 42g carb. (26g sugars, 0 fiber), 3g pro.

CHOCOLATE-DIPPED HAZELNUT MACAROONS

CHOCOLATE-DIPPED HAZELNUT MACAROONS

These pretty cookies with their special flavor and texture are perfect for the holiday season and not that difficult to make.
—Deirdre Cox, Kansas City, MO

Prep: 35 min.
Bake: 15 min./batch + cooling
Makes: 2 dozen

- ⅔ **cup whole hazelnuts, toasted and skins removed**
- ¾ **cup sugar, divided**
- 1 **pkg. (7 oz.) almond paste, crumbled**
- 2 **large egg whites**
- 6 **oz. semisweet chocolate, melted**

1. Preheat oven to 325°. Place hazelnuts and ¼ cup sugar in a food processor; process until nuts are finely ground. Add almond paste, egg whites and remaining sugar; process until blended, about 3 minutes.

2. Cut a small hole in the tip of a pastry bag; insert a large star pastry tip. Fill bag with hazelnut mixture. Pipe 1¼-in. rosettes 2 in. apart onto parchment-lined baking sheets.
3. Bake until light brown, about 12-14 minutes. Cool rosettes on pans 1 minute. Remove to wire racks to cool completely.
4. Dip bottom of each cookie in melted chocolate; allow excess to drip off. Place on waxed paper-lined baking sheets; refrigerate until set, 1 hour.

Note: To toast whole hazelnuts, spread hazelnuts in a 15x10x1-in. baking pan. Bake in a 350° oven 7-10 minutes or until fragrant and lightly browned, stirring the nuts occasionally. To remove skins, wrap hazelnuts in a tea towel; rub with towel to loosen skins.

1 cookie: 134 cal., 8g fat (2g sat. fat), 0 chol., 5mg sod., 13g carb. (11g sugars, 1g fiber), 2g pro.

CRANBERRY PECAN COOKIES

DARK CHOCOLATE BOURBON BALLS

This classic will take you back to Christmases past. The blended taste of bourbon and pecans is irresistible!
—*Taste of Home* Test Kitchen

Prep: 30 min. + chilling
Makes: 4 dozen

- 1¼ cups finely chopped pecans, divided
- ¼ cup bourbon
- ½ cup butter, softened
- 3¾ cups confectioners' sugar
- 1 lb. dark chocolate candy coating, melted

1. Combine 1 cup of pecans and bourbon; let stand, covered, for 8 hours or overnight.
2. Cream the butter and the confectioners' sugar, ¼ cup at a time, until crumbly; stir in the pecan mixture. Refrigerate, covered, until firm enough to shape into 1-in. balls, for about 45 minutes. Place the balls on waxed paper-lined baking sheets. Refrigerate balls until firm, about 1 hour.
3. Dip in the chocolate coating; allow excess to drip off. Sprinkle with the remaining pecans. Let stand until set.

1 bourbon ball: 124 cal., 7g fat (4g sat. fat), 5mg chol., 15mg sod., 16g carb. (15g sugars, 0 fiber), 0 pro.

CRANBERRY PECAN COOKIES

Each delightful little cookie is loaded with cranberries, nuts and a sweet hint of vanilla. But these little gems start with ready-made cookie dough! Let that be your little secret.
—Louise Hawkins, Lubbock, TX

Prep: 10 min. • **Bake:** 10 min./batch
Makes: 3½ dozen

- 1 tube (16½ oz.) refrigerated sugar cookie dough, softened
- 1 cup chopped pecans
- ⅔ cup white baking chips
- ⅔ cup dried cranberries
- 1 tsp. vanilla extract

1. Preheat oven to 350°. In a large bowl, combine the cookie dough, pecans, chips, cranberries and vanilla. Drop by tablespoonfuls about 2 in. apart onto ungreased baking sheets.
2. Bake until lightly browned, 10-12 minutes. Cool 2 minutes before removing from pans to wire racks to cool completely. Store in an airtight container.
1 cookie: 87 cal., 5g fat (1g sat. fat), 4mg chol., 50mg sod., 10g carb. (5g sugars, 0 fiber), 1g pro.

CHOCOLATE-DIPPED STRAWBERRY MERINGUE ROSES

They look sophisticated, but everyone loves these kid-friendly treats. Try crushing them into a bowl of strawberries and whipped cream. Readers of my blog, utry.it, went nuts when I posted that idea.
—Amy Tong, Anaheim, CA

Prep: 25 min.
Bake: 40 min. + cooling
Makes: 2 dozen

- 3 large egg whites
- ¼ cup sugar
- ¼ cup freeze-dried strawberries
- 1 pkg. (3 oz.) strawberry gelatin
- ½ tsp. vanilla extract, optional
- 1 cup 60% cacao Bittersweet chocolate baking chips, melted

1. Place egg whites in a large bowl; let stand at room temperature 30 minutes. Preheat oven to 225°.
2. Place sugar and strawberries in a food processor; process until powdery. Add the gelatin; pulse to blend.
3. Beat egg whites on medium speed until foamy, adding vanilla if desired. Gradually add gelatin mixture, 1 Tbsp. at a time, beating on high after each addition until the sugar is dissolved. Continue beating mixture until stiff glossy peaks form.
4. Cut a small hole in the tip of a pastry bag; insert a #1M star tip. Transfer meringue to the bag. Pipe 2-in. roses 1½ in. apart onto parchment-lined baking sheets.
5. Bake 40-45 minutes or until set and dry. Turn off oven (do not open the oven door); leave the meringues in oven for 1½ hours. Remove from the oven and cool completely on baking sheets.
6. Remove meringues from paper. Dip bottoms in melted chocolate; allow excess to drip off. Place on waxed paper; let stand until set, about 45 minutes. Store the meringues in an airtight container at room temperature.

1 cookie: 33 cal., 1g fat (1g sat. fat), 0 chol., 9mg sod., 6g carb. (5g sugars, 0 fiber), 1g pro
Diabetic exchanges: ½ starch.

CHOCOLATE-DIPPED STRAWBERRY MERINGUE ROSES

PEANUT BUTTER COOKIES

2 cups butter, softened
1 pint vanilla ice cream, softened
4 cups all-purpose flour
2 Tbsp. sugar
2 cans (12 oz. each) apricot and/or raspberry cake and pastry filling
1 to 2 Tbsp. confectioners' sugar, optional

1. In the bowl of a heavy-duty stand mixer, beat butter and ice cream until blended (mixture will appear curdled). Add flour and sugar; mix well. Divide the dough into four portions; cover and refrigerate until easy to handle, about 2 hours.
2. Preheat oven to 350°. On a lightly floured surface, roll out one portion of the dough into a 12x10-in. rectangle; cut the dough into 2-in. squares. Place 1 teaspoon of filling in the center of each one. Overlap 2 opposite corners of dough over the filling; pinch tightly to seal. Place the bundles 2 in. apart on ungreased baking sheets. Repeat with the remaining dough and filling.
3. Bake until the bottoms are lightly browned, 11-14 minutes. Cool 1 minute before removing from pans to wire racks to cool completely. If desired, sprinkle with confectioners' sugar.
Note: This recipe was tested with Solo brand cake and pastry filling. Look for it in the baking aisle.
1 cookie: 60 cal., 3g fat (2g sat. fat), 9mg chol., 27mg sod., 7g carb. (2g sugars, 0 fiber), 1g pro.

PEANUT BUTTER COOKIES

It's truly amazing how much flavor these simple cookies have. I make them often because I always have the ingredients on hand.
—Maggie Schimmel, Wauwatosa, WI

Takes: 30 min. • **Makes:** 2 dozen

1 large egg, room temperature, beaten
1 cup sugar
1 cup creamy peanut butter

1. Preheat oven to 350°. In a large bowl, mix all ingredients. Scoop level tablespoonfuls and roll into balls. Place on ungreased baking sheets and flatten with a fork.
2. Bake for about 18 minutes or until set. Remove to wire racks to cool completely.
1 cookie: 99 cal., 6g fat (1g sat. fat), 8mg chol., 48mg sod., 11g carb. (10g sugars, 1g fiber), 3g pro.

ICE CREAM KOLACHKES

The ice cream in these pastries is a twist on traditional Polish and Czech kolachkes, which are usually filled with poppy seeds, nuts, jam or a mashed fruit mixture. You can use a square cookie cutter to cut the dough.
—Diane Turner, Brunswick, OH

Prep: 1 hour + chilling
Bake: 15 min./batch
Makes: 10 dozen

ICE CREAM KOLACHKES

CHOCOLATE PEANUT BUTTER COOKIES

CHOCOLATE PEANUT BUTTER COOKIES

It's a snap to make a batch of tasty cookies when you use this recipe. My family gobbles them up.
—Mary Pulyer, Port St. Lucie, FL

Prep: 10 min.
Bake: 10 min./batch
Makes: 4 dozen

1   pkg. devil's food cake mix (regular size)
2   large eggs, room temperature
⅓   cup canola oil
1   pkg. (10 oz.) peanut butter chips

1. In a bowl, beat cake mix, eggs and oil (batter will be very stiff). Stir in peanut butter chips.

2. Roll into 1-in. balls. Place on lightly greased baking sheets; flatten slightly. Bake at 350° until a slight indentation remains when lightly touched, about 10 minutes. Cool on pans for 2 minutes before removing to wire racks.

2 cookies: 184 cal., 9g fat (3g sat. fat), 18mg chol., 205mg sod., 22g carb. (12g sugars, 2g fiber), 4g pro.

QUICK & EASY GUMDROPS

These homemade candies are sweet little gummy bites. They're softer than the ones you buy in stores and fun to eat.
—Leah Rekau, Milwaukee, WI

Prep: 25 min. + chilling
Makes: 64 pieces

- 3 envelopes unflavored gelatin
- ½ cup plus ¾ cup water, divided
- 1½ cups sugar
- ¼ to ½ tsp. raspberry extract
  Red food coloring
  Additional sugar

1. In a small bowl, sprinkle gelatin over ½ cup water; let stand for 5 minutes. In a small saucepan, bring sugar and the remaining water to a boil over medium heat, stirring constantly. Add gelatin; reduce heat. Simmer 5 minutes, stirring frequently. Remove from heat; stir in the extract and food coloring as desired.
2. Pour into a greased 8-in. square pan. Refrigerate, covered, until firm, about 3 hours.
3. Loosen the edges of the candy from pan with a knife; turn onto a sugared work surface. Cut into 1-in squares; roll in sugar. Let the squares stand, uncovered, at room temperature until all sides are dry, 3-4 hours, turning every hour. Store gumdrops between layers of waxed paper in an airtight container in refrigerator.
Note: For lemon gumdrops, use lemon extract and yellow food coloring. For orange gumdrops, use orange extract and yellow food coloring plus 1 drop of red food coloring.
1 gumdrop: 19 cal., 0 fat (0 sat. fat), 0 chol., 1mg sod., 5g carb. (5g sugars, 0 fiber), 0 pro.

SALTED NUT SQUARES

A favorite of young and old, this recipe came from my sister-in-law. It's simple to make and delicious. There's no need to keep it warm or cold, so it's perfect for the potluck that has you traveling longer distances.
—Kathy Tremel, Earling, IA

Takes: 15 min. + chilling
Makes: 54 pieces

- 3 cups salted peanuts without skins, divided
- 2½ Tbsp. butter
- 2 cups peanut butter chips
- 1 can (14 oz.) sweetened condensed milk
- 2 cups miniature marshmallows

1. Place half the peanuts in an ungreased 11x7-in. dish; set aside. In a large saucepan, melt butter and peanut butter chips over low heat. Add milk and marshmallows; cook and stir until melted.
2. Pour over the peanuts. Sprinkle with the remaining peanuts. Cover and refrigerate until chilled. Cut into 54 squares (about 1-in.).
1 square: 115 cal., 7g fat (2g sat. fat), 4mg chol., 56mg sod., 10g carb. (8g sugars, 1g fiber), 4g pro.

QUICK & EASY GUMDROPS

PECAN
ROLL-UPS

PECAN ROLL-UPS

Nut lovers alert! The pecans tucked inside these delicate cookies make for especially luscious little bundles.
—Lee Roberts, Racine, WI

Prep: 45 min. + chilling
Bake: 15 min./batch
Makes: 8 dozen

- 1 cup butter, softened
- 1 pkg. (8 oz.) cream cheese, softened
- ¼ tsp. salt
- 2 cups all-purpose flour
- 1¼ cups confectioners' sugar, divided
- 96 pecan halves (about 2 cups)

CHOCOLATE AMARETTI

1. In a large bowl, beat the butter, cream cheese and salt until smooth. Gradually beat in flour. Divide the dough in half; shape each half into a disk. Wrap each in plastic; refrigerate 2 hours or until firm enough to roll.
2. Preheat oven to 350°. Dust a work surface with about 2 Tbsp. confectioners' sugar. Roll one portion of dough into an 18x8-in. rectangle. Cut rectangle crosswise into six 3-in.-wide sections, then cut each section crosswise into eight 1-in.-wide strips. Roll each strip around a pecan half; place 1 in. apart on ungreased baking sheets. Repeat with remaining dough and pecans, dusting work surface with an additional 2 Tbsp. confectioners' sugar.
3. Bake until the bottoms are lightly browned, 12-15 minutes. Remove cookies to wire racks to cool completely.

4. Place remaining confectioners' sugar in a shallow bowl. Roll cookies in sugar, coating well.
Freeze option: Bake and roll cookies in confectioners' sugar as directed. Freeze in freezer containers, separating layers with waxed paper, up to 3 months. Thaw before serving; dust with additional confectioners' sugar.
1 cookie: 51 cal., 4g fat (2g sat. fat), 8mg chol., 30mg sod., 4g carb. (2g sugars, 0 fiber), 1g pro.

CHOCOLATE AMARETTI

These classic almond cookies are like ones you'd find in an Italian bakery. My husband and children always look for them in my holiday baking lineup.
—Kathy Long, Whitefish Bay, WI

Prep: 15 min. • **Bake:** 20 min./batch
Makes: 2 dozen

- 1¼ cups almond paste
- ¾ cup sugar
- 2 large egg whites
- ½ cup confectioners' sugar
- ¼ cup baking cocoa

1. Preheat oven to 350°. In a large bowl, beat almond paste, sugar and egg whites until combined. Combine the confectioners' sugar and cocoa; gradually add to the almond mixture and mix well.
2. Drop by tablespoonfuls 2 in. apart onto parchment-lined baking sheets. Bake until the tops are cracked, 17-20 minutes. Cool for 1 minute before removing from pans to wire racks to cool completely. Store amaretti in an airtight container.
1 cookie: 92 cal., 3g fat (0 sat. fat), 0 chol., 6mg sod., 15g carb. (13g sugars, 1g fiber), 2g pro.

PALMIERS

remaining sugar. Bake until golden brown and glazed, about 3 minutes longer. Remove to wire racks to cool completely. Store pastries in airtight containers.

1 pastry: 83 cal., 3g fat (1g sat. fat), 0mg chol., 34mg sod., 14g carb. (8g sugars, 1g fiber), 1g pro.

YUMMY CRACKER SNACKS

These treats are my family's favorite, and it seems no matter how many batches I make, they always disappear too soon.
—D. Weaver, Ephrata, PA

Prep: 1 hour + chilling
Makes: 4 dozen

- 96   Ritz crackers
- 1   cup creamy peanut butter
- 1   cup marshmallow creme
- 2   lbs. milk chocolate candy coating, melted
      Holiday sprinkles, optional

1. Spread half of the crackers with peanut butter. Spread remaining crackers with the marshmallow creme; place creme side down over the peanut butter crackers, forming a sandwich.

2. Dip the sandwiches in melted candy coating, allowing excess to drip off. Place on waxed paper-lined pans; refrigerate for 15 minutes or until set. If desired, drizzle with additional candy coating and decorate with sprinkles. Store in an airtight container.

1 snack: 170 cal., 10g fat (6g sat. fat), 0 chol., 89mg sod., 19g carb. (14g sugars, 1g fiber), 2g pro.

PALMIERS

It takes just two ingredients to make these impressive but easy-to-do French pastries.
—*Taste of Home* Test Kitchen

Prep: 20 min. • **Bake:** 10 min.
Makes: 2 dozen

- 1   cup sugar, divided
- 1   sheet frozen puff pastry, thawed

1. Preheat oven to 425°. Sprinkle work surface with ¼ cup sugar; unfold the puff pastry sheet on surface. Sprinkle with 2 Tbsp. sugar. Roll into a 14x10-in.
rectangle. Sprinkle with ½ cup sugar to within ½ in. of edges. Lightly press sugar into pastry.

2. With a knife, very lightly score a line crosswise across the middle of the pastry. Starting at one short side, roll up pastry jelly-roll style, stopping at the score mark in the middle. Starting at the other side, roll up pastry jelly-roll style to score mark. Freeze until firm, 20-30 minutes. Cut into ⅜-in. slices.

3. Place slices cut side up 2 in. apart on parchment-lined baking sheets; sprinkle with 1 Tbsp. sugar. Bake for 8 minutes. Turn pastries over and sprinkle with the

CREAM CHEESE COOKIE CUPS

Need a quick dessert? Try these yummy cookie bites. For an even prettier look, use an icing bag to pipe the filling into the cups, then top each with a mini M&M.
—Rachel Blackston, Mauk, GA

Prep: 15 min.
Bake: 10 min. + cooling
Makes: 1 dozen

1 tube (18 oz.) refrigerated chocolate chip cookie dough
4 oz. cream cheese, softened
2 Tbsp. butter, softened
½ tsp. vanilla extract
1¼ cups confectioners' sugar

1. Preheat oven to 350°. Cut cookie dough in half (save one portion for another use). With floured fingers, press 1 Tbsp. of dough onto the bottom and up the sides of 12 ungreased miniature muffin cups. Bake until lightly browned, 8-10 minutes.
2. Using the end of a wooden spoon handle, reshape the puffed cookie cups. Cool for 5 minutes before removing from pan to a wire rack to cool completely.
3. In a small bowl, beat the cream cheese, butter and vanilla until smooth. Gradually beat in the confectioners' sugar. Spoon into cookie cups. Store cookie cups in the refrigerator.

1 cup: 193 cal., 10g fat (5g sat. fat), 21mg chol., 92mg sod., 26g carb. (20g sugars, 0 fiber), 2g pro.

CREAM CHEESE
COOKIE CUPS

TRIPLE FUDGE BROWNIES

BUTTERSCOTCH TOFFEE COOKIES

With its big butterscotch and chocolate flavor, my cookie stands out. I like to enjoy these with a glass of milk or a cup of coffee. It's my fallback recipe when I'm short on time and need to make something delicious fast.

—Allie Blinder, Norcross, GA

Prep: 10 min.
Bake: 10 min./batch + cooling
Makes: 5 dozen

- 2 large eggs, room temperature
- ½ cup canola oil
- 1 pkg. butter pecan cake mix (regular size)
- 1 pkg. (10 to 11 oz.) butterscotch chips
- 1 pkg. (8 oz.) milk chocolate English toffee bits

1. Preheat oven to 350°. In a large bowl, beat eggs and oil until blended; gradually add cake mix and mix well. Fold in chips and toffee bits.
2. Drop by tablespoonfuls 2 in. apart onto greased baking sheets. Bake cookies until golden brown, 10-12 minutes. Cool 1 minute on pans before removing to wire racks to cool completely.

1 cookie: 95 cal., 5g fat (3g sat. fat), 10mg chol., 70mg sod., 11g carb. (3g sugars, 0 fiber), 1g pro.

TRIPLE FUDGE BROWNIES

When you're in a hurry to make dessert, here's a mix of mixes that's convenient and quick. The result is a big pan of rich, fudgy brownies. Friends who ask me for the recipe are delighted that it's so easy.

—Denise Nebel, Wayland, IA

Prep: 10 min. • **Bake:** 30 min.
Makes: 4 dozen

- 1 pkg. (3.9 oz.) instant chocolate pudding mix
- 1 pkg. chocolate cake mix (regular size)
- 2 cups semisweet chocolate chips
  Optional: Confectioners' sugar, vanilla ice cream

1. Preheat oven to 350°. Prepare pudding according to the package directions. Whisk in dry cake mix. Stir in chocolate chips.
2. Pour into a greased 15x10x1-in. baking pan. Bake until top springs back when lightly touched, 30-35 minutes. If desired serve with confectioners' sugar or ice cream.

1 brownie: 91 cal., 3g fat (2g sat. fat), 1mg chol., 86mg sod., 15g carb. (10g sugars, 1g fiber), 1g pro.

**BUTTERSCOTCH
TOFFEE COOKIES**

SHORTCUT COCONUT-PECAN CHOCOLATE TASSIES

You can garnish these cookies with pecan halves or a couple of chocolate chips before baking, Or after they're out of the oven, drizzle a little melted chocolate over them.

—Deb Villenauve, Krakow, WI

Prep: 25 min.
Bake: 10 min./batch + cooling
Makes: 3 dozen

- 1 pkg. chocolate cake mix (regular size)
- ½ cup quick-cooking oats
- 1 large egg, room temperature, lightly beaten
- 6 Tbsp. butter, melted and cooled slightly
- ¾ cup coconut-pecan frosting
  Optional toppings: Pecan halves, melted semisweet chocolate

1. Preheat the oven to 350°. Mix cake mix and oats; stir in egg and melted butter. Shape dough into 1-in. balls. Press onto the bottom and up the sides of greased mini muffin cups.

2. Bake just until set. Cool slightly before removing to wire racks; cool completely.

3. Top each with about 1 tsp. of frosting. If desired, top each with a pecan half or drizzle with melted chocolate.

1 tassie: 94 cal., 4g fat (2g sat. fat), 10mg chol., 105mg sod., 13g carb. (8g sugars, 1g fiber), 1g pro.

TEST KITCHEN TIP
If you love German chocolate cake, you will love these petite, bite-sized versions. It's a little tricky to tell when the cake cups are done baking. When they are set, they will look more matte than glossy.

ROSEMARY SHORTBREAD COOKIES

With the perfect hint of rosemary and a classic buttery texture, these delicate cookies look and taste elegant. That they're very easy to prepare can be our little secret.

—Amavida Coffee, Rosemary Beach, FL

Prep: 30 min. + chilling
Bake: 15 min./batch
Makes: 5½ dozen

- 1 cup butter, softened
- ½ cup confectioners' sugar
- 2 cups all-purpose flour
- 2 Tbsp. minced fresh rosemary
- ½ tsp. sea salt

1. In a large bowl, cream butter and confectioners' sugar until light and fluffy. Combine the flour, rosemary and salt; gradually add to creamed mixture and mix well.
2. Shape dough into two 8¼-in. rolls; wrap each roll in plastic. Refrigerate overnight.
3. Preheat oven to 350°. Cut rolls into ¼-in. slices. Place slices 2 in. apart on ungreased baking sheets.
4. Bake until the edges begin to brown, 11-13 minutes. Cool the cookies on pans for 1 minute before removing to wire racks to cool completely. Store in an airtight container.

1 cookie: 42 cal., 3g fat (2g sat. fat), 7mg chol., 38mg sod., 4g carb. (1g sugars, 0 fiber), 0 pro.

ITALIAN PIGNOLI COOKIES

Cookies are the crown jewels of Italian confections. I can't let a holiday go by without baking these traditional almond cookies rolled in mild pine nuts.

—Maria Regakis, Saugus, MA

Prep: 30 min.
Bake: 15 min./batch
Makes: 2½ dozen

- 1¼ cups (12 oz.) almond paste
- ½ cup sugar
- 4 large egg whites, divided
- 1 cup confectioners' sugar
- 1½ cups pine nuts

1. Preheat oven to 235°. In a small bowl, beat almond paste and sugar until crumbly. Beat in 2 egg whites. Gradually add confectioners' sugar; mix well.
2. Whisk the remaining egg whites in a shallow bowl. Place pine nuts in another shallow bowl. Shape dough into 1-in. balls. Roll each ball in the egg whites and coat with pine nuts. Place 2 in. apart on parchment-lined baking sheets. Flatten slightly.
3. Bake until lightly browned, 15-18 minutes. Cool for 1 minute before removing from pans to wire racks. Store cookies in an airtight container.

1 cookie: 112 cal., 6g fat (1g sat. fat), 0 chol., 7mg sod., 13g carb. (11g sugars, 1g fiber), 3g pro.

ROSEMARY SHORTBREAD COOKIES

BUTTERSCOTCH-RUM RAISIN TREATS

BUTTERSCOTCH-RUM RAISIN TREATS

The holiday flavors of rum raisin rice pudding inspired this recipe. Crispy rice cereal adds crunch, but nuts, toasted coconut, or even candied pineapple could do the job, too.
—Crystal Schlueter, Babbitt, MN

Takes: 20 min.
Makes: 4½ dozen

- 1 pkg. (10 to 11 oz.) butterscotch chips
- 1 pkg. (10 to 12 oz.) white baking chips
- ½ tsp. rum extract
- 3 cups Rice Krispies
- 1 cup raisins

1. Line 56 mini muffin cups with paper liners. In a large bowl, combine butterscotch and white chips. Microwave, uncovered, on high for 30 seconds; stir. Microwave chips in additional 30-second intervals; stir until melted and smooth.
2. Stir in extract, Rice Krispies and raisins. Drop by rounded tablespoonfuls into prepared mini muffin cups. Chill until set.
Freeze option: Freeze cookies in freezer containers, separating layers with waxed paper. To use, thaw before serving.
1 treat: 76 cal., 4g fat (3g sat. fat), 1mg chol., 21mg sod., 11g carb. (9g sugars, 0 fiber), 0 pro.

EASY MEXICAN BROWNIES

EASY MEXICAN BROWNIES

I was hosting a Mexican-themed cocktail party and needed dessert. Dressing up an ordinary brownie mix made life easy and delicious!
—Susan Stetzel, Gainesville, NY

Takes: 30 min.
Makes: 24 brownies

- 1 pkg. fudge brownie mix (13x9-in. pan size)
- 2 tsp. ground cinnamon
- 1 tsp. ground ancho chili pepper
- 2 large eggs
- ½ cup canola oil
- ¼ cup water
- ¾ cup dark chocolate chips

1. Preheat oven to 350°. Whisk together brownie mix and spices. In a separate bowl, whisk eggs, oil and water until blended. Gradually add the chocolate chips and brownie mix to the egg mixture, mixing well. Spread into a greased 13x9-in. baking pan.
2. Bake until a toothpick inserted in center comes out clean (do not overbake), 20-25 minutes. Cool completely in pan on a wire rack.
1 brownie: 173 cal., 10g fat (3g sat. fat), 16mg chol., 92mg sod., 21g carb. (15g sugars, 1g fiber), 2g pro.

& DESSERTS

GINGERBREAD & PUMPKIN
CREAM TRIFLE
P. 230

1

2

3

4

5

EVERY MEAL DESERVES A DESSERT—
AND THESE ARE SIMPLE TO MAKE,
INCREDIBLY TEMPTING AND
DOWNRIGHT DELICIOUS!

LEMON CUSTARD CAKE

GINGERBREAD & PUMPKIN CREAM TRIFLE

(PICTURED ON P. 228)

We wait for these flavors all year long! Stack up the layers in a big trifle bowl, or make minis for everybody at the table.
—Amy Geiser, Fairlawn, OH

Prep: 45 min. + chilling
Makes: 10 servings

- 1 pkg. (14½ oz.) gingerbread cake/cookie mix
- 1 pkg. (3 oz.) cook-and-serve vanilla pudding mix
- ¼ cup packed brown sugar
- 1⅔ cups canned pumpkin pie mix
- 1 carton (8 oz.) frozen whipped topping, thawed
  Optional toppings: Caramel topping, toasted pecans and gingersnap cookies

1. Prepare and bake the cake according to package directions. Cool completely on a wire rack.
2. Prepare pudding mix according to package directions; stir in the brown sugar and pie mix. Transfer to a bowl; refrigerate, covered, 30 minutes.
3. Cut gingerbread into ¾-in. pieces. In a 3-qt. trifle bowl or ten 12-oz. glasses, layer half of each of the cake, pumpkin mixture and whipped topping. Repeat layers. Refrigerate, covered, 4 hours or overnight. Top as desired.
1 serving: 372 cal., 11g fat (6g sat. fat), 23mg chol., 414mg sod., 61g carb. (44g sugars, 2g fiber), 5g pro.

LEMON CUSTARD CAKE

My grandma gave me this recipe, which is nice to whip up for company. This creamy dessert is perfect even for simple meals.
—Sue Gronholz, Beaver Dam, WI

Takes: 15 min.
Makes: 12 servings

- 1 prepared angel food cake (8 to 10 oz.)
- 1 pkg. (3.4 oz.) instant lemon pudding mix
- 1½ cups cold whole milk
- 1 cup sour cream
- 1 can (21 oz.) cherry or strawberry pie filling

Tear cake into bite-sized pieces. Place in a 13x9-in. pan. Combine the pudding mix, milk and sour cream. Beat until thickened, about 2 minutes. Spread over cake. Spoon pie filling on top. Chill until ready to serve.
1 serving: 184 cal., 5g fat (3g sat. fat), 7mg chol., 270mg sod., 31g carb. (18g sugars, 1 fiber), 3g pro.

CRANBERRY PEAR TART

The combination of fresh pears and apple juice give this tart its own distinct appeal. Because it's made with juice instead of sugar, each serving has half the calories of an average slice of apple pie.
—*Taste of Home* Test Kitchen

Prep: 15 min.
Bake: 30 min. + cooling
Makes: 8 servings

1   **sheet refrigerated pie crust**
4   **cups sliced peeled fresh pears (about 4 medium)**
⅓   **cup dried cranberries**
⅓   **cup thawed apple juice concentrate**
1   **tsp. apple pie spice**

1. Preheat oven to 375°. Press crust onto the bottom and up the sides of an ungreased 9-in. tart pan with removable bottom; trim edges. Generously prick the bottom with a fork; set aside.

2. In a large skillet, cook the pears, dried cranberries, apple juice concentrate and apple pie spice over medium heat until the pears are tender. Pour into crust. Bake until the crust is golden brown, 30-35 minutes. Cool the tart on a wire rack.

1 slice: 203 cal., 7g fat (3g sat. fat), 5mg chol., 104mg sod., 35g carb. (17g sugars, 3g fiber), 1g pro. **Diabetic exchanges:** 1½ starch, 1½ fat, ½ fruit.

CRANBERRY PEAR TART

PUFFED APPLE PASTRIES

Store-bought puff pastry makes a crunchy nest for holding sweet apples. Add a touch of cinnamon and spice, and dessert is done.
—*Taste of Home* Test Kitchen

Takes: 25 min. • **Makes:** 6 servings

- 1 pkg. (10 oz.) frozen puff pastry shells
- 1 can (21 oz.) apple pie filling
- ½ tsp. ground cinnamon
- ¼ tsp. ground nutmeg
  Vanilla ice cream, optional

1. Bake pastry shells according to the package directions. Meanwhile, in a small saucepan, combine the apple pie filling, cinnamon and nutmeg; mix well. Cook and stir the mixture over medium-low heat until heated through, 3-4 minutes.

2. Remove tops from the pastry shells; fill with the apple mixture. Replace tops. Serve warm, with ice cream if desired.

1 serving: 332 cal., 14g fat (3g sat. fat), 0 chol., 179mg sod., 49g carb. (20g sugars, 3g fiber), 3g pro.

PUFFED APPLE PASTRIES

BLUEBERRY ANGEL DESSERT

Make the most of angel food cake, pie filling and whipped topping by creating this light dessert that doesn't keep you in the kitchen for hours. It's the perfect way to end a summer meal. You can mix things up by using other flavors of pie filling, like cherry or peach.
—Carol Johnson, Tyler, TX

Prep: 10 min. + chilling
Makes: 12 servings

- 1 pkg. (8 oz.) cream cheese, softened
- 1 cup confectioners' sugar
- 1 carton (8 oz.) frozen whipped topping, thawed
- 1 prepared angel food cake (8 to 10 oz.), cut into 1-in. cubes
- 2 cans (21 oz. each) blueberry pie filling

In a large bowl, beat cream cheese and confectioners' sugar until smooth; fold in whipped topping and cake cubes. Spread evenly into an ungreased 13x9-in. dish; top with blueberry pie filling. Refrigerate, covered, at least 2 hours before serving.

1 serving: 384 cal., 10g fat (7g sat. fat), 21mg chol., 223mg sod., 70g carb. (50g sugars, 3g fiber), 3g pro.

Lemon Custard Angel Dessert: Replace cream cheese mixture with 3.4-oz. package instant lemon pudding mix beaten with 1½ cups milk and 1 cup sour cream until thickened. Fold in the cake cubes; top with strawberry pie filling.

**BLUEBERRY
ANGEL DESSERT**

STRAWBERRY SHORTCAKE STACKS

STRAWBERRY SHORTCAKE STACKS

When a wonderful friend brought me a pint of strawberries, I didn't want to just eat them straight (tempting as it was). Instead, I made strawberry shortcake with my own pretty, elegant spin. These light and airy puff pastry stacks let the fruit shine.

—Jenny Dubinsky, Inwood, WV

Prep: 25 min.
Bake: 15 min. + cooling
Makes: 12 servings

- 1 sheet frozen puff pastry, thawed
- 4 cups fresh strawberries, sliced
- ¼ cup plus 3 Tbsp. sugar, divided
- 1½ cups heavy whipping cream
- ½ tsp. vanilla extract

1. Preheat oven to 400°. On a lightly floured surface, roll puff pastry to a 10-in. square; cut into 12 rectangles (approx. 3x2½-in.). Place on ungreased baking sheets. Bake pastry until golden brown, 12-15 minutes. Remove to wire racks; cool completely.

2. In a large bowl, toss the sliced strawberries with ¼ cup sugar. Let stand 30 minutes, stirring occasionally. In another bowl, beat the cream until it begins to thicken. Add vanilla and remaining sugar; beat until stiff peaks form.

3. To serve, split the pastries horizontally in half. Top each bottom half with 2 Tbsp. whipped cream and 1 Tbsp. strawberries; replace top half. Top with the remaining whipped cream and sliced strawberries.

1 serving: 246 cal., 16g fat (8g sat. fat), 34mg chol., 76mg sod., 23g carb. (11g sugars, 2g fiber), 3g pro.

LEMON CREME BRULEE

Here's a refreshing, tangy twist on a classic. Don't have the kitchen torch traditionally used for creme brulee? Simply pop the ramekins under the broiler.

—Sara Scheler, Pewaukee, WI

Prep: 15 min.
Bake: 45 min. + chilling
Makes: 5 servings

- 3 **cups heavy whipping cream**
- 6 **large egg yolks, room temperature**
- ½ **cup plus 5 tsp. sugar, divided**
- ½ **tsp. salt**
- 2 **Tbsp. grated lemon zest**
- ½ **tsp. lemon extract**

1. Preheat oven to 325°. In a large saucepan, heat cream until bubbles form around sides of pan; remove from heat. In a large bowl, whisk egg yolks, ½ cup sugar and salt until blended but not foamy. Slowly stir in the hot cream. Stir in lemon zest and extract.

2. Place five 6-oz. broiler-safe ramekins in a baking pan large enough to hold them without touching. Pour the egg mixture into ramekins. Place pan on oven rack; add very hot water to pan to within ½ in. of top of ramekins. Bake until a knife inserted in the center comes out clean (centers will still be soft) 45-50 minutes.

3. Immediately remove ramekins from the water bath to a wire rack; cool 10 minutes. Refrigerate until cold.

4. To caramelize topping with a kitchen torch, sprinkle custards evenly with the remaining sugar. Hold torch flame about 2 in. above the custard surface; move the flame slowly across the custard until the sugar is evenly caramelized. Refrigerate for 30-60 minutes before serving.

5. To caramelize topping in a broiler, preheat broiler and place ramekins on a baking sheet; let stand at room temperature 15 minutes. Sprinkle custards evenly with remaining sugar. Broil 3-4 in. from heat until the sugar is caramelized, 2-3 minutes. Refrigerate for 30-60 minutes before serving.

1 serving: 652 cal., 57g fat (35g sat. fat), 384mg chol., 285mg sod., 29g carb. (28g sugars, 0 fiber), 7g pro.

LEMON CREME BRULEE

PEAR BUNDT CAKE

PEAR BUNDT CAKE

Next time you make cake from a mix, try this easy and delicious recipe. The finely chopped pears and syrup add sweet flavor and prevent the cake from drying out. And since there's no added oil, this cake is surprisingly low in fat.
—Veronica Ross, Columbia Heights, MN

Prep: 15 min.
Bake: 50 min. + cooling
Makes: 16 servings

- 1 can (15 oz.) reduced-sugar sliced pears
- 1 pkg. white cake mix (regular size)
- 2 large egg whites, room temperature
- 1 large egg, room temperature
- 2 tsp. confectioners' sugar

1. Preheat oven to 350°. Drain pears, reserving the syrup; chop pears. Place pears and syrup in a large bowl; add the cake mix, egg whites and egg. Beat on low speed for 30 seconds. Beat on high for 4 minutes.
2. Coat a 10-in. fluted tube pan with cooking spray and dust with flour. Add batter.
3. Bake until a toothpick inserted in the center comes out clean, 50-55 minutes. Cool 10 minutes before removing from pan to a wire rack to cool completely. Dust with confectioners' sugar.
1 slice: 163 cal., 4g fat (1g sat. fat), 13mg chol., 230mg sod., 30g carb. (0 sugars, 1g fiber), 2g pro.
Diabetic exchanges: 2 starch, 1 fat.

BLUEBERRY ICE CREAM

BLUEBERRY ICE CREAM

The wild blueberries on our property spark many recipe ideas, and this is one of the best! Our children, grandchildren and great-grandchildren think this is tops for summer taste.
—Alma Mosher, Mohannes, NB

Prep: 15 min. + chilling
Process: 20 min./batch + freezing
Makes: about 1¾ qt.

- 4 cups fresh or frozen blueberries
- 2 cups sugar
- 2 Tbsp. water
- 4 cups half-and-half cream

1. In a large saucepan, combine the blueberries, sugar and water. Bring to a boil. Reduce heat; simmer, uncovered, until the sugar is dissolved and the berries are softened. Press the mixture through a fine-mesh strainer into a bowl; discard the pulp. Stir in cream. Cover and refrigerate overnight.
2. Fill the cylinder of ice cream freezer two-thirds full; freeze according to the manufacturer's directions. (Refrigerate any remaining mixture until ready to freeze.)
3. Transfer the ice cream to freezer containers, allowing headspace for expansion. Freeze until firm, 2-4 hours. Repeat with any remaining ice cream mixture.
½ cup: 226 cal., 7g fat (5g sat. fat), 34mg chol., 35mg sod., 37g carb. (34g sugars, 1g fiber), 3g pro.

**CARAMELIZED
PEARS**

HEAVENLY
ANGEL FOOD CAKE

*This tall, pretty layer cake with
luscious chocolate filling couldn't
be easier to put together. Every
airy bite melts in the mouth.*
—Teri Roberts, Hilliard, OH

Prep: 20 min.
Bake: 35 min. + chilling
Makes: 12 servings

  1   pkg. (16 oz.) angel food
      cake mix
 24   large marshmallows
  6   milk chocolate candy bars
      with almonds (1.45 oz.
      each), chopped
 ⅔   cup whole milk
  1   carton (12 oz.) frozen
      whipped topping,
      thawed, divided

1. Bake the cake according to
package directions, using an
ungreased 10-in. tube pan. Cool.
2. For filling, in a small saucepan,
combine marshmallows, candy
bars and milk. Cook and stir over
low heat until the marshmallows
are melted. Transfer to a small
bowl; cool to room temperature.
Fold in ¾ cup whipped topping.
3. Cut cake horizontally into three
layers. Place bottom layer on a
serving plate; spread with a third
of the filling. Repeat layers twice.
Refrigerate for at least 1 hour.
4. Frost top and sides of cake with
the remaining whipped topping.
1 slice: 382 cal., 12g fat (8g sat.
fat), 5mg chol., 306mg sod.,
62g carb. (38g sugars, 1g fiber),
6g pro.

CARAMELIZED PEARS

*After picking an abundant crop
of pears, a friend suggested
warming them with butter and
brown sugar. This tasty recipe
was the result! We like them over
vanilla bean ice cream. You can try
the same technique with apples,
peaches or plums, too.*
—Sue Gronholz, Beaver Dam, WI

Takes: 20 min. • **Makes:** 3 cups

 ½   cup packed brown sugar
 ¼   cup butter, cubed
 ¼   tsp. ground cinnamon
  4   cups chopped peeled
      ripe pears
      Vanilla ice cream, optional

In a large skillet, combine brown
sugar, butter and cinnamon. Cook
over medium heat until sugar is
dissolved, stirring occasionally,
4-5 minutes. Add the pears; cook
and stir until the pears are tender,
5-10 minutes longer. Serve over
ice cream if desired.
¼ cup: 96 cal., 4g fat (2g sat. fat),
10mg chol., 33mg sod., 16g carb.
(13g sugars, 1g fiber), 0 pro.

SHOOFLY CUPCAKES

These old-fashioned molasses cupcakes were my grandmother's specialty. To keep them from disappearing too quickly, she would store them out of sight—but we always figured out her hiding places!

—Beth Adams, Jacksonville, FL

Prep: 15 min.
Bake: 20 min. + cooling
Makes: 2 dozen

- 4 cups all-purpose flour
- 2 cups packed brown sugar
- ¼ tsp. salt
- 1 cup cold butter, cubed
- 2 tsp. baking soda
- 2 cups boiling water
- 1 cup molasses

1. Preheat oven to 350°. In a large bowl, combine flour, brown sugar and salt. Cut in the butter until crumbly. Set aside 1 cup for the topping. Add baking soda to the remaining crumb mixture. Stir in water and molasses.
2. Fill paper-lined muffin cups two-thirds full. Sprinkle with reserved crumb mixture. Bake until a toothpick inserted in center comes out clean, 20-25 minutes. Let cool for 10 minutes before removing from pans to wire racks to cool completely.

1 cupcake: 248 cal., 8g fat (5g sat. fat), 20mg chol., 219mg sod., 43g carb. (26g sugars, 1g fiber), 2g pro.

★ ★ ★ ★ ★ **READER REVIEW**

"Excellent cupcakes! I made the recipe as written, no changes, to retain the authentic shoofly taste and was not disappointed!"

KRISTINECHAYES
TASTEOFHOME.COM

SHOOFLY CUPCAKES

BAKED CUSTARD WITH CINNAMON

Mother used to make this comforting custard when I was growing up on the farm. It was wonderful after a chilly evening of doing chores. Now I fix it for my husband and four sons.
—Mary Kay Morris, Cokato, MN

Prep: 10 min.
Bake: 50 min. + cooling
Makes: 4 servings

- 2 large eggs
- 2 cups whole milk
- ⅓ cup sugar
- ¼ tsp. salt
  Dash ground cinnamon
  Dash ground nutmeg

1. In a small bowl, whisk eggs, milk, sugar and salt. Pour into 4 ungreased 8-oz. custard cups; sprinkle tops with the cinnamon and nutmeg.
2. Place in a 13x9-in. baking pan; pour hot water in pan to a depth of ¾ in. Bake, uncovered, at 350° until a knife inserted in the center comes out clean, 50-55 minutes. Remove the cups to a wire rack to cool. Serve warm or chilled. Store in the refrigerator.
1 serving: 177 cal., 7g fat (3g sat. fat), 123mg chol., 239mg sod., 23g carb. (22g sugars, 0 fiber), 7g pro.

BAKED CUSTARD WITH CINNAMON

COCONUT-LAYERED POUND CAKE

If you love chocolate, almonds and coconut, this cake is for you. It comes together in a flash and tastes like an Almond Joy candy bar!
—Linda Nichols, Steubenville, OH

Takes: 10 min. • **Makes:** 8 servings

- 1 pkg. (7 oz.) sweetened shredded coconut
- 1 can (14 oz.) sweetened condensed milk
- ½ cup chopped almonds, toasted
- 1 loaf (16 oz.) frozen pound cake, thawed
- 1 cup chocolate fudge frosting

Mix coconut, milk and almonds. Cut cake horizontally into four layers. Place bottom layer on a serving plate; top with half the coconut mixture, one cake layer and ½ cup frosting. Repeat layers. Refrigerate, covered, until serving.
Note: To toast nuts, bake in a shallow pan in a 350° oven for 5-10 minutes or cook in a skillet over low heat until lightly browned, stirring occasionally.
1 slice: 715 cal., 35g fat (19g sat. fat), 98mg chol., 426mg sod., 93g carb. (72g sugars, 3g fiber), 10g pro.

COCONUT-LAYERED POUND CAKE

GRILLED ANGEL FOOD CAKE WITH STRAWBERRIES

GRILLED ANGEL FOOD CAKE WITH STRAWBERRIES

One night I goofed, accidentally using the balsamic butter I save for grilling chicken on my pound cake. What a delicious mistake that my entire family loved! For a patriotic look, add a drizzle of blueberry syrup.

—Tammy Hathaway, Freeman Township, ME

Takes: 15 min. • **Makes:** 8 servings

2 cups sliced fresh strawberries
2 tsp. sugar
3 Tbsp. butter, melted
2 Tbsp. balsamic vinegar
8 slices angel food cake (about 1 oz. each)
    Optional: Reduced-fat vanilla ice cream and blueberry syrup

1. In a bowl, toss strawberries with sugar. In another bowl, mix butter and vinegar; brush over the cut sides of the cake.

2. On a greased rack, grill cake, uncovered, over medium heat until golden brown, 1-2 minutes on each side. Serve cake with strawberries and, if desired, ice cream and blueberry syrup.

1 cake slice with ¼ cup strawberries: 132 cal., 5g fat (3g sat. fat), 11mg chol., 247mg sod., 22g carb. (4g sugars, 1g fiber), 2g pro. **Diabetic exchanges:** 1½ starch, 1 fat.

QUICK & EASY BAKLAVA SQUARES

I love baklava but rarely indulged because it takes so much time to make. Then a friend gave me this simple recipe. Now I make these squares for family, friends and co-workers for special gatherings and holiday gifts.
—Paula Marchesi, Lenhartsville, PA

Prep: 20 min.
Bake: 30 min. + cooling
Makes: 2 dozen

- 1 lb. (4 cups) chopped walnuts
- 1½ tsp. ground cinnamon
- 1 pkg. (16 oz., 14x9-in. sheets) frozen phyllo dough, thawed
- 1 cup butter, melted
- 1 cup honey

1. Preheat oven to 350°. Coat a 13x9-in. baking dish with cooking spray. Combine walnuts and cinnamon.

2. Unroll phyllo dough. Layer two sheets of phyllo in the prepared dish; brush with butter. Repeat with six more sheets of phyllo, brushing every other one with butter. (Keep remaining phyllo covered with a damp towel to prevent it from drying out.)

3. Sprinkle ½ cup nut mixture in dish; drizzle with 2 Tbsp. honey. Add two more phyllo sheets, brushing with butter; sprinkle another ½ cup nut mixture and 2 Tbsp. honey over phyllo. Repeat layers six times. Top with the remaining phyllo sheets, brushing every other one with butter. Using a sharp knife, score the surface to make 24 squares. Bake squares until golden brown and crisp, 25-30 minutes. Cool on a wire rack 1 hour before serving.

1 square: 294 cal., 21g fat (6g sat. fat), 20mg chol., 145mg sod., 26g carb. (13g sugars, 2g fiber), 5g pro.

TART CHERRY PIE

My aunt and I are diabetic, and we both enjoy this yummy, fruity pie. Our friends even request it for dessert when they come to visit.
—Bonnie Johnson, DeKalb, IL

Prep: 15 min. + cooling
Makes: 8 servings

- 2 cans (14½ oz. each) pitted tart cherries
- 1 pkg. (3 oz.) cook-and-serve vanilla pudding mix
- 1 pkg. (.3 oz.) sugar-free cherry gelatin
   Sugar substitute equivalent to 4 tsp. sugar
- 1 pie crust (9 in.), baked

Drain cherries, reserving juice; set cherries aside. In a large saucepan, combine the cherry juice and dry pudding mix. Cook and stir until mixture comes to a boil and is thickened and bubbly. Remove from the heat; stir in the gelatin powder and sweetener until dissolved. Stir in cherries; transfer to pie crust. Cool completely. Store in the refrigerator.

1 piece: 174 cal., 7g fat (3g sat. fat), 5mg chol., 162mg sod., 25g carb. (11g sugars, 1g fiber), 2g pro. **Diabetic exchanges:** 1 starch, 1 fat, ½ fruit.

QUICK & EASY BAKLAVA SQUARES

**EASY FRESH
STRAWBERRY PIE**

EASY FRESH STRAWBERRY PIE

For my mother's 70th birthday, I made two of these strawberry pies instead of a cake. Since it was mid-May in Texas, the berries were perfect. It was a memorable occasion for the whole family.
—Josh Carter, Birmingham, AL

Prep: 20 min. + cooling
Bake: 15 min. + chilling
Makes: 8 servings

- 1 pastry shell (9 in.), unbaked
- ¾ cup sugar
- 2 Tbsp. cornstarch
- 1 cup water
- 1 pkg. (3 oz.) strawberry gelatin
- 4 cups sliced fresh strawberries
  Whipped cream, optional

1. Line unpricked crust with a double thickness of heavy-duty foil. Bake at 450°. for 8 minutes. Remove foil; bake 5 minutes longer. Cool on a wire rack.
2. Meanwhile, in a small saucepan, combine the sugar, cornstarch and water until smooth. Bring to a boil; cook and stir until thickened, about 2 minutes. Remove from the heat; stir in the gelatin until dissolved. Refrigerate until slightly cooled, 15-20 minutes.
3. Arrange the strawberries in crust. Pour gelatin mixture over berries. Refrigerate until set. Serve with whipped cream if desired.
1 slice: 264 cal., 7g fat (3g sat. fat), 5mg chol., 125mg sod., 49g carb. (32g sugars, 2g fiber), 2g pro.

QUICK ICEBOX SANDWICHES

QUICK ICEBOX SANDWICHES

My mother liked making these cool, creamy treats when I was growing up in the States because she could make them so quickly. Now my three kids enjoy them!
—Sandy Armijo, Naples, Italy

Prep: 20 min. + freezing
Makes: 2 dozen

- 1 pkg. (3.4 oz.) instant vanilla pudding mix
- 2 cups cold whole milk
- 2 cups whipped topping
- 1 cup miniature semisweet chocolate chips
- 24 whole graham crackers, halved

1. For filling, combine pudding mix and milk according to package directions; refrigerate until set. Fold in the whipped topping and chocolate chips.
2. Place 24 graham cracker halves on a baking sheet; top each with about 3 Tbsp. of filling. Place another graham cracker half on top. Wrap each sandwich individually in plastic; freeze until firm, about 1 hour. Serve frozen.
1 sandwich: 144 cal., 5g fat (3g sat. fat), 3mg chol., 162mg sod., 23g carb. (13g sugars, 1g fiber), 2g pro.

BLUEBERRY LEMON TRIFLE

COOKIE ICE CREAM PIE

This crunchy, creamy treat is the ultimate freezer dessert. Whip it up and serve to company—or the neighborhood kids!
—Debbie Walsh, Madison, WI

Prep: 25 min. + freezing
Makes: 8 servings

- 10 Oreo cookies, crushed
- 3 Tbsp. butter, melted
- 14 whole Oreo cookies
- ½ gallon white chocolate raspberry truffle ice cream, softened and divided
- ½ cup prepared fudge topping, divided
  Fresh raspberries, optional

1. In a small bowl, combine crushed cookies and butter; press onto bottom of a 9-in. pie plate. Stand whole cookies up around the edges, pressing lightly into crust. Freeze until set, about 1 hour.
2. For filling, spread half of the ice cream over the crushed cookies. Drizzle with ¼ cup of the fudge topping. Freeze until set, about 1 hour. Spread the remaining ice cream on top. Drizzle with the remaining fudge topping. Freeze several hours or overnight.
3. Garnish with fresh raspberries if desired. Let stand at room temperature for 15 minutes before cutting.
1 piece: 763 cal., 45g fat (24g sat. fat), 201mg chol., 448mg sod., 81g carb. (62g sugars, 3g fiber), 11g pro.

BLUEBERRY LEMON TRIFLE

A refreshing lemon filling and fresh blueberries give this sunny dessert sensation plenty of color. Don't worry about heating up the oven—this trifle doesn't need to be baked.
—Ellen Peden, Houston, TX

Prep: 15 min. + chilling
Makes: 14 servings

- 3 cups fresh blueberries, divided
- 2 cans (15¾ oz. each) lemon pie filling
- 2 cups lemon yogurt
- 1 prepared angel food cake (8 to 10 oz.), cut into 1-in. cubes
- 1 carton (8 oz.) frozen whipped topping, thawed
  Lemon slices and fresh mint, optional

1. Set aside ¼ cup blueberries for garnish. In a large bowl, combine pie filling and yogurt.
2. In a 3½-qt. serving or trifle bowl, layer a third of each of the cake cubes, lemon mixture and blueberries. Repeat layers twice more. Top with whipped topping. Cover and refrigerate for at least 2 hours. Garnish with the reserved blueberries and, if desired, lemon slices and fresh mint leaves.
1 serving: 230 cal., 4g fat (3g sat. fat), 2mg chol., 235mg sod., 44g carb. (27g sugars, 1g fiber), 3g pro.

MINISTER'S DELIGHT

A friend gave me this recipe several years ago. She told me that a local minister's wife fixed it every Sunday, so she named it accordingly.

—Mary Ann Potter, Blue Springs, MO

Prep: 5 min. • **Cook:** 2 hours
Makes: 12 servings

- 1 can (21 oz.) cherry or apple pie filling
- 1 pkg. yellow cake mix (regular size)
- ½ cup butter, melted
- ⅓ cup chopped walnuts, optional

Place the pie filling in a 1½-qt. slow cooker. Combine the cake mix and butter (mixture will be crumbly); sprinkle over filling. Sprinkle with walnuts if desired. Cover and cook on low for 2-3 hours. Serve in bowls.

1 serving: 304 cal., 12g fat (6g sat. fat), 20mg chol., 357mg sod., 48g carb. (31g sugars, 1g fiber), 2g pro.

★ ★ ★ ★ ★ **READER REVIEW**

"This 'cobbler' comes out great when baked, too. I used a 13x9-in. baking dish at 350° for 30 minutes. This is such a comforting dessert to warm the soul."

TRAMAR TASTEOFHOME.COM

MINISTER'S DELIGHT

EASY PISTACHIO BUNDT CAKE

Mixes make this light cake easy. Go for the pistachios on top— the extra crunch is worth it!
—Dina Crowell, Fredericksburg, VA

Prep: 15 min.
Bake: 35 min. + cooling
Makes: 12 servings

- 1   pkg. yellow cake mix (regular size)
- 1   pkg. (3.4 oz.) instant pistachio pudding mix
- 4   large eggs, room temperature
- 1½ cups water
- ¼   cup canola oil
- ½   tsp. almond extract
- Confectioners' sugar
- Finely chopped pistachios, optional

1. Preheat oven to 350°. Grease and flour a 10-in. fluted tube pan.
2. In a large bowl, combine first 6 ingredients; beat on low speed for 30 seconds. Beat on medium for 2 minutes. Transfer to the prepared pan.
3. Bake 35-40 minutes or until a toothpick inserted in center comes out clean. Cool in pan 10 minutes before removing to a wire rack to cool completely.
4. Dust with confectioners' sugar. If desired, sprinkle with pistachios.
Note: To remove cakes easily, use solid shortening to grease plain and fluted tube pans.

1 slice: 266 cal., 10g fat (2g sat. fat), 62mg chol., 416mg sod., 41g carb. (24g sugars, 0 fiber), 4g pro.

S'MORES CRESCENT ROLLS

Here's how to score indoor s'mores: Grab crescent dough and Nutella. Then invite the kids to help with this rolled-up version of the campfire classic.
—Cathy Trochelman, Brookfield, WI

Takes: 25 min. • **Makes:** 8 servings

- 1   tube (8 oz.) refrigerated crescent rolls
- ¼   cup Nutella, divided
- 2   whole graham crackers, broken up
- 2   Tbsp. milk chocolate chips
- ⅔   cup miniature marshmallows

1. Preheat oven to 375°. Unroll crescent dough; separate into 8 triangles. Place 1 tsp. of Nutella at the wide end of each triangle; sprinkle with the broken graham crackers, chocolate chips and marshmallows. Starting from the wide end, roll up and place on ungreased baking sheets, point side down; curve to form crescents. Bake until golden brown, 9-11 minutes.
2. In a microwave, warm the remaining Nutella to reach a drizzling consistency; spoon over the rolls. Serve warm.
1 roll: 201 cal., 10g fat (3g sat. fat), 1mg chol., 256mg sod., 25g carb. (12g sugars, 1g fiber), 3g pro.

EASY PISTACHIO BUNDT CAKE

S'MORES
CRESCENT
ROLLS

**TURTLE
PRALINE TART**

TURTLE
PRALINE TART

*This rich dessert is my own
creation, and I'm very proud
of it. It's easy enough to make
for everyday meals but special
enough to serve to guests—
or take to a potluck.*
—Kathy Specht, Clinton, MT

Prep: 35 min. + chilling
Makes: 16 servings

  1 **sheet refrigerated pie crust**
 36 **caramels**
  1 **cup heavy whipping cream,
     divided**
 3½ **cups pecan halves**
  ½ **cup semisweet chocolate
     chips, melted**

1. Unroll pie crust on a lightly
floured surface. Transfer to
an 11-in. fluted tart pan with
removable bottom; trim edges.
2. Line crust with two sheets of
heavy-duty foil. Bake at 450° for
8 minutes. Remove foil; bake until
light golden brown, 5-6 minutes
longer. Cool on a wire rack.

3. In a large saucepan, combine
caramels and ½ cup cream. Cook
and stir over medium-low heat
until caramels are melted. Stir in
pecans. Spread filling evenly into
crust. Drizzle with the melted
semisweet chocolate.
4. Refrigerate until set, about
30 minutes. Whip remaining
cream; serve with tart.
1 slice: 335 cal., 24g fat (4g sat.
fat), 4mg chol., 106mg sod.,
31g carb. (19g sugars, 3g fiber),
4g pro.

STRAWBERRY-CITRUS FREEZER POPS

I knew that clementines and strawberries would create a luscious combination in a fruit pop, and these are just as tasty as I anticipated!
—Colleen Ludovice, Wauwatosa, WI

Prep: 20 min. + freezing
Makes: 10 pops

- 2 cups fresh strawberries, sliced
- 6 Tbsp. water
- 1 Tbsp. sugar
- 10 freezer pop molds or paper cups (3 oz. each) and wooden pop sticks
- 2 cups clementine segments (about 10), seeded if necessary
- 6 Tbsp. orange juice

1. Place strawberries, water and sugar in a food processor; pulse until combined. Divide among molds or cups. Top with foil and insert sticks through foil. Freeze until firm, about 2 hours.
2. Wipe food processor clean. Add clementines and orange juice; pulse until combined. Spoon over strawberry layer. Freeze, covered, until firm.
1 pop: 82 cal., 0 fat (0 sat. fat), 0 chol., 3mg sod., 20g carb. (16g sugars, 3g fiber), 1g pro. **Diabetic exchanges:** 1 fruit.

STRAWBERRY-CITRUS FREEZER POPS

LEMON PLUM SORBET

This brightly flavored fruit sorbet is delicious and refreshing whether served plain or on top of a slice of angel food cake.
—Eirianedd Simpson, Pahrump, NV

Prep: 25 min. + freezing
Makes: 6 servings

- 8 medium plums
- 2 cups sugar
- 1 cup water
- ⅓ cup lemon juice
- 2 tsp. grated lemon zest

1. In a large saucepan, bring 8 cups water to a boil. Add plums; cover and boil for 30-45 seconds. Drain and immediately place in ice water. Drain and pat dry. When cool enough to handle, remove skins. Cut in half; remove pits.
2. In a small saucepan, bring sugar and 1 cup water to a boil. Cook and stir until the sugar is dissolved. Add lemon juice and zest; set aside to cool.
3. Place the plums in a food processor; add sugar syrup. Cover and process until smooth, 2-3 minutes. Transfer puree to an 8-in. square dish. Freeze until the edges begin to firm, about 1 hour; stir. Freeze until firm, about 2 hours longer.
4. Just before serving, transfer to a food processor; cover and process for 2-3 minutes or until mixture is smooth.
¾ cup: 310 cal., 1g fat (0 sat. fat), 0 chol., 0 sod., 79g carb. (76g sugars, 1g fiber), 1g pro.

MINI SWEET
POTATO PIES

MINI SWEET POTATO PIES

My 2-year-old son helped me create this recipe one day. It was the first day he told me "I love you!" I will always remember making these with him.
—Emily Butler, South Williamsport, PA

Prep: 45 minutes
Bake: 25 min. + cooling
Makes: 2 dozen

- 2 large sweet potatoes, peeled and cut into ¾-in. cubes
- 2 sheets refrigerated pie crust, room temperature
- 1 cup packed brown sugar, divided
- ¼ cup all-purpose flour
- 3 Tbsp. cold unsalted butter, cubed

1. Preheat oven to 400°. Place the sweet potatoes in a greased 15x10x1-in. baking pan; bake until tender, 35-40 minutes.
2. On a work surface, unroll one crust. Using a 2½-in. round cutter, cut out 12 circles. Press circles onto bottoms and up sides of 12 nonstick mini muffin cups. Repeat with second crust. Chill until filling is ready.
3. In a food processor, pulse flour, butter and ¼ cup brown sugar until crumbly; set aside for the topping. Add the baked sweet potatoes and remaining brown sugar to food processor; pulse until almost smooth. Fill crust-lined cups three-fourths full. Sprinkle with topping.
4. Decrease oven setting to 325°.

Bake until crust is golden brown, 20-24 minutes. Cool 5-10 minutes before removing from pan to a wire rack.

1 mini pie: 156 cal., 6g fat (3g sat. fat), 7mg chol., 67mg sod., 25g carb. (12g sugars, 1g fiber), 1g pro.

CREAMY HAZELNUT PIE

I'd always been a huge fan of peanut butter. Then I tried Nutella—I was hooked! I even adapted one of my favorite pie recipes for that ingredient.
—Lisa Varner, El Paso, TX

Prep: 10 min. + chilling
Makes: 8 servings

CREAMY HAZELNUT PIE

- 1 pkg. (8 oz.) cream cheese, softened
- 1 cup confectioners' sugar
- 1¼ cups Nutella, divided
- 1 carton (8 oz.) frozen whipped topping, thawed
- 1 chocolate crumb crust (9 in.)

1. Beat the cream cheese, confectioners' sugar and 1 cup of Nutella until smooth. Fold in whipped topping. Spread evenly into crust.
2. Warm the remaining Nutella in microwave for 15-20 seconds; drizzle over pie. Refrigerate at least 4 hours or overnight.

1 piece: 567 cal., 33g fat (13g sat. fat), 32mg chol., 224mg sod., 65g carb. (51g sugars, 2g fiber), 6g pro.

INDEX